THERMOPOLIS

BIG HORN

N

RANGE

WIND RIVER

1830
1838
RIVERTON

AGIE R.

LANDER
1829

POPO

SWEETWATER RIVER

South Pass

IC CK.

N RIVER

Rendezvous Sites

0   10   20   30   40
Scale 1:1,000,000

RENDEZVOUS SITES:
1825-1840

OMING

COLORADO

Rocky Mountain Rendezvous:
A History of the Fur Trade Rendezvous
1825-1840

Fred R. Gowans

Rocky Mountain

A History of the Fur Trade Rendezvous
1825-1840

Fred R. Gowans

GIBBS·SMITH
P
PUBLISHER

Rendezvous

Copyright 1985 by Fred R. Gowans

Published by Gibbs M. Smith, Inc.
Peregrine Smith Books
P.O. Box 667
Layton, UT 84041

Library of Congress Cataloging in Publication Data

Gowans, Fred R., 1936 –
  Rocky Mountain rendezvous.

  Reprint. Originally published: Provo, Utah: Brigham Young
University, c1976.
  Bibliography: p. 221.
  1. West (U.S.) – History – To 1840. 2. Fur trade – West (U.S.)
– History – 19th century. 3. Frontier and pioneer life – West
(U.S.) 4. Indians of North America – West (U.S.)
I. Title.
[F592.G68 1985]   978'.02   84-27586
ISBN 0-87905-193-0

Book design and illustrations by Stuart Heimdal.
Maps and photographs by Fred R. Gowans.

Cover illustration: **The "Rendezvous," Near Green River, Oregon**
by Alfred Jacob Miller, Picture Division, Public Archives of
Canada, Ottawa, C-439. Back cover illustration: **Breakfast at
Sunrise** by Alfred Jacob Miller, C-424.

06 05 04 03 12 11 10 9 8

DEDICATED
TO
MY PARENTS
FLOYD D. GOWANS
RACHEL HILL GOWANS

MAPS

PHOTOGRAPHS

CONTENTS

PREFACE

Hundreds of articles and books have been written about the American fur trade and the men who made its history. The sole purpose of this work is to look at one small part of this era of Western Americana – THE RENDEZVOUS. By use of detailed maps and pictures of the actual rendezvous sites plus the journals, diaries and letters of those who attended the annual festival of the mountains, the author is hopeful that the reader may acquire a better understanding and appreciation of this monumental event. One of the most noted students of the American fur trade and the first to write a definitive work on the subject was Hiram Martin Chittenden. Let his words provide the background of what gave birth to the fur trade rendezvous:

The rendezvous was one of the most interesting developments of the fur trade in the Rocky Mountains. It arose from the necessity of carrying the trade into regions remote from navigable rivers, where boats could not carry the annual merchandise nor bring back the furs. The transportation was done by annual caravans from the States, and rendezvous were appointed for each year at points convenient for the trappers and Indians to meet the traders. These meetings were great events and form one of the most picturesque features of early frontier life in the Far West.

(From: **Life, Letters and Travels of Father DeSmet 1801-1873,** p. 216.)

INTRODUCTION

In 1822 a partnership was entered into between William H. Ashley and Andrew Henry that was to have a great impact on the American fur trade. In April of that year, Henry led a group of men to the mouth of the Yellowstone River and started construction of a fort, later named for him. Another group of men under the direction of Daniel Moore, following Henry up the Missouri, wrecked their boat and lost more than $10,000 worth of cargo. On receiving word of the disaster, Ashley outfitted another boat and, taking personal command, arrived at the mouth of the Yellowstone in October.

Ashley returned to St. Louis during the winter while Henry remained at Fort Henry to direct field operations. His men moved further up the Missouri to the mouth of the Musselshell and ascended the Yellowstone to the mouth of the Powder River. The following spring Jedediah Smith was sent down river by Henry to notify Ashley that they would need supplies for the coming year. Upon receiving Henry's request, Ashley assembled the necessary supplies and set out for the Yellowstone. The supply boats, however, were attacked by the Arikaras and Ashley lost 15 men and a large amount of cargo.

In spite of this setback, the partners regrouped their forces and sent out two main trapping expeditions. The first group under Henry's command returned to the Yellowstone and, feeling that the post at the Yellowstone was strategically in an unsuitable location, moved up the Yellowstone to the mouth of the Bighorn River and erected the second Fort Henry. From this location, Henry sent trappers to the southwest toward the mountains and the land of the Crow nation.

Ashley's second group, led by Jedediah Smith, left Fort Kiowa on the Missouri in September of 1823 and headed west. They arrived at the Crow villages and found Henry's men already encamped there. Both groups wintered together among the Crow in the Wind River Valley. In the spring of 1824, the men traveled westward into the Green River country and found a paradise of beaver. When the spring hunt was over, the furs were taken back to St. Louis by Thomas Fitzpatrick and James Clyman while the majority of the trappers remained in the mountains to trap. The report that the two trappers brought to St. Louis concerning the rich beaver country around the Green River indicated a far more valuable source of beaver than Ashley ever dreamed of finding.

In November of 1824, Ashley organized the first supply train to the Central Rockies to supply the trappers so that they could remain in the mountains. With the distribution of these supplies in 1825 at a pre-selected site the fur trade rendezvous was born.

With this new plan of operation, Ashley was not dependent upon the Indian trade. His own men could remain the year around in the mountains, trapping the rivers and streams of the Rocky Mountains. Neither was there a need for a trading post since the annual rendezvous could handle both the distribution of supplies and the procuring of the valuable beaver pelts.

Pawnee Indians Watching the Caravan. 1867, by A. J. Miller, Public Archives of Canada, C-431.

RANDAVOUZE CREEK RENDEZVOUS
1825

William Ashley left Fort Atkinson on November 3, 1824, to guide a supply train to the first rendezvous. He overtook twenty-five of his trappers on November 25th. These men had left earlier, taking with them fifty pack horses, one wagon and a team. The wagon was later abandoned due to heavy snow. Their route was up the Platte to its south fork, up the south fork to Cache la Poudre, up Cache la Poudre to the Platte, west to Pacific Creek, and down the Big Sandy, to their destination at the Green River. They arrived there on April 19, 1825.

Ashley dispersed his men to the surrounding mountains to trap, with an understanding that he would mark the rendezvous site on his descent of the Green River. Ashley wrote:

> ... *The place of deposite as aforesaid, will be the place of randavoze for all our parties on or before the 10th July next & that place may be known — Trees will be pealed standing the most conspicuous near the Junction of the rivers. Sould such a point be without timber I will raise a mound of Earth five feet high or Set up rocks the top of which will be made red with vermillion thirty feet distant from the same — and one foot below the serface of the earth a northwest direction will be deposited a letter communicating to the parties any thing that I may deem necessary ...*[1]

While descending the Green River, Ashley cached his supplies at three different locations. The first was on Wednesday, April 29, 1825, at Bridger Bottom, six miles below Buckboard Wash and fourteen miles above Henry's Fork. There they left:

> 2 bags coffee
> hams goods

    3 pack powder - 11 sqt
    2 Tobacco
    3 B. lead
    horse shoes
    Beads large & small
    2 packs sugar -
    1 pack cloth with some knives therein -
    1 pack 7 doz Knives[2]

The second cache was on Monday, May 18, 1825, two or three miles below the mouth of Ashley Fork. There they left:

2½ Kegs Tobacco	150 lbs
14 doz Knives	
2 peaces scarlett Cloth	
2 ditto Blue Stroud	
3 Bags coffee	200 lbs
Bale & Bag Sugar	130 lbs
3 packs beaver	50 skins
pack of beads assorted	
vermillion	
assortment of Indian trinkett, mockerson alls do.	
2 Bags gun powder	150 lbs
3 Bars lead	120 lbs
Bag Flint	1000
Bag Salt	10 lbs
pack cloths -	
pack containing a variety of Indian trins-ketts -	
Ribbons Binding & C	
axes hoes & C[3]	

The third cache was on Thursday, May 21, 1825, at the mouth of White River on the location of the Provost winter camp of 1824-25. They here:

"... cached the cargo of my canoes..."[4]

Ashley indicated two different rendezvous locations:

(1) *Saturday, May 2, 1825*
   ... proceeded down the river about 6 miles & Encamped in a beautiful bottom where I made sign for the different parties to Randavouze...[5]

(2) Sunday, May 3, 1825
> *descended the river — about 4 miles & Encamped at the Entrance of a small creek on the West Side with bs E&W (Henrys Fork) its 60 feet wide ... there is much beaver sign on small river, beauteful bottoms on which is a considerable small willow (and some distance above) large timber — finding this a much more suitable place for a Randavouze I have made marks indicative of my intention to Randavouze here & in consequence of which have given the name of Randavouze Creek ...*[6]

Minnie Maud Creek (Nine Mile Creek) was the farthest point south to which Ashley traveled. Here he left the river and traveled north to the Duchesne River, then turned west traveling up the Duchesne to the Strawberry River and on to Red Creek, where he met Etienne Provost who was trapping out of Taos. Ashley and Provost returned to the junction of the Strawberry and Duchesne Rivers. There Ashley talked Provost into returning to the Green River and digging up his cache at Ashley Fork. Ashley most likely had retrieved his own cache at White River before his ascent of the Green River.

Taking one of Ashley's men to point out the cache, Provost returned to the Green River to get Ashley's cache and then returned to the confluences of the Strawberry and Duchesne Rivers where Ashley was encamped. With the return of Provost, the company traveled up the Strawberry to its source and then north across Kamas Valley to the Weber River and down the Weber to Chalk Creek.

Provost left Ashley at this point and descended the Weber to the Great Salt Lake, where he traded with Euteaw Indians before rejoining Ashley a few days later. Ashley ascended Chalk Creek to Bear River, went down the Bear a few miles before turning east to the Big Muddy, and then descended the Big Muddy to the point where it turns to the east. Instead of going east, however, Ashley turned southwest and traveled to Henry's Fork. He followed Henry's to the rendezvous site that he had selected on the Green River, arriving there about June 29th or 30th. The actual date given in Ashley's journal for the buying and selling of supplies and furs at the rendezvous was July 1, 1825.

> *On the 1st day of July, all the men in my employ or with whom I had any concern in the Country, together with*

17

twenty nine who had recently withdrawn from the Hudson's Bay Company, making in all 120 men, were assembled in two camps near each other about 20 miles distant from the place appointed by me as a general rendezvous ...[7]

James Beckwourth described the rendezvous as follows:

... On arriving at the rendezvous, we found the main body of the Salt Lake party already there with the whole of their effects. The general would open none of his goods, except tobacco, until all had arrived, as he wished to make an equal distribution; for goods were then very scarce in the mountains, and hard to obtain.

When all had come in, he opened his goods, and there was a general jubilee among all at the rendezvous. We constituted quite a little town, numbering at least eight hundred souls, of whom one half were women and children. There were some among us who had not seen any groceries, such as coffee, sugar &c., for several months. The whisky went off as freely as water, even at the exorbitant price he sold it for. All kinds of sports were indulged in with a heartiness that would astonish more civilized societies.[8]

For some years the exact location of the 1825 Rendezvous had been in question. From Ashley's statement, we know that the rendezvous was held 20 miles from the confluences of Henry's Fork and Green River. This puts the rendezvous either 20 miles up Green River or 20 miles up Henry's Fork. The site 20 miles up the Green River, however, is barren and dry with no appeal for a rendezvous. In fact, Ashley would have passed this area in descending the Green River and had not marked it as a site for the rendezvous. However, after leaving the Big Muddy on his return to the rendezvous site, Ashley would have descended Henry's Fork to its mouth, passing over beautiful rich grass land, which lay 20 miles from the confluences of Henry's Fork and Green River. Upon his arrival at the earlier designated rendezvous site, where his men were waiting for him, Ashley relocated the rendezvous 20 miles up Henry's Fork to the lush grass land on the bench between Burnt Fork and Birch Creek.

Ashley gives the number present at the rendezvous as 120 with the following breakdown: Hudson's Bay Company deserters, 29 men; Etienne Provost, 13; Jedediah Smith, 7; Ashley, 25; and John H. Weber, 25 to 30. This leaves a discrepancy of 16 to 21 men. The difference could very likely be in the number accredited to Provost. For on Saturday, June 7th, Ashley met Provost near Red Creek and recorded in his journal that Provost's party consisted of 12 men, not including Provost. However, on Saturday, May 16th, while descending the Green River, Ashley had encountered two of Provost's men and indicated in his journal that Provost's party consisted of 20 to 30 men. If these figures are accurate, this makes an additional 7 to 17 men. The difference in number could also be the presence of free trappers or the presence of some local Indians at the first rendezvous. The actual number is impossible to ascertain.

According to his journal, Ashley left the rendezvous site with 50 men on July 2, 1825, and started for St. Louis. Therefore, the formal rendezvous lasted only one day. However, the mountainmen who gathered at the specified site had waited for several days for Ashley to arrive.

Ashley's journal contains some interesting facts about the 1825 Rendezvous; for example, prices for the trading goods were as follows:

> *Coffee - $1.50 per pound*
> *Sugar - $1.50 per pound*
> *Tobacco - $3.00 per pound*
> *powder - $2.00 per pound*
> *fish hooks - $1.50 per dozen*
> *flints - $1.00 per dozen*
> *Scissors - $2.00 each*
> *Knive - $2.50 each*
> *Blue Cloth - $5.00 per yard*
> *Scarlett - $6.00 per yard*
> *lead - $1.00 per pound*
> *Blanketts - $9.00 each three point North West blanket*
> *buttons - $1.50 per dozen*[9]

Although there seemed to be a standard price for each item, often the prices would vary in dealings with different people. For example, sugar varied from $1.00 per pound to $2.00 per pound. Tobacco usually sold for $3.00 per pound, but sold to some for $2.00. Ashley usually paid $3.00 per pound for beaver as a standard amount, yet some mountainmen received only $2.00. It appears from the account books that those who went to work for Ashley in 1822-23 were paid $2.00 per pound. Probably their agreement at that time specified that amount. A free trapper received $5.00 per pound. According to Beckwourth's account, liquor was available at the 1825 Rendezvous. His account may not be reliable, however, since Ashley's detailed list of supplies does not include any mention of liquor. In any case, Ashley changed that factor in procuring supplies for the 1826 Rendezvous.

On July 2, 1825, the trappers loaded the fur packs on the horses and started for the Bighorn River by way of South Pass. Ashley took 20 of the men to dig up a cache of 45 packs left, probably by Jedediah Smith in 1824, further east on the Sweetwater River. While separated from the main group, Ashley and his men were attacked by Blackfeet. They sent for help from the main group who were taking a more direct route to the Bighorn River. With their reinforcement, Ashley was able to escape and reunite his men.

They arrived on the Bighorn on August 7, 1825. There they constructed boats and loaded their furs for the descent of the Bighorn and Yellowstone rivers. With the furs safely loaded for river travel, half of the men, approximately 25, returned with the horses to the mountains. Exactly how many men went with Ashley and how many remained to spend another year in the mountains is not known. However, from 24 to 28 men (depending on whose account is used) traveled with Ashley to the mouth of the Yellowstone.

The point of embarkation for the river trip was where the Wind River emerges from the mountains and becomes the Bighorn River (now Thermopolis, Wyoming). One of the main reasons that Ashley chose that route was his knowledge of the Atkinson-O'Fallon Expedition, which was then on the upper Missouri making treaties with the Indians. Ashley met this expedition at the mouth of the Yellowstone on August 19, 1825.

The furs were floated down the Missouri on the boats Mink, Muskrat and Rackoon. Ashley and his company arrived at St. Louis on October 4, 1825. It was on this trip down the Missouri that Ashley took into partnership Jedediah Smith to replace Andrew Henry who was quitting the mountain life. Thus, the Ashley-Henry Company was dissolved and the Ashley-Smith Company organized.

The value of the furs which Ashley brought into St. Louis

varies according to which report is used. Different newspapers estimate the number of packs from 80 to 100 and the value from $40,000 to $50,000. In a letter to the American Fur Company, O.N. Bustwick stated the total weight at 9,700 pounds, packed in 100 packs with a value of $48,000. Atkinson's journal also mentions 100 packs.

The packs assembled at the rendezvous and brought out by horse to the Bighorn River weighed about 50 pounds. Ashley's 1825 ledgers contain a listing of the packs with their weight and the number of furs in each bundle. The 50 pound packs were reapportioned for shipping by the Atkinson-O'Fallon Expedition into the 100 pound bundles that arrived in St. Louis. Some interesting facts about Ashley's packs are available. From a random sampling of 21 packs, the average number of skins in each pack was 32 and the average weight of each pack was 52 pounds. Therefore, the average weight of each skin was 1.64 pounds, worth $4.92 at $3.00 per pound.

Without question, the summer rendezvous was the most important annual gathering of the mountainmen. However, from the time that the streams froze over until the spring thaw (approximately December 1 to March 1), most of the mountainmen gathered in a pre-selected setting to give each other some degree of companionship during the long and cold winter days. The mountainmen referred to this gathering as Winter Quarters. The first location for the annual winter quarters was Willow Valley (Cache Valley) where John H. Weber and his men had spent the winter of 1824-25 previous to the 1825 Rendezvous.

Because of the hard winter, the mountainmen removed to Salt Lake Valley sometime during the winter and situated themselves in two camps at the mouth of the Weber and Bear Rivers. James Beckwourth estimated the encampment at 600-700 men, including Indians. Peter Skene Ogden was told by some Snake Indians on March 24, 1826, that they had spent the winter with Americans. The Indians numbered about 20 lodges. According to the few available accounts, William Sublette seems to have been in charge of the winter encampment.

During the late winter and early spring of 1826, the mountainmen encamped by the Great Salt Lake were the first to explore the shoreline by boat. With the coming of spring, the mountainmen took to the streams to trap. They planned to meet again in a few months at the summer rendezvous.

21

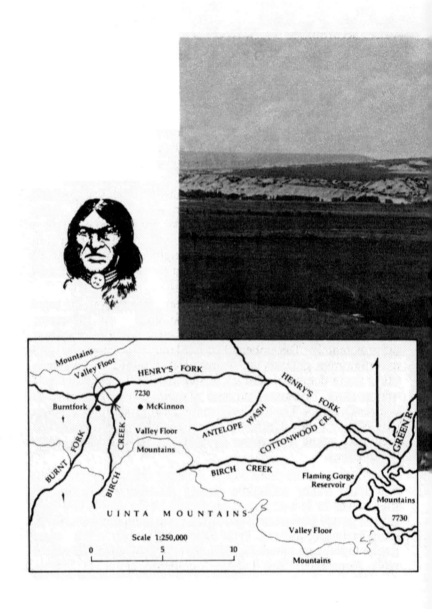

RANDAVOUZE CREEK RENDEZVOUS
1825

The picture is taken looking in a northwest direction. Birch Creek is in the foreground with trees and brush covering the banks of the river. Henry's Fork is located at the base of the bluffs in the background, flowing from the extreme left to the extreme right in the picture. Burnt Fork is located in the background at the extreme left, flowing into Henry's Fork. The junction of Burnt Fork and Henry's Fork is identified by trees and heavy brush. The bench between Burnt Fork and Birch Creek was the location of the 1825 Rendezvous. Today native-grass hay fields cover most of the rendezvous site.

MAP INFORMATION

The circles on the maps depict the area seen in the pictures and also establish the central location of the rendezvous. It is impossible, however, to be exact in representing the total area covered in any given rendezvous. The tip of the arrow attached to the circle represents the position and direction in which the picture was taken.

WILLOW VALLEY RENDEZVOUS
1826

A supply train under the command of William Ashley left St. Louis on March 8, 1826, with 26 men bound for the 1826 Rendezvous. Jedediah Smith and Robert Campbell with 60 men and 160 mules had left for the mountains in late October or early November of 1825 with $20,000 worth of supplies. They had sent word back to Ashley that they were having troubles and that they were snowed in on the Republican Fork and needed more mules, having lost one-third of their herd. Ashley caught up with Smith and Campbell at Grand Island on April 1, 1826. There Ashley sent Jedediah Smith and Moses Harris ahead to make arrangements for the rendezvous in Willow Valley (Cache Valley).

The route to the 1826 Rendezvous was not the same as the route taken in 1825 by way of the South Fork of the Platte. Instead, the supply train stayed on the North Platte to present-day Casper, Wyoming, following the Sweetwater over South Pass and on to the Green River. The trip was hard; many men were not able to endure the hardship. In fact, between 20 and 30 men deserted because of the horrible conditions. After arriving at the Green River, the supply train continued on to Ham's Fork. There 60 to 75 mountainmen, having received word from Smith and Harris of the approaching supply train, rode out to meet it.

From Ham's Fork the company traveled to the Bear River, following its course north past Bear Lake. They then followed the big bend south, back to Willow Valley, arriving sometime in late May or early June. Ashley noted that it took 78 days to make the trip, arriving on May 25, 1826, while Jedediah Smith recorded the arrival as sometime in June.

The exact location of the rendezvous in Willow Valley is impossible to determine since none of the participants of the 1826 festivities left any information pertaining to the precise location. The journal of William Ashley and portions of Robert Campbell's journal and letters, which represent the majority of the information now available concerning the 1826 Rendezvous, were edited by Dale Morgan and published under the title, **The West of William Ashley.** The book contains a map showing the location of the 1826 Rendezvous in the south end of Willow Valley five miles south of the confluence of Blacksmith's Fork and the Logan River. Also, in **Jedediah Smith and the Opening of the West,** Morgan states:

> Cache Valley was the place appointed for the second great summer rendezvous. Accounts of the American fur trade have usually placed this rendezvous in the valley of the Great Salt Lake, but it is apparent that Cache Valley was the locale, the vicinity of present Hyrum.[1]

Morgan's opinion is based on Jedediah Smith's journal entries of July 1st and 2nd, 1827, while he was traveling along the shore of the Great Salt Lake and traversing the Wasatch Range enroute to the 1827 rendezvous at Little Lake (Bear Lake).

> *July 1st 25 Miles North along the shore of the Lake Nothing material occurred.*
>
> *2nd 20 Miles North East Made our way to the Cache. But Just before arriving there I saw some indians on the opposite side of the creek. It was hardly worth while as I thought, to be any wise careful, so I went directly to them and found as near as I could judge by what I knew of the language to be a band of the Snakes. I learned from them that the Whites, as they term our parties, were all assembled at the little Lake, a distance of about 25 Miles. There was in this camp about 200 Lodges of indians and as the were on their way to the rendevous I encamped with them.*
>
> *3rd I hired a horse and a guide and at three O Clock arrived at the rendezvous. My arrival caused a considerable bustle in camp, for myself and party had been given up as lost. A small Cannon brought up from St. Louis was loaded and fired for a salute.*[2]

From the directions and distances given in Smith's journal Morgan suggests that Smith traveled through present day Box Elder Canyon over Sardine Pass into the south end of Willow Valley and to the Cache near the mouth of Blacksmith's Fork Canyon. Morgan's theory would have Smith follow Blacksmith's Fork Canyon over the mountains to reach the rendezvous at Little

Lake on July 3rd. This proposed route of Smith's from the Great Salt Lake to the rendezvous site is certainly feasible and probably correct. However, Morgan's whole theory is based upon the assumption that the cache was located at the site of the 1826 Rendezvous. This certainly makes sense but still there is no proof. In 1967 a portion of Jedediah Smith's journal was found in St. Louis and published in 1977. The journal gives valuable information concerning Smith's activities on the Bear River after the close of the 1826 Rendezvous. Smith recorded that he left the big bend of the Bear River (Soda Springs, Idaho) and

> ... *started for cache or willow valley to which place I was under the necessity of going to procure some things from our cache and to make some repairs on our Guns for at that place we had a sett of Black smith tools. crossing Bear River and making several days at quick traveling I arrived at the Cache on the 15th of August. Found every thing safe at the cache had some coal Burned a forge erected and my work underway as fast as possible. took such things as I wanted from the Cache and on the 18th of August I struck over west on to the Big Salt Lake ...*[3]

Harrison G. Rogers was the clerk on Smith's southwest expedition and his day book lists the items taken from the cache which shows that it contained a large portion of Ashley's 1826 supplies. Even though the new journal substantiates the existence of a cache and its contents in the south end of Willow Valley there still remains the question of the exact location of the 1826 Rendezvous. The north end of Willow Valley must also be considered as a possible site of the rendezvous since we know that John H. Weber and his men spent the winter of 1824-25 on Cub Creek in the present area of Cove, Utah. This location was evidently picked by Weber because it could provide his men with an ample supply of food, water and shelter. It was not uncommon

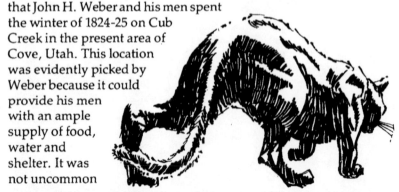

for the mountainmen to hold their summer rendezvous and winter quarters at the same location because of its natural setting. As the mountainmen descended the Bear River into Willow Valley with the supply train in 1826, they would have arrived at Cub Creek first. Morgan's suggested location was still twenty-five more miles to the south. Knowing that the Cove location was adequate for the rendezvous there would have been ample reason for Ashley to have selected the site. Consequently, either of the locations could have been the site for the 1826 Rendezvous. However, from the information available at this time the Blacksmith's Fork site would be the most logical, because of the cache location. Hopefully, future research will be able to pinpoint this site.

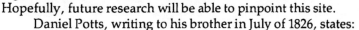

Daniel Potts, writing to his brother in July of 1826, states:

> ... *this valley has been our chief place of rendezvous and wintering ground. Numerous streams fall in through this valley, which, like the others, is surrounded by stupendous mountains, which are unrivalled for beauty and serenity of scenery. You here have a view of all the varieties, plenty of ripe fruit, an abundance of grass just springing up, and buds beginning to shoot, while the higher parts of the mountains are covered with snow, all within 12 or 15 miles of this valley. The river passes through a small range of mountains and enters the valley that borders on the Great Salt Lake* ...[4]

James Beckwourth leaves the following description of the rendezvous:

> *The absent parties began to arrive, one after the other, at the rendezvous. Shortly after, General Ashley and Mr. Sublet came in, Accompanied with three hundred pack mules, well laden with goods and all things necessary for the mountaineers and the Indian trade. It may well be supposed that the arrival of such a vast amount of luxuries from the East did not pass off without a general celebration. Mirth, songs, dancing,*

A

B

28

WILLOW VALLEY RENDEZVOUS
1826, 1831

Picture A is taken looking in a southeast direction near the Idaho-Utah State line, toward the small farming community of Cove, Utah situated near the junction of Cub Creek and the Bear River. The small community of Cove is located in the left-center portion of the picture at the base of the Wasatch Range. Picture B is taken looking in a northeast direction toward Blacksmith's Fork. The city of Hyrum, Utah and Blacksmith's Fork Canyon can be seen in the right-center portion of the picture. The 1831 Rendezvous was also scheduled to be held in Willow Valley but the supply train under the command of Thomas Fitzpatrick failed to arrive. Presently farm lands cover most of the area.

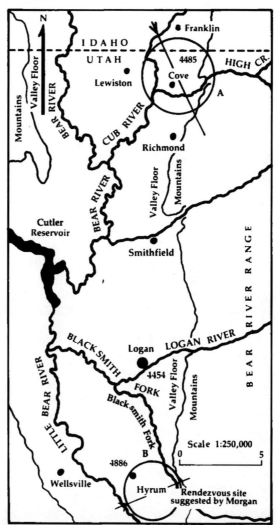

shouting, trading, running, jumping, singing, racing, target-shooting, yarns, frolic, with all sorts of extravagances that white men or Indians could invent, were freely indulged in. The unpacking of the medicine water contributed not a little to the heightening of our festivities.

We had been informed by Harris, previous to the arrival of the general, that General Ashley had sold out his interest in the mountains to Mr. Sublet, embracing all his properties and possessions there. He now intended to return to St. Louis, to enjoy the fortune he had amassed by so much toil and suffering, and in which he had so largely shared in person.[5]

According to Robert Campbell, the rendezvous lasted only a couple of weeks, but Daniel Potts states that the men celebrated the 4th of July by firing their guns and making toasts. It would appear that the rendezvous was much longer than two weeks since Ashley was still on the Bear River as late as July 18, 1826. If Ashley were right in assuming that he arrived on May 25th and if he were still on Bear River as of July 18th, he was in the area of the rendezvous for almost eight weeks. Of course, it is possible that the date of May 25th is wrong and that Jedediah Smith was correct in stating that it was June. Also, the rendezvous could have broken up much earlier than July 18th. Potts actually could have been with a group of trappers on July 4th after the break up of the rendezvous. So the length of the rendezvous is still in question. Furthermore, because of the lack of documents, there is no information on the prices of supplies at the rendezvous or on the amount paid for beaver. However, the amounts paid at the 1826 Rendezvous were likely much the same as those of the 1825 Rendezvous.

On July 18, 1826, on Bear River, after leaving the rendezvous, Ashley sold out his interest in the fur company to Jedediah Smith, David Jackson and William Sublette. Ashley was probably enroute back to St. Louis when the transaction took place. The story that Ashley sold out in Salt Lake Valley is not likely true since little evidence exists to show that Ashley ever saw the Great Salt Lake Valley or even the lake itself.

The terms of the agreement gave the new owners Ashley's merchandise, which was to be paid for with beaver at the 1827 Rendezvous. Ashley was either to pay $3.00 per pound for beaver at the 1827 Rendezvous or take the furs to St. Louis for the owners and get the best price available there. However, Ashley would charge $1.12½ per pound for transportation charges. These transactions were to be completed by July 1, 1827. Ashley was to see that supplies were at the 1827 Rendezvous, to be located at the south end of Bear Lake, by July 1st. The supplies were to cost between $7,000 and $15,000. The partners were to notify Ashley by March 1, 1827, concerning the exact amount of supplies. Ashley also obtained in the agreement the right to send his own trappers with the supply train and the stipulation that the firm of Smith, Jackson and Sublette could only buy their supplies from Ashley.

With the agreement in hand and the firm of Smith, Jackson and Sublette owing him $7,821, Ashley returned to St. Louis by route of South Pass and the Platte River, arriving at St. Louis in late September. The trip took 70 days. One account places the arrival on September 9, 1826. This, however, is too early since the earliest time that Ashley could have departed from the rendezvous was mid-July and 70 days were needed to make the trip. Furthermore, the newspaper accounts in St. Louis of Ashley's return were dated as late as September 21st and September 28th.

The value and amount of the furs brought to St. Louis by Ashley is recorded at 125 packs worth $60,000. This would indicate that each pack was valued at $480.00. This is very close to the 1825 value per pack. This puts the weight of each pack at about 100 pounds which represented the weight per pack most readily accepted. There is one reference to the 1826 catch weighing 12,000 pounds. This would be agreeable to the 100-pound weight per pack.

The fall was spent by the mountainmen trapping in both the north and central Rockies. As the streams began to freeze over, the mountainmen started for their annual winter gathering. Winter quarters was again in Willow Valley, and the winter itself was quite mild. On New Year's Day, 1827, William Sublette and Moses "Black" Harris started east from Willow Valley to confirm their agreement with Ashley concerning the supplies to be taken on the 1827 Rendezvous. The trek of Sublette and Harris was with intense suffering. They did not arrive in St. Louis until March 4, 1827. Although they were three days late, Ashley honored their agreement.

During winter quarters, Daniel Potts with five men left Willow Valley to explore the country to the south. They explored as far south as the Sevier River, returning just prior to the summer rendezvous. In March the mountainmen left Willow Valley and returned to the business of trapping, hoping to have an excellent catch to take to the rendezvous at Bear Lake that summer.

SWEET LAKE RENDEZVOUS
1827

During the fall of 1826, Ashley worked on arrangements with the firm of Bernard Pratte and Company to help supply the 1827 Rendezvous. By December of 1826, when the arrangements were finalized, Bernard Pratte and Company had become the western department of John Jacob Astor's American Fur Company. On March 8, 1827, Ashley advertised in a St. Louis newspaper for fifty men to go to the mountains. Their wages were to be $110 for one year's service. Consequently, forty-six men and supplies, valued at $22,447.14, left St. Louis on April 12, 1827, with James Bruffee and Hiram Scott in charge. The company also had in its possession a cannon mounted on wheels. This four pounder was the first wheeled vehicle to cross South Pass. The purpose of taking the four pounder was probably both for protection of the supply train and for use at the rendezvous. The cannon was taken back with the returning supply train, since there would have been no reason to leave it in the mountains. It would have been more a nuisance than a help to the mountainmen. There is some evidence to indicate that it also made the round trip to the 1828 Rendezvous. Incidentally, one source claims that Ashley left for the mountains in 1827 with the supplies but returned to St. Louis because of illness.

While in St. Louis, William Sublette obtained from Superintendent of Indian Affairs William Clark a two-year license to trade with the Indians. Sublette also took to the mountains with him his young brother, Pinckney Sublette. Unfortunately, the young lad was killed during his first winter in the mountains.

The route to the rendezvous was the same as the route taken in 1826 and which later became the standard route of the supply trains to and from the rendezvous. This well-traveled route, used by the supply trains during the 1820's and 1830's, was to become the eastern part of the famous Oregon Trail.

The mountainmen and Indians started to gather at the south end of Bear Lake in June of 1827. The agreement of 1826 had stated "... *at or near the west end of the little lake of Bear River* ..."[1] At about the same time as the arrival of the supply train, the trappers and Indians gathered at the rendezvous were attacked by the Blackfeet. Daniel Potts records:

> ... *A few Days previous to my arival at this place a party of about 20 Black feet approchid the Camp and killed a Snake and his squaw the alarm was immediately given and the Snakes Utaws and Whites sallied forth for Battle the enemy fled to the Mountain to a small concavity thickly groon with small timber surrounded by open ground In this engagement the squaws where busily engaged in throwing up batterys an dragging off the dead there was only six whites engaged in this battle who immediately advanced within Pistol shot and you may be assured that almost every shot counted one The loss of the Snakes was three killed and the same wounded that of the Whites one wounded and two narrowly made their escape that of the Utaws was none though who gained great applause for their bravery the loss of the enemy is not known six were found dead on the ground besides a great number where carried off on Horses ...*[2]

Beckwourth also gives an account of the attack on the rendezvous:

> *Two days after the arrival of the general, the* tocsin *again sounded through our whole camp, "The Black Feet! the Black Feet!" On they came, making the very earth tremble with the tramps of their fiery warhorses. In their advance they surprised three men and two women belonging to the Snakes, who were out some distance from camp, gathering roots. The whole five were instantly overtaken, killed, and scalped.*
>
> *As soon as the alarm was given, the old prophet came to our camp and, addressing Mr. Sublet, said,*
>
> *"Cut Face, three of my warriors and two women have just been killed by the Black Feet. You say that your warriors can fight — that they are great braves. Now let me see them fight, that I may know your words are true."*
>
> *Sublet replied, "You shall see them fight, and then you will know that they are all braves — that I have no cowards among my men, and that we are all ready to die for our Snake friends."*
>
> *"Now, men," added he, turning to us, "I want every brave man to go and fight these Black Feet, and whip them, so*

*that the Snakes may see that we can fight, and let us do our best
before them as a warning to them. Remember, I want none to
join in this battle who are not brave. Let all cowards remain in
camp."*

*... There were over three hundred trappers mounted in a
few moments, who, with Captain Sublet at their head, charged
instantley on the enemy.*

*... After six hours' fighting, during which time a number
of the enemy were slain, we began to want nourishment ... The
fruits of our victory were one hundred and seventy-three scalps,
with numerous quivers of arrows, war-clubs, battle-axes, and
lances ... The trappers had seven or eight men wounded, but
none killed. Our allies lost eleven killed in battle.*

*... As usual on all such occasions, our victory was
celebrated in camp, and the exercises lasted several days,
conformably to Indian custom.*[3]

Robert Campbell who was present at the time of the attack
gives a more reliable account than Blackwourth:

*... the Blackfeet attacked the Snakes and the Snake warriors
with William Sublette went out to assist them when Tullock
was wounded on the wrist, and his hand withered from the
effects of the wound ... Sublette behaved bravely. I staid in camp
in charge of everything. The families of those killed disposed of
all the bodies. One of them placed a buffalo robe on Sublette's
tent and said to him, "You are a great warrior. I seen it. My
'bonich' behaved cooly."*[4]

The exact time of the arrival of the supply train is not
known. According to Daniel Potts, writing his brother on July 8th
from the rendezvous, the supply train had arrived just a few days
prior. Jedediah Smith arrived at the rendezvous on July 3rd from
his trip to California, and he was saluted by the firing of the
cannon. The agreement of 1826 indicated that the supplies would
be at the rendezvous prior to July 1, 1827, and the deadline was
evidently met. Most likely, although this is conjecture, the
supply train got to the south end of Bear Lake by following the
present Route 3 from Bear River to Laketown, Utah.

The agreement of 1826 guaranteed that to the firm of Smith,
Jackson and Sublette, Ashley would provide supplies at the
following prices:

Gunpowder - $1.50 per pound
Lead - $1.00 per pound
Shot - $1.25 per pound

Blanketts - $9.00 each
Scarlet cloth - $6.00 per yard
Beaver traps - $9.00 each
Sugar - $1.00 per pound
Coffee - $1.25 per pound
Flour - $1.00 per pound
¼ Rum reduced - $13.50 per gallon
Flint - $.50 per dozen
Tobacco - $3.00 per pound
Bridles - $7.00 each
Spurs - $2.00 pair
Flannel - $1.50 per yard
Blue cloth - $5.00 per yard

Daniel Potts states, *"There is a poor prospect of making much here, owing to the evil disposition of the Indians and the exorbitant prices of goods. For example,*

Powder - $2.50 per pound
Lead - 1 50
Coffee - 2 00
Sugar - 2 00
Tobacco - 2 00
. . .
Blankets (three point) - 15 00
. . .
Scarlett cloth (course) do - 10 00
. . .
Horses cost from 150 dollars to 300, and some as high as 500."[5]

By comparing the two lists, it is apparent that the new partnership made good money on their markup.

Bruffee and Scott, acting for Ashley, purchased the following skins:

7,400⅓ pds of beaver @ $3.00 per pound
95 pds of castor @ $3.00 per pound
102 otter skins @ $2.00 each

A total of $22,690 was accredited to the Smith, Jackson and Sublette Company for the furs. With the supplies costing $22,447.14, it would appear that the profit was slim. But, as mentioned above, the profit was made from the sales on supplies. The partnership did well enough to pay off in full the $7,821 owed to Ashley from the debt accrued at the 1826 Rendezvous. It had been a good season for the new company.

The rendezvous broke up on July 13, 1827, with some of the mountainmen leaving earlier. Potts recorded that he and his group were pulling out on July 9th. Jedediah Smith left the rendezvous headed for California to meet the men he had left with the furs. This trip would end in disaster, with 25 men killed and most of the profits lost. However, Smith was able to sell his 1,568 pounds of beaver for $2.50 per pound at San Francisco harbor to Captain John Bradshaw who was enroute to Boston. Smith was not to return to the summer rendezvous until 1829.

As the supply train descend on the Platte, Hiram Scott, who had taken ill enroute to the rendezvous, became so bad that he was left behind with two companions who were to escort him to civilization. Bruffee promised to wait downstream at the bluffs on the Platte River. Scott and his two companions finally arrived at the meeting spot in deplorable condition. Bruffee was not there; he had moved on. In desperation, Scott's two escorts abandoned him and left him there by the bluffs to die. Today, the location where he was deserted bears his name, Scotts Bluff, Nebraska.

Bruffee arrived at Lexington, Missouri, on October 1, 1827. Ashley met him at Lexington, having supplies valued at approximately $20,000 ready to send back to the mountains. Sublette and Jackson spent about five days in Lexington and left with the new supplies for the mountains. Information is lacking, but it appears that these supplies did not reach the mountainmen until spring. There was to be no spring supply train.[6]

Upon his arrival at St. Louis, Ashley sold the furs obtained from Bruffee to B. Pratte and Company for $33,270.72, getting $4.37½ per pound, a nice profit of $10,580.72. **The Missouri Observer,** dated October 17, 1827, placed the value of the furs at $60,070. It would also appear that B. Pratte and Company had a sizeable profit.

Another event was taking place in the late summer of 1827 which was to have an impact on the rendezvous. Joshua Pilcher, Lucien B. Fontenelle, W. H. Vanderburgh, Charles Bent and Andrew Drips organized a fur company and left Council Bluffs late in the summer of 1827. They lost their horses to raiding Crow Indians east of South Pass. Out of necessity they cached their supplies near South Pass and wintered on Green River.

Winter Quarters (1827-1828) had three major locations. The old routine of everyone getting together in one location was not as evident. There was, however, still a major gathering place at Willow Valley. But records reveal that some mountainmen were located at Bear Lake and some others at the mouth of the Bear and Weber Rivers at the Great Salt Lake. Also, Robert Campbell and David Jackson spent the winter in Flathead country. The winter was very severe. Peter Skene Ogden was snowed in near Snake

River south of present day Blackfoot, Idaho. His records reveal that the mountainmen were starving to death on Bear River, that they had no supplies. This record agrees with the earlier statement that the supplies sent out by Ashley in October did not find their way to the mountainmen until spring. The mountainmen were jubilant to have spring arrive in 1828 and eagerly awaited the rendezvous to be held again at Sweet Lake.

Prairie on Fire. 1867, by A. J. Miller, Public Archives of Canada, C-432.

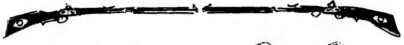

As the mountainmen gathered for the 1828 Rendezvous at the south end of Bear Lake, some degree of excitement was gone. There would be no supply train this year since the supplies had been brought out late in the fall by William Sublette and David Jackson. The supplies, valued at about $20,000, had reached the mountains in November, but most trappers had not received them until early spring. Some did not obtain supplies until the summer rendezvous. But even without the supply train, the mountainmen still anxiously awaited the rendezvous.

A group of trappers under the direction of Robert Campbell, enroute to the rendezvous from Flathead country, had a run in with the Indians just a few miles north of the rendezvous site. As in 1827, the rendezvous started off with a battle with the Blackfeet. William Ashley wrote concerning the encounter:

> ... Mr. Campbell had a valuable collection of furs, and intended, about this time, setting out to join the rest of the Americans. This circumstance induced Mr. C. to use all possible expedition on his march. Notwithstanding, when within a few miles of the rendezvous, he discovered two or three hundred Indians in pursuit of him: he and party succeded in reaching some rocks near at hand, which seemed to offer a place of safety. The Indians, who proved to be Blackfoot warriors, advanced, but were repulsed with the loss of several of their men killed; they would, no doubt, have ultimately succeeded in cutting off the whites, had they not have been so near the place of rendezvous, where, in addition to 60 or 70 white men, there were several hundred Indians friendly to them, and enemies to the Blackfoots. This fact was communicated to the assailants by a Flathead Indian, who happened to be with Mr. Campbell, and who spoke the Blackfoot language. At

the same time, the Indians saw two men, mounted on fleet horses, pass through their lines, unhurt, to carry the information of Mr. C's situation to his friends. This alarmed the Indians, and produced an immediate retreat. Lewis Bolduc, being an inactive man, was overtaken and killed before he had reached the rocks. Several others were wounded, while defending themselves among the rocks. The party lost about five thousand dollars worth of beaver furs, forty horses, and a small amount of merchandise.[1]

Daniel Potts at the rendezvous site recorded the following:

A party of about one hundred Blackfeet mounted attacked thirty odd of our hunters with their familys this engagement lasted for upwards of three hours when a couple of our men mounted two of their swiftest horses dashed through their ranks of the horrid tribe where the balls flew like hail and arrived with express at our camp in less than one hour a distance of more than sixteen miles In this we had one man killed & two wounded one child lost. that of the enemy six or eight killed and wounded ...[2]

Robert Campbell also leaves an account of the attack:

... Campbell relates that his party was attacked by the Blackfeet when about 18 miles from the head of the lake, after being joined by four trappers from rendezvous the night before. "My cook, who had the tents packed on the horses was found killed early in the morning. I led the party and got to a willow spring and prepared for defence." After a four-hour fight, ammunition got so dangerously low that Campbell in company with "a little Spaniard" undertook to break through the besiegers to obtain help from the camp at the south end of Bear Lake ... Campbell got through the ring of foes, and soon was galloping back with reinforcements and ammunition. The Blackfeet had disappeared by the time of his return. "We lost half a dozen horses in the fight, but got off safely, except with the loss of one man killed and two or three wounded ..."[3]

James Beckwourth was not one of the two riders who risked their lives. Of course he suggests that he was, giving a vivid description of his bravery:

Immediate assistance must be had, and it could come from

no other place than our camp. To risk a message there seemed to subject the messenger to inevitable death; yet the risk must be encountered by some one ... I was wounded, but not severly; and, at a time so pressing, I hardly knew that I was wounded, at all. I said, "Give me a swift horse, and I will try to force my way. Do not think I am anxious to leave you in your perilous position."

"You will run the greatest risk," said they. "But if you go, take the best horse."

Campbell then said that two had better go, for there might be a chance of one living to reach the camp. Calhoun volunteered to accompany me, if he had his choice of horses, to which no one raised any objection. Disrobing ourselves, then, to the Indians costume, and tying a handkerchief round our heads, we mounted horses fleet as the wind, and bade the little band adieu. "God bless you!" shouted the men; the women cried, "The Great Spirit preserve you, my friends." Again we dashed through the ranks of the foe before they had time to comprehend our movement. The balls and arrows flew around us like hail, but we escaped uninjured. Some of the Indians darted in pursuit of us, but, seeing they could not overtake us, returned to their ranks ... My companion and I returned with the first party, and, breaking once more through the enemy's line, rode back into the willows, amid the cheers of our companions and the loud acclamations of the women and children, who now breathed more freely again. The Indians were surprised at seeing a re-inforcement and their astonishment was increased when they saw a whole line of men coming to our assistance. They instantly gave up the battle and commenced a retreat. [4]

The rendezvous was held during the first part of July. Since there had been no supply train, it was up to the owner to get the furs back to St. Louis. This would be added work for the partners but would also mean higher profit. Ashley had been paying $3.00 per pound for beaver in the mountains, but now the partners would receive $5.00 per pound in St. Louis. The furs accumulated at the rendezvous represented 70 packs, consisting of:

7,710½ pounds of beaver
49 otter skins

27 pounds of castoreum

73 muskrat skins

Sublette sold the furs in St. Louis. They brought a total of $35,810.75; so after paying Ashley for the fall supplies, the firm had a surplus of $16,000.

Also arriving at the 1828 Rendezvous was Joshua Pilcher and Company, supplied by the American Fur Company, with their few supplies. They had uncached their supplies at South Pass and found them destroyed by water. They did succeed in salvaging some supplies and at the rendezvous were fortunate to trade for 17 packs of beaver. Pilcher remained in the mountains while his associates traveled with their furs back to St. Louis. They accompanied William Sublette who left the rendezvous about August 1st and arrived in St. Louis on October 6, 1828.

Sublette spent the winter of 1828-1829 in St. Louis making arrangements for the spring supply train.

The exact location for winter quarters is not known. But it probably was around the Big Horn and Powder River country near their confluences with the Yellowstone River. It is known that David Jackson and Thomas Fitzpatrick had gone north to Flathead Lake for the winter and that Jedediah Smith was spending the winter at Fort Vancouver with Hudson's Bay officials.

Joshua Pilcher, after sending his associates with their meager catch east with William Sublette, followed David Jackson north to Flathead Lake. He was giving the fur business one more chance. He tried to get backing from Hudson's Bay Company but failed. Most of his men joined Jackson's employ and Pilcher soon retired from the fur trade, returning to St. Louis. Also during the winter of 1828-29, James Beckwourth began his illustrious life and career with the Crow Indians.

William Ashley in a letter to Governor John Miller of Missouri on December 24, 1828, cited some interesting figures in regard to the fur trade:

> *The party of American hunters in that region, formerly in my employ consisted of about one hundred men, the proceeds of their labour, during the four years before mentioned exceed two hundred thousand dollars, notwithstanding repeated heavy losses by Indian depredations, which is not included in this Estimate — two*

thirds of this amt. have been lodged, & circulated in Missouri, in exchange for articles for the traders, the production of the state, the purchase of mules from our Santa Fe traders, & paid to men in different capacities employed in the business, who are generally citizens of Missouri — During the same period of four years, from the best information I could obtain, the Hudson Bay Compy has had employed in the same business & upon the same Territory claimed by the U States west of the R Mountains, about six hundred men, & we may reasonable suppose their success to have been equal to the one hundred in my employ, should that have been the case, the proceeds of their business in the course of the four years, has exceeded twelve hundred thousand dollars — Six or — Eight hundred thousand of which, had those operations been confined to our own Citizens would have circulated in this State.[5]

In a copy of this letter Ashley added to these figures:

"... They (Hudson's Bay Company) have much experience in the business; and as much may be expected from their exertions as from any other persons, with the same amt. of capital." He also estimates the proceeds of their labor for the past four years, over and beyond the losses, as exceeding "Two hundred & twenty thousand Dollars." Valuing the Hudson's Bay Company proceeds at "Thirteen hundred thousand dollars,..."[6]

Ashley also made some comments on the number of deaths which occurred during the preceding years:

...he (William Sublette) *reports the loss of eight of his party killed by the Indians last year — & 4 missing who no doubt have been also killed. I have recently heard of the loss of eight men more destroyed in the same way who together with 19 others have accompanied Mr. Smith down the river Rio Colarado of the West — ...*[7]

According to Ashley's figures 39 people had been killed. This figure is wrong, however. Smith had lost ten men to the Mojave Indians in 1827 which Ashley could have known about and fifteen to the Umpquas in 1828 which he could not have yet received word on. Eleven other men had been killed for a total of 36.

SWEET LAKE RENDEZVOUS
1827, 1828

The picture is taken from the hills just east of Laketown, Utah, looking in a northwest direction. Bear Lake is in the background extending north across the Utah-Idaho border. The flat fertile land pictured at the south end of Bear Lake was the location of the 1827 and 1828 Rendezvous. Farm land covers most of the rendezvous site today.

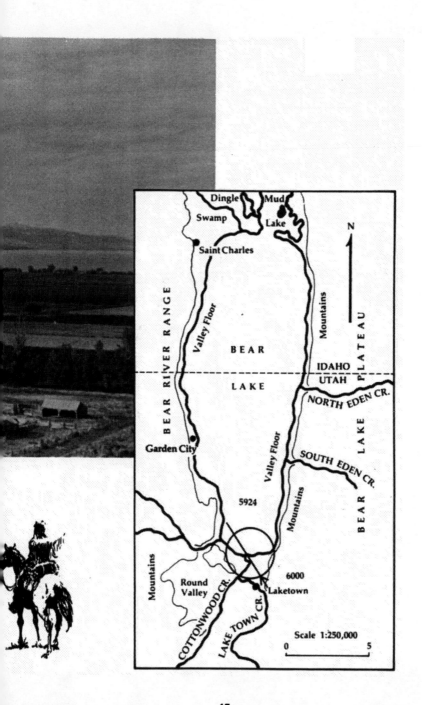

Dingle
Swamp
Mud
Lake

Saint Charles

BEAR RIVER RANGE

Valley Floor

BEAR

LAKE

Mountains

N

PLATEAU

IDAHO
UTAH

NORTH EDEN CR.

Garden City

Valley Floor

SOUTH EDEN CR.

5924

Mountains

BEAR LAKE

Mountains

Round
Valley

COTTONWOOD CR.

LAKE TOWN CR.

6000
Laketown

Scale 1:250,000

0   5

Thus with the close of 1828, plans were being prepared that would culminate with William Sublette bringing the supply train to the mountains in the spring. Also the trappers who were scattered throughout the mountains were actively trapping the streams and rivers and making plans for their annual festival in the mountains.

POPO AGIE-PIERRE'S HOLE RENDEZVOUS
1829

William Sublette left St. Louis with a supply train on March 7th, bound for the 1829 Rendezvous. The supplies he carried were valued at approximately $9,500. He had 55 men in his company, including such men as Joe Meek, Robert Newell and George Ebberts, who were going to the mountains for the first time. Also across half a continent, Jedediah Smith was leaving Fort Vancouver on March 12, 1829, enroute to Flathead Lake where he would meet his partner, David Jackson. Jackson had not seen Smith since the 1827 Rendezvous.

The route west to the rendezvous was the usual until just east of South Pass. Here the caravan turned north to the Popo Agie, meeting Robert Campbell and his men, who were returning from their spring hunt in Crow country, at the present site of Lander, Wyoming, between the first and middle of July. Thomas Fitzpatrick was with Campbell. He had gone to Flathead Lake with Jackson in the fall of 1828. Most likely Fitzpatrick brought Jackson's fall and spring catch to Campbell. Thus, Campbell had in his possession the total catch of the mountainmen under the employ of Smith, Jackson and Sublette. The meeting on the Popo Agie had been pre-arranged between Sublette and Campbell in the fall of 1828. This meeting can be considered the first Rendezvous of 1829 but was not the major gathering.

Joe Meek leaves us an excellent description of this rendezvous and all rendezvous in general:

The Summer rendezvous was always chosen in some valley where there was grass for the animals, and game for the camp. The plains along the Popo Agie, besides furnishing these necessary bounties, were bordered by picturesque mountain ranges, whose naked bluffs of red sandstone glowed in the morning and evening sun with a mellowness of coloring charming to the eye of the Virginia recruit. The waving grass of

47

the plain, variegated with wild flowers; the clear summer heavens flecked with white clouds that threw soft shadows; the lodges of the Booshways, around which clustered the camp in motley garb and brilliant coloring; gay laughter, and the murmur of soft Indian voices, all made up a most spirited and enchanting picture, in which the eye of an artist could not fail to delight.

But as the goods were opened the scene grew livelier. All were eager to purchase, most of the trappers to the full amount of their year's wages; and some of them, generally free trappers, went in debt to the company to a very considerable amount, after spending the value of a year's labor, privation, and danger, at the rate of several hundred dollars in a single day.[1]

Meek also leaves some interesting information on free trappers in comparison to the hired trappers:

The difference between a hired and a free trapper was greatly in favor of the latter. The hired trapper was regularly indentured and bound not only to hunt and trap for his employers, but also to perform any duty required of him in camp. The booshway, or the trader, or the partisan, had him under his command, to make him take charge of load and unload the horses, stand guard, cook, hunt fuel, or, in short, do any and every duty. In return for this toilsome service he received an outfit of traps, arms and ammunition, horses, and whatever his service required. Besides his outfit, he received no more than three or four hundred dollars a year as wages. There was also a class of free trappers for, and who were obliged to agree to a certain stipulated price for their furs before the hunt commenced. But the genuine free trapper regarded himself as greatly the superior of the foregoing classes. He had his own horses and accoutrements, arms, and ammunition. He took what route he thought fit, hunted and trapped when and where he chose; traded with the Indians; sold his furs to whoever offered highest for them; dressed flauntingly, and generally had an Indian wife and half-breed children.[2]

Sublette sent forty men under the command of his brother Milton back to the Big Horn and Yellowstone River country to prepare for the fall hunt. In the meantime, Campbell returned to St. Louis with 45 packs of beaver. Campbell then traveled to Scotland because of family problems, not again to return to the mountains until 1832. Campbell received $22,476 in St. Louis for the year's catch which consisted of:

4,076 lbs of beaver at $5.25 per pound
7 otter skins at $3.00 per pound
14 lbs of castoreum at $4.00 per pound

Thomas Fitzpatrick and Robert Newell were sent west by Sublette to find David Jackson and his men. With the distribution of supplies to the trappers completed and Campbell enroute to St. Louis, Sublette left the Popo Agie, following the Wind River to its source and crossing To-gwo-tee-a Pass to Buffalo Fork onto the Snake River and into Jackson Hole.

According to Meek, Sublette met Jackson in Jackson Hole while Smith was in Pierre's Hole. Newell, however, states that both Jackson and Smith met in Pierre's Hole. Whichever account is true, Sublette continued on to Pierre's Hole by way of Teton Pass, arriving there on August 20, 1829, where the general rendezvous was held. According to Newell, there were 175 men present. If this number is an accurate figure, there must have been several free trappers present.

This rendezvous was, without doubt, a special occasion for Jedediah Smith. Most everyone present thought him dead. The meeting of old friends and the stories that followed, relating the history of the last two years, took many nights around the campfires. Smith also had in his possession a draft for $2,400 which represented all that was left of those unfortunate two years.

Joseph Meek leaves the following description concerning the rendezvous in Pierre's Hole:

> ... found time to admire the magnificent scenery of the valley, which is bounded on two sides by broken and picturesque ranges, and overlooked by that magnificent group of mountains, called the Three Tetons, towering to a height of fourteen thousand feet. This emerald cup set in its rim of amethystine mountains was so pleasant a sight to the mountain-men that camp was moved to it without delay, where it remained until some time in September, recruiting its animals and preparing for the fall hunt.

> Here again the trappers indulged in their noisy sports and rejoicing, ostensibly on account of the return of the long-absent Booshway.[3]

49

The rendezvous broke up in late September. There is some evidence to show that Smith had convinced his partners at the rendezvous that they should trap the east side of the Rockies and leave the west side to the Hudson's Bay Company. It is very possible that Smith had made this commitment at Fort Vancouver to Hudson's Bay officials in return for the friendship they had demonstrated to him during the winter of 1828-9.

After the fall hunt, winter quarters was located on the Wind River as it emerges from the Wind River Mountains, with about 200 people present. Here on December 24th, Jedediah Smith wrote his famous letter to his brother which revealed his religious feelings. All three partners were present until the first of January, 1830, when William Sublette left on snowshoes for St. Louis, taking Moses Harris, his old traveling companion, with him. They arrived in St. Louis in the middle of February.

Joe Meek describes winter quarters as follows:

> This was the occasion when the mountain-men "lived fat" and enjoyed life: a season of plenty, of relaxation; of amusement, of acquaintanceship with all the company, of gayety, and of "busy idleness." Through the day, hunting parties were coming and going, men were cooking, drying meat, making moccasins, cleaning their arms, wrestling, playing games, and, in short, everything that an isolated community of hardy men could resort to for occupation, was resorted to by these mountaineers. Nor was there wanting, in the appearance of the camp, the variety, and that picturesque air imparted by a mingling of the native element; for what with their Indian allies, their native wives, and numerous children, the mountaineers' camp was a motley assemblage, and the trappers themselves, with their affectations of Indian coxcombry, not the least picturesque individuals.

> The change wrought in a wilderness landscape by the arrival of the grand camp was wonderful indeed. Instead of Nature's superb silence and majestic loneliness, there was the sound of men's voices in boisterous laughter, or the busy hum of conversation; the loud-resounding stroke of the axe; the sharp report of the rifle; the neighing of horses, and braying of mules; the Indian whoop and yell; and all that not unpleasing confusion of sound which accompanies the movements of the creature of man. Over the plain, only dotted until now with shadows of clouds, or the transitory passage of the deer, the

50

antelope, or the bear, were scattered hundreds of lodges and immense herds of grazing animals ...

If the day was busy and gleesome, the night had its charms as well. Gathered about the shining fires, groups of men in fantastic costumes told tales of marvelous adventures, or sung some old remembered song, or were absorbed in games of chance. Some of the better educated men, who had once known and loved books, but whom mishap in life had banished to the wilderness, recalled their favorite authors, and recited passages once treasured, now growing unfamiliar; or whispered to some chosen confrere the saddened history of his earlier years, and charged him thus and thus, should ever-ready death surprise himself in the next spring's hunt.

It will not be thought discreditable to our young trapper, Joe, that he learned to read by the light of the campfire. Becoming sensible, even in the wilderness, of the deficiencies of his early education, he found a teacher in a comrade, named Green, and soon acquired sufficient knowledge to enjoy an old copy of Shakespeare which with a Bible, was carried about with the property of the camp.[4]

Sometime in January the location for winter quarters was moved over to Powder River due to the severe winter and lack of buffalo. Powder River offered both buffalo and better forage for their animals. The fall catch was cached at Wind River to be dug up next summer when the rendezvous would be held in that location. The mountainmen remained at their winter quarters on Powder River until April. With the coming of spring, the trappers were wading the cold icy streams in search of beaver to be sold at the summer rendezvous.

POPO AGIE RENDEZVOUS
1829

A portion of the 1829 Rendezvous was held on the banks of the Popo Agie River, which flows northeast from the Wind River Range. The picture is taken just east of Lander, Wyoming, looking north. The Popo Agie River is located in the background. On the flat bench areas surrounding the river, a portion of the 1829 Rendezvous was held. Most of the rendezvous site today is in permanent pasture and hay.

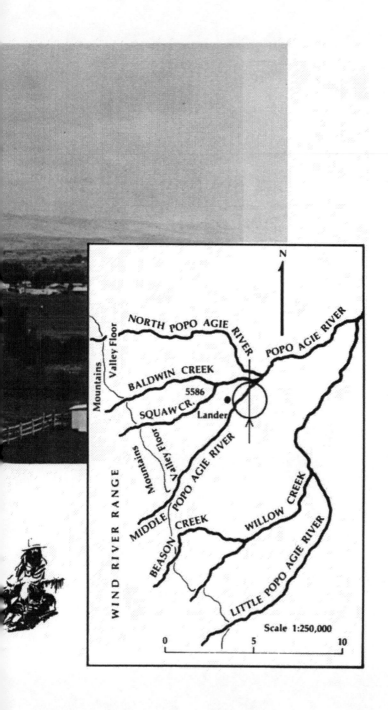

N

NORTH POPO AGIE RIVER

POPO AGIE RIVER

Valley Floor

Mountains

BALDWIN CREEK

5586

SQUAW CR.

Lander

Mountains

Valley Floor

MIDDLE POPO AGIE RIVER

WILLOW CREEK

BEASON CREEK

WIND RIVER RANGE

LITTLE POPO AGIE RIVER

Scale 1:250,000

0   5   10

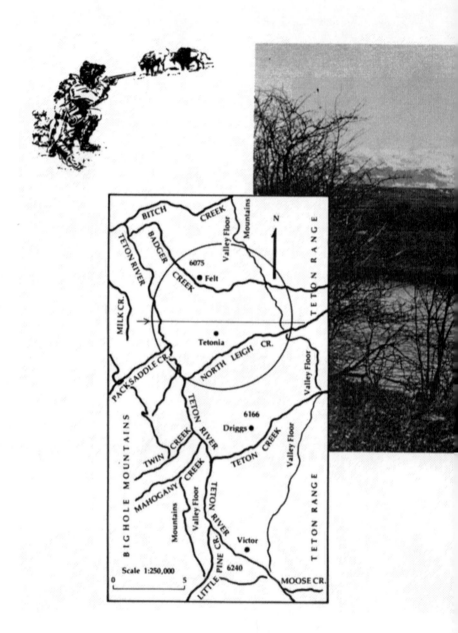

PIERRE'S HOLE RENDEZVOUS
1829, 1832

The picture is taken looking east across Pierre's Hole with the Grand Tetons and the small communities of Felt and Tetonia, Idaho, in the background and the Teton River in the foreground. Pierre's Hole is located at the western base of the Teton Range which straddles the Wyoming - Idaho State line. This beautiful valley surrounded by mountains was a favorite gathering place for the mountainmen and was the site of the 1829 and 1832 Rendezvous. Farm lands cover most of the rendezvous site today.

WIND RIVER RENDEZVOUS
1830

The wagon train that left St. Louis in April of 1830 under the direction of William Sublette was unique. There were ten wagons drawn by five mules each, two Dearborn carriages drawn by one mule each, and twelve head of cattle and one milch cow. Over the last few years, the mountainmen must have wondered if wagons could follow the route up the Platte and over South Pass. The cannon had been brought out in 1827 with no difficulty. So this year Sublette was going to find out. Accompanying Sublette and the wagons west were 81 new recruits, all mounted on mules.

Also in the spring of 1830, the American Fur Company offered the first real rivalry to the firm of Smith, Jackson and Sublette. In February, under the direction of Lucien Fontenelle, Andrew Drips and Joseph Robidoux, the supply train for the American Fur Company left St. Louis. Accompanying the supply train was Warren A. Ferris. It was never to reach the rendezvous or make contact with the free trappers.

Before leaving St. Louis, Sublette renewed his license with William Clark on April 14, and on April 16 reviewed his accounts with Ashley. The firm of Smith, Jackson and Sublette had credit of over $28,000 at the close of 1829. As the supply train pulled out, they were carrying supplies valued at almost $30,000. It was to be a big year. Sublette recorded:

… *our route from St. Louis was nearly due west to the western limits of the State; and thence along the Santa Fe trail about forty miles; from which the course was some degrees north of west, across the waters of the Kanzas and up the Great Platte river, to the Rocky Mountains, and to the head of Wind River, where it issues from the mountains.*[1]

Upon their return to St. Louis in the fall, the partners wrote a letter to the Secretary of War telling him of the feasibility of this route to the Pacific Ocean. Once enroute to the mountains, the caravan butchered eight of the twelve cattle for meat. However, the milch cow arrived safely at the rendezvous, providing a different sort of drinking liquid for the mountainmen assembled there.

Enroute to the rendezvous, the supply train arrived at a landmark, on the Sweetwater on July 4, 1830. Today this landmark bears the name given at that time, "Independence Rock." The rendezvous was held, as Sublette stated at *"the head of Wind River, where it issues from the mountains."*[2] This site is today's Riverton, Wyoming, at the confluences of the Wind River and the Popo Agie River. The site was the same as the location of the Wind River cache of the previous December. William Sublette arrived with supplies in the middle of July. There was a large gathering at the rendezvous.

Meek describes the rendezvous as follows:

... Beaver the currency of the mountain, was plenty that year, and goods were high accordingly. A thousand dollars a day was not too much for some of the most reckless to spend on their squaws, horses, alcohol, and themselves. For "alcohol" was the beverage of the mountaineers. Liquors could not be furnished to the men in that country. Pure alcohol was what they "got tight on;" and a desperate tight it was, to be sure![3]

The fall and spring catch was the biggest yet, consisting of 170 packs of beaver valued at $84,499.14. After paying the $29,177.15 owed for the spring supplies, the partners had left $17,604.33 apiece, plus the $28,160 still on Ashley's books as credit. Yet even with this fantastic year, the partners could see that the future of the fur trade was in question. It was time to get out.

On August 4, 1830, the firm of Smith, Jackson, and Sublette sold out their interest to the partnership of Thomas Fitzpatrick, James Bridger, Milton Sublette, Henry Fraeb and Jean Gervais. The partners called their new company the Rocky Mountain Fur Company. The company was "born in-debt" to the amount of $15,532.22, which was due to Smith, Jackson and Sublette by November 1, 1831.

As mentioned earlier, the American Fur Company came to the mountains under the direction of Fontenelle, Drips and Robidoux. They arrived at the Green River on June 21st. They searched for the rendezvous and the free trappers but did not

A

B

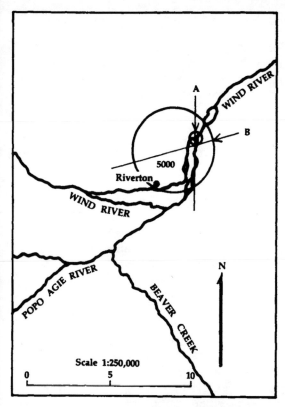

WIND RIVER RENDEZVOUS
1830, 1838

The Rendezvous of 1830 and 1838 were held adjacent to the junction of the Popo Agie River (Little Wind River) and the Wind River. Picture A is taken looking south at the confluence of the Popo Agie (left) and the Wind River (right). Picture B is taken looking southwest. The community of Riverton, Wyoming, can be seen in the background at the extreme left. The heavy brush and timber running through the center of the picture is found on the banks of the rivers before and after their confluences. In the foreground a dirt road can be seen running into the trees at the center-right of the picture. The junction of the rivers is located at approximately where the dirt road enters the trees. On the adjacent plains surrounding the rivers, the Rendezvous of 1830 and 1838 were held. Most of the rendezvous site today remains uncultivated.

find them. They finally cached their supplies and went to the fall hunt. This group spent the winter in Willow Valley with Fraeb and Gervais of the Rocky Mountain Fur Company and some free trappers. With the transfer of ownership, Smith, Jackson, Sublette and 70 men left the mountains in August with their ten wagons and the two Dearborn carriages filled with beaver and the one milch cow.

Before leaving the mountains, men were sent to uncache some furs on the Bighorn River. Then following the usual route, they arrived in St. Louis on October 10, 1830. Smith, Jackson and Sublette turned their catch over to Ashley in November. Ashley advanced the partners $23,000 since it would take almost six months for them to completely settle their fur sales. They needed the funds to commence their new endeavor in the Santa Fe Trade.

As the rendezvous broke up, the mountainmen divided into different groups to trap during the fall, planning to assemble at winter quarters in December. The general winter rendezvous was at the mouth of Powder River on the Yellowstone River. Fitzpatrick, Bridger, and Milton Sublette were there while Fraeb and Gervais wintered in Willow Valley. There were about 200 men at the Yellowstone location.

In early March, Fitzpatrick started out for St. Louis to represent the Rocky Mountain Fur Company in obtaining supplies for the 1831 Rendezvous. Fitzpatrick was taking over the role that William Sublette had played for the last four years. His route was by water, down the Bighorn to the Yellowstone and on to the Missouri, following it to St. Louis, arriving there in early May, 1831.

WILLOW VALLEY RENDEZVOUS
1831

When Thomas Fitzpatrick arrived in Lexington in early May of 1831, he was too late to make arrangements for supplies through the firm of Smith, Jackson and Sublette. They had already left for Santa Fe. Since Smith, Jackson and Sublette had not received word from the Rocky Mountain Fur Company, they left St. Louis thinking that no word was being brought in that spring concerning supplies for the rendezvous. They also figured that if the Rocky Mountain Fur Company really needed supplies, they could work out arrangements from Santa Fe. Fitzpatrick had no alternative but to follow them to Santa Fe and purchase supplies there. It is possible that Smith had left the firm of Smith, Jackson and Sublette and that the caravan that Fitzpatrick traveled to Santa Fe with was under the direction of Jackson and Sublette. While crossing the Cimarron Desert, Jedediah Smith was killed by Comanches. It was also while enroute to Santa Fe that Fitzpatrick found the young Arapahoe Indian boy he named Friday. The caravan arrived in Santa Fe on July 4, 1831. While there, Sublette and Jackson ended their partnership. Jackson continued on to California and Sublette returned to St. Louis. Arrangements were also made for Fitzpatrick to get supplies and for the Rocky Mountain Fur Company, if they so desired, to sell their furs to Jackson's and Sublette's agent, David Waldo, in Santa Fe at $4.25 per pound to pay off the $15,532.22. However, payment had to be made before December 31, 1831.

Leaving Santa Fe with $6,000.00 worth of supplies and heading north, Fitzpatrick employed the services of Kit Carson at Taos. The entire party consisted of about 40 men. They traveled along the front range of the Rockies to North Platte, arriving there in September. Fraeb, who was out searching for his partner, found Fitzpatrick near the Sweetwater. After a few days of encampment together to catch up on the news from the mountains and Santa Fe, Fitzpatrick turned the supplies over to Fraeb and turned east on the ninth of September. Fitzpatrick was certain that the supplies of 1832 would be on time. As Fitzpatrick traveled east, he met trappers at Laramie Creek. This meant more competition for the Rocky Mountain Fur Company. Fraeb turned west to find the mountainmen and to distribute the so terribly needed supplies. At this point, let us drop back to early summer and the mountainmen who were gathering for the rendezvous.

There is a question as to the location of the 1831 Rendezvous. Both Willow Valley and Green River are suggested. It is very possible that both locations had mountainmen eagerly waiting for the supply train. However, there seems to be more evidence that the Willow Valley location was to be the site of the general rendezvous. Once again Joe Meek gives us a description of the rendezvous:

> It was expected that Fitzpatrick would have arrived from St. Louis with the usual annual recruits and supplies of merchandise, in time for the summer rendezvous; but after waiting for some time in vain, Bridger and Sublette determined to send out a small party to look for him. The large number of men now employed, had exhausted the stock of goods on hand. The camp was without blankets and without ammunition; knives were not be had; traps were scarce; but worse than all the tobacco had given out, and alcohol was not! In such a case as this, what could a mountain-man do?[1]

After waiting several weeks and finally realizing that Fitzpatrick was not going to show up, the mountainmen left for the fall hunt without the supplies that they were so desperately in need of. Fraeb set out to find his partner. He had been told by a Crow medicine man that Fitzpatrick was alive but on the wrong trail. After finding Fitzpatrick, Fraeb spent the fall getting the supplies into the hands of the trappers. As Ferris reports:

> Fraeb arrived ... and camp presented a confused scene of rioting, and debauchery for several days, after which however the kegs of alcohol were again bunged, and all become tranquil.
>
> The men provided themselves with lodges, and made preparations for passing the winter as comfortable as possible![2]

Fitzpatrick arrived in St. Louis in early fall to make arrangements for the spring supplies. There had been no furs brought in this year, but they had been cached in the mountains and would be taken back in 1832 by William Sublette.

Winter quarters was held on the Salmon River, with many Flathead and Nez Perce Indians present. Ferris records:

... We purchased all the dried meat the Indians could spare, together with robes, and "appishimous" in addition to our former stock of bedding. Our arrangements completed, we had nothing to do, but to make the time pass as easily as possible. We assembled at each others lodges, and spent the evening merrily, by listening to good humoured stories, and feasting on the best the country afforded, with the frequent addition of a large kettle of coffee, and cakes.[3]

Events were also taking place in the late fall and winter on the part of the American Fur Company that would create keen competition during 1832. Fifty men from Fort Union spent the winter in Willow Valley and forty-eight American Fur Company men under Andrew Drips spent the winter around Laramie Creek.[4]

PIERRE'S HOLE RENDEZVOUS
1832

When Thomas Fitzpatrick arrived in St. Louis in the fall of 1831, he had neither furs nor money and was, consequently, in no position to make arrangements for the supply train in 1832. Fortunately for him, William Sublette advanced sufficient money to pay his winter expenses. However, because of his plight, he was unable to make a very good deal with Sublette to obtain supplies for the coming spring. Sublette took advantage of this situation and, during the winter, set in motion the arrangements that would culminate with a signed agreement at Pierre's Hole in July of 1832, giving him the controlling power as a supplier to the Rocky Mountain Fur Company.

On April 25, 1832, Sublette renewed his license with William Clark, Superintendent of Indian Affairs. He also received a permit to take whiskey into Indian country to be used by his "boatmen." Evidently almost any excuse could be and was used to get around the laws restricting the importing of whiskey to Indian country.

Sublette left St. Louis with 50 men in late April of 1832. Traveling with the supply train were Thomas Fitzpatrick and Robert Campbell. Sublette also took to the rendezvous his younger brother, Andrew Sublette. At Independence they were joined by Nathaniel Wyeth and company.

The supply train pulled out of Independence on May 13, 1832, with 35 men and 300 head of stock. At Laramie Creek it met trappers belonging to the party of John Gantt and Jefferson Blackwell. Fitzpatrick had met Gantt and Blackwell in 1831 at Laramie Creek when he was returning to St. Louis, and Blackwell had accompanied him east. When Fitzpatrick informed the trappers that their leader's firm was bankrupt, the men, under the direction of A.C. Stephens, sold their 120 beaver skins to Fitzpatrick and went on to the rendezvous with the supply train. The historian for this group of trappers was Zenas Leonard, who left an excellent history concerning his visit to the rendezvous.

Fitzpatrick cached the furs at Laramie Creek and set out alone ahead of the supply train to check out the location of Indian tribes with an understanding to meet Sublette on July 2nd at a specified location. Sublette continued with the supplies, crossing South Pass and on toward Green River. Before reaching the Green, Sublette made contact with some American Fur Company trappers and had a run-in with Blackfeet Indians. Joe Meek describes the skirmish as follows:

... camp was suddenly aroused at midnight by the simultaneous discharge of guns and arrows, and the frightful whoops and yells with which the savages made an attack. Nobody was wounded, however; but on springing to arms, the Indians fled, taking with them a few horses which their yells had frightened from their pickets. These marauders were Blackfeet, ... [1]

Nathaniel Wyeth adds this information:

This night at about 12 ock. we were attacked by Indians probably the Blackfoot. They approached within 50 yds. and fired about 40 shots into camp and some arrows they wounded three animals got 5 from Mr. Sublette One from an Independent hunter and 4 which I left out of camp for better feed mine were all poor and sore backed and useless. [2]

On his way to the rendezvous, Sublette ascended the Green River to Hoback River Canyon and followed it into Jackson Hole. From there, he crossed over Teton Pass into Pierre's Hole. Although the mountainmen had assembled there, they had not seen Fitzpatrick. However, he arrived later the same day with two Iroquois half-breeds who had found him almost dead. Fitzpatrick told a tale of nearly meeting death at the hands of Indians, of subsequent escape and flight and of another near escape from death from fatigue and exposure.

The mountainmen had begun to assemble in Pierre's Hole in June. This beautiful valley is named after Pierre Tevanitagon, an Iroquois who originally came to the mountains with the Northwest Fur Company. The weather was cold with rain, snow, and hail into July. Gathered at the rendezvous in 1832 were several different companies including the American Fur Company, the Hudson's Bay Company, the Rocky Mountain Fur Company plus some independent companies such as Bean-

Sinclair. Nathaniel Wyeth, who was to become an interesting figure in the fur trade in the next few years, was also present. In addition, B. L. E. Bonneville, on leave from the army, arrived with his men on Green River. Bonneville remained on the Green and constructed Fort Bonneville near the confluence of Horse Creek and Green River. His fort became known among the mountainmen as "Fort Nonsense," since the winters were so cold and severe that it was almost impossible for the mountainmen to remain in that area. However, the fort proved to be in a strategic location since six rendezvous would be held in that area during the next eight years.

There was keen rivalry among the trappers gathered for the rendezvous, particularly between the American Fur Company and the Rocky Mountain Fur Company. Even though several different companies were located in Pierre's Hole, they remained in separate camps. The festivities of a rendezvous did not completely break down the memories of the previous months when feelings and competition for furs and territory ran exceedingly high.

The American Fur Company trappers were awaiting their supplies which were being brought by Fontennelle from the east and Etienne Provost from Fort Union, which was located at the mouth of the Yellowstone River. With the return of some trappers who had gone to look for the anxiously-awaited supplies, word was brought of the approaching supply train of Sublette and Fitzpatrick. Provost and Fontennelle were not to be found. Sublette's train was the only one to appear at the rendezvous, arriving there on July 8, 1832. The trappers at the rendezvous, under the direction of Vanderburgh and Drips, waited for their supplies in vain. Provost had made it no further than Green River where he made contact with Fontennelle and Bonneville.

Approximately 1000 people, including Nez Perce and Flathead, and between 2000 and 3000 horses and mules gathered at the summer rendezvous, which was one of the largest and most picturesque ever to be held in the mountains. Several of the trappers and army personnel there left accounts of the rendezvous. One of the most complete is that of Joe Meek who leaves the following description:

All the parties were now safely in. The lonely mountain valley was populous with the different camps. The Rocky Mountain and American companies had their separate camps; Wyeth had his; a company of free trappers, fifteen in number, led by a man named Sinclair, from Arkansas, had the fourth; the Nez Perces and Flatheads, the allies of the Rocky Mountain company, and the friends of the whites, had their lodges along all the streams; so that altogether there could not have been less than one thousand souls, and two or three thousand horses and mules gathered in this place.

"When the pie was opened then the birds began to sing." When Captain Sublette's goods were opened and distributed among the trappers and Indians, then began the usual gay carousal; and the "fast young men" of the mountains outvied each other in all manner of mad pranks. In the beginning of their spree many feats of horsemanship and personal strength were exhibited, which were regarded with admiring wonder by the sober and inexperienced New Englanders under Mr. Wyeth's command. And as nothing stimulated the vanity of the mountainmen like an audience of this sort, the feats they performed were apt to astonish themselves. In exhibitions of the kind, the free trappers took the lead, and usually carried off the palm, like the privileged class that they were.

But the horse-racing, fine riding, wrestling, and all the manlier sports, soon degenerated into the baser exhibitions of a "crazy drunk" condition. The vessel in which the trapper received and carried about his supply of alcohol was one of the small camp kettles. "Passing around" this clumsy goblet very freely, it was not long before a goodly number were in the condition just named, and ready for any mad freak whatever. It is reported by several of the mountainmen that on the occasion of one of these "frolics," one of their number seized a kettle of alcohol, and poured it over the head of a tall, lank, redheaded fellow, repeating as he did so the baptismal ceremony. No sooner had he concluded than another man with a lighted stick, touched him with the blaze, when in an instant he was enveloped in flames. Luckily some of the company had sense enough to perceive his danger, and began beating him with pack-saddles to put out the blaze. But between the burning and the beating, the unhappy wretch nearly lost his life, and never recovered from the effects of his baptism by fire.

Beaver being plenty in camp, business was correspondingly lively, there being a great demand for goods.

67

When his demand was supplied, as it was in the course of about three weeks, the different brigades were set in motion. One of the earliest to move was a small party under Milton Sublette, including his constant companion, Meek. With this company, no more than thirty in number, Sublette intended to explore the country to the south-west, then unknown to the fur companies, and to preceed as far as the Humboldt river in that direction.[3]

Warren Ferris adds some information about the exact location of the rendezvous, *"On the 8th sublett arrived, and halted in the middle of the hole, with the R.M.F. Co., for whom he brought one hundred mules, laden with merchandise."*[4] In addition to the descriptions of the rendezvous given by Meek and Ferris, Nathaniel Wyeth leaves the following description:

... arrived at the rendezvous of the hunters of this region here we found about 120 lodges of the Nez Perces and about 80 of the Flatheads a company of trappers of about 90 under Mr. Dripps of the firm of Dripps & Fontennelle connected with the American Fur Co. Many independent Hunters and about 100 men of the Rocky Mountain Fur Co. under Mess Milton Sublette and Mr. Frapp. I remained at this encampment until the 17th during which time all my men but 11 left me to these I gave such articles as I could spare from the necessities of my own Party and let them go. While here I obtained 18 Horses in exchange for those which were worn out and for a few toys such as Beads Bells red and Blue cloth, Powder and Balls fish hooks vermillion old Blankets We also supplied ourselves with Buffaloe robes we have now a good outfit and here we found plenty of meat which can be had of the Indians for a trifle[5]

Robert Newell leaves the following record:

Met all hunters these parts Vanderburgh Drips & Co with about 175 men William Sublette arived with Supplies for our Camp Mr. fitzpatrick who was with Sublette left to come to us but was chased by the indians and Detained and Just escaped death come to us. this is to be Remembered to be the largest party of whites ever Seen together north west or west of the yellow stones mouth or even thare except our American Troops (aug 1832) up the above date I think our number to exceed 350 but not much but in all whites and indians all sorts and kinds of men about 600, (a crimmage with the Black feet —)

Into Rondezvous got our Supplies and Scattered in the following courses to our profession[6]

Zenas Leonard is most specific about the location and the beauty of the scene:

> *There was at this rendezvous at this time, about 400 white people, who lived in constant intercourse with the Flatheads and "Nez Perces," or Pierced Nose tribes, which latter consists of 1000 warriors, ... This valley is situated on the river of the same name, and is from 70 to 80 miles in length, with a high mountain on the east and west — each so high that it is impossible to pass over them, and is from eight to ten miles wide. The river runs immediately through the centre, with a beautiful grove of timber along either bank; from this timber to the mountain, a distance of four or five miles, there is nothing but a smooth plain. This meadow or prairie is so perfectly level that a person may look up or down as far as the eye will reach without meeting anything to obstruct the sight, until the earth and sky appear to meet.*[7]

Captain Bonneville, who was not at the rendezvous but later had contact with several trappers who were present, leaves this account:

> *The valley called Pierre's Hole is about thirty miles in length and fifteen in width, bounded to the west and south by low and broken ridges, and overlooked to the east by three lofty mountains, called the three Tetons, which domineer as landmarks over a vast extent of country.*
>
> *A fine stream, fed by rivulets and mountain springs, pours through the valley toward the north, dividing it into nearly equal parts. The meadows on its borders are broad and extensive, covered with willow and cotton-wood trees, so closely interlocked and matted together as to be nearly impassable.*
>
> *In this valley was congregated the motely populace connect with the fur trade. Here the two rival companies had their encampments, with their retainers of all kinds: traders, trappers, hunters, and half-breeds, assembled from all quarters, awaiting their yearly supplies, and their orders to start off in new directions. Here, also, the savage tribes connected with the trade, the Nez Perces or Chopunnish Indians, and Flatheads, had pitched their lodges beside the streams, and with their squaws, awaited the distribution of goods and finery. There was, moreover, a band of fifteen free trappers, commanded by a gallant leader from Arkansas, named*

69

Sinclair, who held their encampment a little apart from the rest. Such was the wild and heterogeneous assemblage, amounting to several hundred men, civilized and savage, distributed in tents and lodges in the several camps.

> *The arrival of Captain Sublette with supplies put the Rocky Mountain Fur Company in full activity. The wares and merchandise were quickly opened, and as quickly disposed of to trappers and Indians; the usual excitement and revelry took place, after which all hands began to disperse to their several distinations.*[8]

One other interesting account is that given by George Nidever:

> *We arrived at Pierre's Hole just before 4th of July [1832]. On our way we had crossed several mountains, and the last one just before reaching Pierre's Hole. Morning found us wading through the snow on its top and by evening we were in the midst of green grass and summer weather at its foot. At Pierre's Hole we found already arrived some 50 or more hunters and trappers. A few days later, a company of 150 trappers under Wm. Sublette arrived from St. Louis bringing supplies. The second in command, Fitzpatrick, they had lost while crossing Green River. Having gone in advance to reconnoitre, he was cut off by the Indians and so hard pressed that he was obliged to abandon his horse and take to the rocks. His companions supposed him killed.*

A week or so after the arrival of the company, a trapper by name of Poe and I went out for a short hunt, and met Fitzpatrick crossing the Lewis Fork. He was mounted, having by the merest chance caught a horse saddled and bridled, that had escaped from one of the men at Pierre's Hole and wandered to where he was found by Fitzpatrick. Fitzpatrick was shoeless, hatless, and almost naked. In crossing a river his powder horn was lost, and this rendered useless his gun and pistols, which he threw away. For ten days or thereabouts he had wandered about, having in that time eaten of no food excepting a very small piece of dried meat. We piloted him back to camp.

Other hunters, singly and by small companies, continued to arrive at the rendezvous until they numbered in all about 500. This was the favorite rendezvous for trappers West of the Rocky Mts. and had been the center of a rich beaver country. At this time, however, it was well nigh trapped out. The companies then at the rendezvous were, as near as I can remember, William Sublette's, of 150 men — they had come out expressly for trading purposes and returned with about 100 men to St. Louis when the rendezvous broke up; Milton Sublette's, a brother of Wm., composed of about 30 men; Frapp's company, also about 30 men; Wyatt's (Wyeth's) company of emigrants of about 12 to 16, who were going to the mouth of the Columbia to explore (the) country; Perkin's company of about 3 to 5 men.

Our own company had also got together again, making some 14 or 15 more. When we separated on the Green River, the majority of them finally agreed to make a hunt on the Platte River, but having found the country filled with Indians and lost one of their men by them, they turned back. The rest of the trappers at the rendezvous were a class that hunted singly in parts of the Mts. free from the Indians, or in unorganized bands and with no recognized leader; many of these men never leaving the mountains. At the yearly rendezvous they would exchange their pelts for what few supplies they required and then return to the mountains.[9]

Because of the keen competition being given the Rocky Mountain Fur Company by the American Fur Company, the Rocky Mountain Fur Company offered to split up the territory but the American Fur Company declined the offer.

The rendezvous started to break up on July 17th. But, as the mountainmen pulled out, a battle ensued. Joe Meek leaves this account:

71

One of the earliest to move was a small party under Milton Sublette, including his constant companion, Meek. With this company, no more than thirty in number, Sublette intended to explore the country to the south-west, then unkown to the fur companies, and to proceed as far as the Humboldt River in that direction.

On the 17th of July they set out toward the south end of the valley, and having made but about eight miles the first day, camped that night near a pass in the mountains. Wyeth's party of raw New Englanders, and Sinclair's free trappers, had joined themselves to the company of Milton Sublette, and swelled the number in camp to about sixty men, many of them new to the business of mountain life.

Just as the men were raising camp for a start the next morning, a caravan was observed moving down the mountain pass into the valley. No alarm was at first felt, as an arrival was daily expected of one of the American company's partisan's, Fontenelle, and his company. But on reconnoitering with a glass, Sublette discovered them to be a large party of Blackfeet, consisting of a few mounted men, and many more, men, women, and children, on foot. At the instant they were discovered, they rushed down like a mountain torrent into the valley, flourishing their weapons, and fluttering their gay blankets and feathers in the wind. There was no doubt as to the warlike intentions of the Blackfeet in general, nor was it for a moment to be supposed that any peaceable overture on their part meant anything more than that they were not prepared to fight at that particular juncture; therefore let not the reader judge too harshly of an act which under ordinary circumstances would have been infamous. In Indian fighting, every men is his own leader, and the bravest take the front rank. On this occasion there were two of Sublette's men, one a half-breed Iriquois, the other a Flathead Indian, who had wrongs of their own to avenge, and they never let slip a chance of killing a Blackfoot. These two men rode forth alone to meet the enemy, as if to hold a "talk" with the principal chief, who advanced to meet them, bearing the pipe of peace. When the chief extended his hand, Antonio Godin, the half-breed, took it, but at the same moment he ordered the Flathead to fire, and the chief fell dead. The two trappers galloped back to camp, Antoine bearing for a trophy the scarlet blanket of his enemy.

This action made it impossible to postpone the battle, as the dead chief had meant to do by peaceful overtures, until the warriors of his nation came up. The Blackfeet immediately betook themselves to a swamp formed by an old beaver dam, and thickly overgrown with cottonwood and willow, matted together with tough vines. On the edge of this dismal covert the warriors skulked, and shot with their guns and arrows, while in its very midst the women employed themselves in digging a trench and throwing up a breastwork of logs, and whatever came to hand. Such a defence as the thicket afforded was one not easy to attack; its unseen but certain dangers being sufficient to appal the stoutest heart.

Meantime, an express had been sent off to inform Captain Sublette of the battle, and summon assistance. Sinclair and his free trappers, with Milton Sublette's small company, were the only fighting men at hand. Mr. Wyeth, knowing the inefficiency of his men in an Indian fight, had them to take care of themselves, but charged them not to appear in open field. As for the fighting men, they stationed themselves in a ravine, where they could occasionally pick off a Blackfoot, and waited for reinforcements.

Great was the astonishment of the Blackfeet, who believed they had only Milton Sublette's camp to fight, when they beheld first one party of white men and then another; and not only whites; but Nez Perce and Flatheads came galloping up the valley. If before it had been a battle to destroy the whites, it was now a battle to defend themselves. Previous to the arrival of Captain Sublette, the opposing forces had kept up only a scattering fire, in which nobody on the side of the trappers had been either killed or wounded. But when the impetuous captain arrived on the battle-field, he prepared for less guarded warfare. Stripped as if for the prize-ring, and armed cap-a-pie, he hastened to the scene of action, accompanied by his intimate friend and associate in business, Robert Campbell.

At sight of the reinforcements, and their vigorous movements, the Indians at the edge of the swamp fell back within their fort. To dislodge them was a dangerous undertaking, but Captain Sublette was determined to make the effort. Finding the trappers generally disinclined to enter the thicket, he set the example, together with Campbell, and thus induced some of the free trappers, with their leader, Sinclair, to emulate his action. However, the others took courage at this, and advanced near the swamp, firing at random at their invisible foe, who, having the advantage of being able to see them, inflicted some wounds on the party.

The few white "braves" who had resolved to enter the swamp, made their wills as they went, feeling that they were upon perilous business. Sublette, Campbell, and Sinclair succeeded in penetrating the thicket without alarming the enemy, and came at length to a more open space from whence they could get a view of the fort. From this they learned that the women and children had retired to the mountains, and that the fort was a slight affair, covered with buffalo robes and blankets to keep out prying eyes. Moving slowly on, some slight accident betrayed their vicinity, and the next moment a shot struck Sinclair, wounding him mortally. He spoke to Campbell,

requesting to be taken to his brother. By this time some of his men had come up, and he was given in charge to be taken back to camp. Sublette then pressed forward, and seeing an Indian looking through an aperture, aimed at him with fatal effect. No sooner had he done so, and pointed out the opening to Campbell, than he was struck with a ball in the shoulder, which nearly prostrated him, and turned him so faint that Campbell took him in his arms and carried him, assisted by Meek out of the swamp. At the same time one of the men received a wound in the head. The battle was now carried on with spirit, although from the difficulty of approaching the fort, the firing was very irregular.

The mountaineers who followed Sublette, took up their station in the woods on one side of the fort, and the Nez Perces, under Wyeth, on the opposite side, which accidental arrangement, though it was fatal to many of the Blackfeet in the fort, was also the occasion of loss to themselves by the cross-fire. The whites being constantly reinforced by fresh arrivals from the rendezvous, were soon able to silence the guns of the enemy, but they were not able to drive them from their fort, where they remained silent and sullen after their ammunition was exhausted.

Seeing that the women of the Nez Perces and Flatheads were gathering up sticks to set fire to their breastwork of logs, an old chief proclaimed in a loud voice from within, the startling intelligence that there were four hundred lodges of his people close at hand, who would soon be there to avenge their deaths, should the whites choose to reduce them to ashes. This harangue, delivered in the usual high-flown style of Indian oratory, either was not clearly understood, or was wrongly interpreted, and the impression got abroad that an attack was being made on the great encampment. This intelligence occasioned a diversion, and a division of forces; for while a small party was left to watch the fort, the rest galloped in hot haste to the rescue of the main camp. When they arrived, they found it had been a false alarm, but it was too late to return that night, and the several camps remained where they were until the next day.

Meantime the trappers left to guard the fort remained stationed within the wood all night, firmly believing they had their enemy "corraled," as the horsemen of the plains would say. On the return, in the morning, of their comrades from the main camp, they advanced cautiously up to the breastwork of logs, and behold! Not a buffalo skin nor red blanket was to be seen! Through the crevices among the logs was seen an empty fort. On making this discovery there was much chagrin among the white trappers, and much lamentation among the Indian allies, who had abandoned the burning of the fort expressly to save for themselves the fine blankets and other goods of their hereditary foes.

From the reluctance displayed by the trappers, in the beginning of the battle, to engage with the Indians while under cover of the woods, it must not be inferred that they were lacking in courage. They were too well informed in Indian modes of warfare to venture recklessly into the den of death, which a savage ambush was quite sure to be. The very result which attended the impetuosity of their leaders, in the death of Sinclair and the wounding of Captain Sublette, proved them not over cautious.

On entering the fort, the dead bodies of ten Blackfeet were found, besides others dead outside the fort, and over thirty horses, some of which were recognized as those stolen from Sublette's night camp on the other side of the mountains, besides those abandoned by Fitzpatrick. Doubtless the rascals had followed his trail to Pierre's Hole, not thinking, however, to come upon so large a camp as they had found at last. The savage garrison which had so cunningly contrived to elude the guard set upon them, carried off some of their wounded, and, perhaps, also some of their dead; for they acknowledged afterwards a much larger loss than appeared at the time. Besides Sinclair, there were five other white men killed, one half-breed, and seven Nez Perces. About the same number of whites and their Indian allies were wounded.

An instance of female devotion is recorded by Bonneville's historian as having occurred at this battle. On the morning following it, as the whites were exploring the thickets about the fort, they discovered a Blackfoot woman leaning silent and motionless against a tree. According to Mr. Iving, whose fine feeling for the sex would incline him to put faith in this bit of romance, "their surpise at her lingering here alone, to fell into the hands of her enemies, was dispelled when they saw the corpse of a warrior at her feet. Either she was so lost in grief as not to perceive their approach, or a proud spirit kept her silent and motionless. The Indians set up a yell on discovering her, and before the trappers could interfere, her mangled body fell upon the corpse which she had refused to abandon." This version is true in the main incidents, but untrue in the sentiment. The woman's leg had been broken by a ball, and she *was unable to move from the spot where she leaned. When the trappers approached her, she stretched out her hands supplicatingly, crying out in a wailing voice, "kill me! kill me! O white men, kill me!" — But this the trappers had no disposition to do. While she was entreating them, and they refusing, a ball from some vengeful Nez Perce or Flathead put an end to her sufferings.*

Still remembering the threats of the Blackfoot chief, that four hundred lodges of his brethren were advancing on the valley, all the companies returned to rendezvous, and remained for several days, to see whether an attack would take place. But if there had ever been any such intention on the part of the Blackfoot nation, the timely lesson bestowed on their advance guard had warned them to quit the neighborhood of the whites.

Captain Sublette's wound was dressed by Mr. Wyeth's physician, although it hindered his departure for St. Louis for some time, it did not prevent his making his usual journey later in the season. It was well, perhaps, that he did not set out earlier, for of a party of seven who started for St. Louis a few days after the battle, three were killed in Jackson's Hole, where they fell in with the four hundred warriors with whom the Blackfoot chief threatened the whites at the battle of Pierre's Hole. From the story of the four survivors who escaped and returned to camp, there could no longer be any doubt that the big village of the Blackfeet had actually been upon the trail of Capt. Sublette, expecting to overtake him. How they were disappointed by the reception met with by the advance camp, has already been related. [10]

This battle left a deep impression on the chroniclers who were present or who later got a second-hand version of it. The Appendix includes some selected variant versions of the fight.

An agreement was entered into by the Rocky Mountain Fur Company with William Sublette on July 25, 1832, at the rendezvous. The agreement was signed by Thomas Fitzpatrick in behalf of the company. Fitzpatrick was, without question, the business brains behind the Rocky Mountain Fur Company. The agreement contained the following financial stipulation: (1) the Rocky Mountain Fur Company owed $15,620.00 for 1832 supplies; (2) the Rocky Mountain Fur Company owed $20,812.41 for previous debts; and (3) the Rocky Mountain Fur Company owed $10,318.47 for orders and notes due men going to St. Louis.

In further compliance with the agreement, Sublette would transport the furs at a cost of 50¢ per pound to St. Louis at the risk of the Rocky Mountain Fur Company and would sell the furs in St. Louis. Consequently, the company turned over to Sublette 169 packs of beaver weighing 13,719 pounds, 247 pounds of beaver castor and some muskrat and otter pelts. These furs represented two years of fatiguing and dangerous work in the mountains.

Sublette left the rendezvous on July 30th with 60 men, including Robert Campbell. He left Pierre's Hole by way of Teton Pass and ascended the Gros Ventre River over Union Pass. He then descended the Wind River, crossing over to the Sweetwater River and onto the Platte, arriving at Lexington on September 21, 1832, and at St. Louis on October 3, 1832. Surprisingly he was not bothered by Indians on his return trip to the States. Sublette had been requested by the Rocky Mountain Fur Company to contact Ashley, who was now a Senator from Missouri, to see if pressure could be brought upon other fur companies that were encroaching on what the Rocky Mountain Fur Company felt was its territory.

Sublette was able to sell the beaver furs for $58,305.75 at $4.25 per pound. He also received $1,204.06 for the castor. Even with nearly $60,000 received by Sublette from the sale of the furs, the Rocky Mountain Fur Company was still in debt. The agreement signed on July 25th placed the company in debt $46,750 plus a freight bill of $7,171.61, the dealer's commission, and a bill still owed to William Sublette since the formation of the Rocky Mountain Fur Company, with its interest. The Rocky Mountain Fur Company was $5,400 in the red. There were still three packs of beaver not sold which represented about 240 pounds or $1,020 but not enough to pay off the debt.

After Sublette left Pierre's Hole, Vanderburgh and Drips, knowing of Fontennelle's and Provost's presence on the Green River, left the rendezvous on August 2nd to seek them on the Green and to obtain supplies. They immediately set out on the heels of the Rocky Mountain Fur Company trappers. On August 12th Fontennelle and thirty of his men took their furs to the Yellowstone River to ship them to St. Louis. The fall hunt was a continual game of hide and seek between the two companies. The Rocky Mountain Fur Company had the knowledge of the land and the expertise in trapping, but the American Fur

Company had the money and time to make life miserable for its competitor. They had made their intentions clear at the rendezvous when they had turned down the offer to divide the territory between the two companies. Why should they take half when it was but a matter of time until they could have it all.

Fitzpatrick and Bridger purposely led the American Fur Company into Blackfoot country trying to either lose the trappers or let the Blackfeet take care of them. The guise evidently worked for the trappers were attacked. In the melee, Vanderburgh was killed and Jim Bridger wounded in the back by an arrow. The arrowhead remained there until 1835 when Dr. Marcus Whitman removed it at the 1835 Rendezvous. While in Blackfoot country, Fitzpatrick cached all of his supplies on the Salmon River.

Winter quarters was held near the forks of the Salmon River with approximately 90 Rocky Mountain Fur Company trappers present, including all of the partners. Bonneville was at the winter rendezvous busily engaged in building a fort. Ferris leaves the following description of the fort:

This miserable establishment, consisted entirely of several log cabins, low, badly constructed, and admirably situated for besiegers only, who would be sheltered on every side, by timber, brush etc.

I was undeceived, at sight, respecting this "fort" which I had been informed was to be a permanent post for trading with the Indians: but its exposed situation, and total want of pickets, proved that it was only intended for a temporary shelter for the company, during the winter. [11]

Also present was the American Fur Company and numerous Flathead and Nez Perce Indians. Because of the lack of food for the horses and mules, the largest portion of the mountainmen moved their camps in January to the mouth of the Portneuf River, near present day Pocatello, Idaho.

During the winter in St. Louis, William Sublette and Robert Campbell became business partners. They were making plans to challenge the American Fur Company's monopoly on the upper Missouri River in the coming year.

The spring hunt was highly competitive, almost warlike competition, between the two companies. The five partners were feeling the ever-heavy hand of the American Fur Company. It was becoming a pressure with which they could not cope.

GREEN RIVER (SISKEEDEE-AGIE)[1] RENDEZVOUS
1833

After the formation of their St. Louis Fur Company during the winter of 1832-33, William Sublette and Robert Campbell embarked on the very difficult task of challenging the American Fur Company on the upper Missouri. With the arrival of spring weather, Sublette traveled up the Missouri by boat, taking supplies and materials to build posts adjacent to the American Fur Company forts. He was successful in erecting a dozen posts during the spring, summer and fall of 1833. Meanwhile, accompanied by forty to fifty men, including Sir William Drummond Stewart, Charles Larpenteur, Edmund Christy and Ben Harrison, the son of William H. Harrison, who was soon to be President of the United States, Campbell left Lexington, Missouri, in early May, enroute to the rendezvous with yearly supplies valued at $15,000.

Campbell's companions were of a varied sort. The wealthy Scotsman, Stewart, made several trips to the mountains to hunt. Edmund Christy, hoping to make money in the fur business, would join forces with the Rocky Mountain Fur Company at the rendezvous. Ben Harrison had been sent west by his father in the hopes that he would find a cure for his drinking problems. Charles Larpenteur would spend the next forty years as a fur trader on the upper Missouri.

Thomas Fitzpatrick, knowing that no arrangements had been made by the Rocky Mountain Fur Company for supplies, sent Henry Fraeb east to meet the yearly supply train which, they hoped, had left Missouri in early  spring. If, however, Fraeb did not encounter the supply train, he was authorized by the company to continue on to St. Louis and purchase supplies. As a matter of fact, he met Campbell near the mouth of Laramie Creek and made negotiations for the purchase of the supplies. With the transaction completed, Fraeb and Campbell continued to the rendezvous. Don Berry states in **A Majority of Scoundrels** that Fitzpatrick rode out to meet Campbell to turn over the company furs. This seems very unlikely since Campbell traveled on to the rendezvous and stayed there three weeks. There was no need for the exchange to take place prior to the rendezvous. If Fitzpatrick did ride out to meet Campbell, it most likely was to approve the negotiations between Fraeb and Campbell.

The route taken by the supply train after it left the Platte was up the Sweetwater River and across South Pass, then northwest to the confluence of the Green River and Horse Creek, arriving there on July 5, 1833. Fontenelle and Drips, who were to bring the supplies for the American Fur Company, arrived on July 8th. Several narratives taken from the writing of the mountainmen and travelers who were present at the rendezvous give in detail the location and activities of the 1833 Rendezvous.

Nathaniel Wyeth's excellent journal answers many questions concerning the rendezvous. One of the most important being that the central gathering place of the 1833 Rendezvous was at Fort Bonneville. But as the rendezvous progressed the American Fur Company moved approximately five miles downstream, to the junction of Green River and Horse Creek. The Rocky Mountain Fur Company was still five miles further downstream. Consequently, the rendezvous was spread out for about ten miles along the Green. Wyeth reports:

> *15th July. Made E.S.E. 12 miles to Green river and to Mr. Bonnevilles fort day clear and fine. Found here collected Capt. Walker, Bonneville, Cerry, of one Co. Dripps and Fonetenelle of the Am. Fur Co. Mr. Campbell just from St. Louis, Mess. Fitzpatric, Gervais, Milton Sublette of the Rocky Mountain Fur Co. and in all the Cos. about 300 whites and a small village of Snakes here I got letters from home. During the last year among all the Cos there had been in all about 25 men killed two of my original party with them, viz Mr More & O'Neil. (O'Neal?)*
>
> *16th. Same camp.*

GREEN RIVER RENDEZVOUS
1833, 1835, 1836, 1837, 1839, 1840

The Green River Rendezvous site was located adjacent to the confluence of Horse Creek and Green River. Picture A is taken looking northeast. Horse Creek is in the foreground and Green River in the center, running from left to right. The junction can be seen at the right center of the picture. Portions of the Green River rendezvous were held adjacent to Fort Bonneville which was five miles north up Green River. Picture C is taken looking north. Both the stone marker and historical sign, which are now located on the old site of Fort Bonneville, can be seen in the center of the picture. The bluff, running from the center of the picture to the extreme right in the background, is referred to by several travelers and mountainmen in describing the terrain surrounding the Fort. The rendezvous of 1833 had three sites along the Green River. The site downstream from the junction of Horse Creek and Green River is shown in Picture B looking southeast. Across these vast fertile benches six rendezvous were held. Elegant rich hay fields cover most of the rendezvous site today.

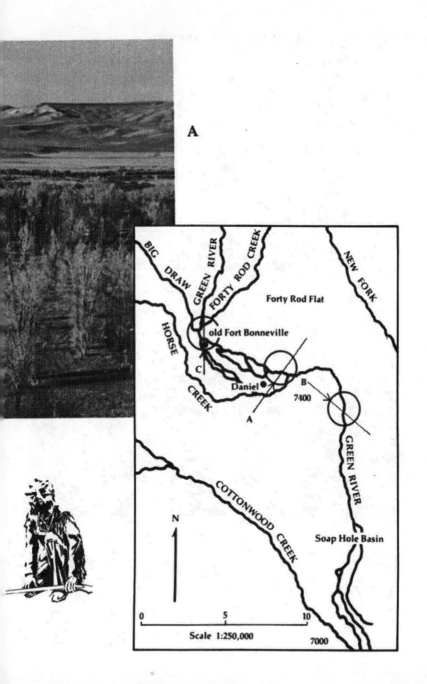

A

BIG DRAW

GREEN RIVER

FORTY ROD CREEK

NEW FORK

Forty Rod Flat

HORSE CREEK

old Fort Bonneville

C

Daniel

B

7400

A

GREEN RIVER

COTTONWOOD CREEK

N

Soap Hole Basin

0   5   10

Scale 1:250,000

7000

B

C

> *17th. Moved 10 miles down the river S.E. it is here a*
> *large and rapid stream and to be forded only in a few places.*
> *Here we were followed by the Snake village we encamped with*
> *the Rocky Mountain Fur Co.*
>
> *18th to the 24 remained at the same camp during which*
> *time the weather was pleasant and warm for several nights we*
> *were an(n)oyed by mad dogs or wolves which I cannot say but*
> *believe the latter as one was killed. I think one animal did the*
> *whole mischief as when men were bitten at one camp none were*
> *at the other about nine persons were bitten at Dripps &*
> *Fontenelles camp and three at ours. D. & Fs. camps is 4 miles*
> *above us on the same side of the river we hope he was not mad as*
> *no simtons have yet appeared.*[2]

Captain Bonneville refers to the lower camps downstream
from his fort where he and his employees gathered. Bonneville
also leaves an excellent account of the activities at the rendezvous
and the details of the attack upon the camps by rabid wolves.

> *The Green River Valley was at this time the scene of one of*
> *those general gatherings of traders, trappers, and Indians, that*
> *we have already mentioned. The three rival companies, which,*
> *for a year past had been endeavoring to out-trade, out-trap and*
> *out-wit each other, were here encamped in close proximity,*
> *awaiting their annual supplies. About four miles from the*
> *rendezvous of Captain Bonneville was that of the American Fur*
> *Company, hard by which, was that also of the Rocky Mountain*
> *Fur Company.*
>
> *After the eager rivalry and almost hostility displayed by*
> *these companies in their late campaigns, it might be expected*
> *that, when thus brought in juxtaposition, they would hold*
> *themselves warily and sternly aloof from each other, and,*
> *should they happen to come in contact, brawl and bloodshed*
> *would ensue.*
>
> *No such thing! Never did rival lawyers, after a wrangle*
> *at the bar, meet with more social good humor at a circuit dinner.*
> *The hunting season over, all past tricks and manoeuvers are*
> *forgotten, all feuds and bickerings buried in oblivion. From the*
> *middle of June to the middle of September, all trapping is*
> *suspended; for the beavers are then shedding their furs and their*
> *skins are of little value. This, then is the trapper's holiday,*
> *when he is all for fun and frolic, and ready for a saturnalia*
> *among the mountains.*
>
> *At the present season, too, all parties were in good*
> *humor. The year had been productive. Competition, by*

threatening to lesson their profits, had quickened their wits, roused their energies, and made them turn every favorable chance to the best advantage; so that, on assembling at their respective places of rendezvous, each company found itself in possession of a rich stock of peltries.

The leaders of the different companies, therefore, mingled on terms of perfect good fellowship; interchanging visits, and regaling each other in the best style their respective camps afforded. But the rich treat for the worthy captain was to see the "chivalry" of the various encampments, engaged in contests of skill at running, jumping, wrestling, shooting with the rifle, and running horses. And then their rough hunters' feastings and carousals. They drank together, they sang, they laughed, they whooped; they tried to out-brag and out-lie each other in stories of their adventures and achievements. Here the free trappers were in all their glory; they considered themselves the "cocks of the walk," and always carried the highest crest. Now and then familiarity was pushed too far, and would effervesce into a brawl, and a "rough and tumble" fight; but it all ended in cordial reconsiliation and maudlin endearment.

The presence of the Shoshonie tribe contributed occasionally to cause temporary jealousies and feuds. The Shoshonie beauties became objects of rivalry among some of the amorous mountaineers. Happy was the trapper who could muster up a red blanket, a string of gay beads, or a paper of precious vermilion, with which to win the smiles of a Shoshonie fair one.

The caravans of supplies arrived at the valley just at this period of gallantry and good fellowship. Now commenced a scene of eager competition and wild prodigality at the different encampments. Bales were hastily ripped open, and their motley contents poured forth. A mania for purchasing spread itself throughout the several bands - munitions for war, for hunting, for gallantry, were seized upon with equal avidity - rifles, hunting knives, traps, scarlet cloth, red blankets, garish beads, and glittering trinkets, were bought at any price and scores run up without any thought how they were ever to be rubbed off. The free trappers, especially, were extravagant in their purchases. For a free mountaineer to pause at a paltry consideration of dollars and cents, in the attainment of any object that might strike his fancy, would stamp him with the mark of the beast in the estimation of his comrades. For a trader to refuse one of these free and flourishing blades a credit, whatever unpaid scores might stare him in the face, would be a flagrant affront scarcely to be forgiven.

Now succeeded another outbreak of revelry and extravagance, The trappers were newly fitted out and arrayed, and dashed about with their horses caparisoned in Indian style. The Shoshonie beauties also flaunted about in all the colors of the rainbow. Every freak of prodigality was indulged to its fullest extend, and in a little while most of the trappers, having squandered away all their wages, and perhaps run knee-deep in debt, were ready for another hard campaign in the wilderness.

During this season of folly and frolic, there was an alarm of mad wolves in the two lower camps. One or more of these animals entered the camps for three nights successively, and bit several of the people.

Captain Bonneville relates the case of an Indian, who was a universal favorite in the lower camp. He had been bitten by one of these animals. Being out with a party shortly afterwards, he grew silent and gloomy, and lagged behind the rest as if he wished to leave them. They halted and urged him to move faster, but he entreated them not to approach him, and, leaping from his horse, began to roll frantically on the earth, gnashing his teeth and foaming at the mouth. Still he retained his senses, and warned his companions not to come near him, as he should not be able to restrain himself from bitting them. They hurried off to obtain relief, but on their return he was nowhere to be found. His horse and his accoutrements remained upon the spot. Three or four days afterwards a solitary Indian, believed to be the same, was observed crossing a valley, and pursued; but he darted away into the fastnesses of the mountains, and was seen no more.

Another instance we have from a different person who was present in the encampment. One of the men of the Rocky Mountain Fur Company had been bitten. He set out shortly afterwards in company with two white men on his return to the settlements. In the course of a few days he showed symptoms of hydrophobia, and became raving toward night. At length, breaking away from his companions, he rushed into a thicket of willows where they left him to his fate![3]

Warren Ferris' narrative is excellent in describing the terrain around Fort Bonneville and details concerning the fort.

With a single companion, I departed on the morning of the

7th, (June) to ascertain if any of our long absent friends who left us at "Pierre's Hole," with John Gray nearly a year since, had arrived at "horse creek," the appointed place of rendezvous. Passing down the plains of Green river, twenty miles, we discovered several squaws scattered over the prairie engaged in digging roots, who informed us that a party of whites and Snakes, were now at Bonneville's fort, a few miles below. We continued on our way down, and found at the place indicated by our informants, Capt. Walker with some of his men, also John Gray, and a small party headed by Fallen and Vanderburgh, who received an outfit from Wm. H. Vanderburgh, in Pierre's Hole last year ... Some fifty or sixty lodges of Snakes lay encamped about the fort, and were daily exchanging their skins and robes, for munitions, knives, ornaments, etc., with the whites, who kept a quantity of goods opened for the purpose of trading in one of the block houses, constituting a part of the fort. This establishment was doubtless intended for a permanent trading post, but its projector, who has, however, since changed his mind, and quite abandoned it. From the circumstance of a great deal of labor having been expended in its construction, and the works shortly after their completion deserted, it is frequently called, "Fort Nonsense." It is situated in a fine open plain, on a rising spot of ground, about three hundred yards from Green River on the west side, commanding a view of the plains for several miles up and down that stream. On the opposite side of the fort about two miles distant, there is a fine willowed creek, called "Horse Creek," flowing parallel with Green river, and emptying into it about five miles below the fortification. The river from the fort, in one direction, is terminated by a bold hill rising to the height of several hundred feet on the opposite side of the creek, and extending in a line parallel with it.

Again on the east side of the river, an abrupt bank appears rising from the water's edge, and extending several miles above and below, till the hills, jutting in on the opposite side of the river; finally conceal it from the sight. The fort presents a square enclosure, surrounded by posts or pickets firmly set in the ground, of a foot or more in diameter, planted close to each other, and about fifteen feet in length. At two of the corners, diagonally opposite to each other, block houses of unhewn logs are so constructed and situated, as to defend the square outside of the pickets, and hinder the approach of an enemy from any quarter. The prairie in the vicinity of the fort is covered with fine grass, and the whole together seems well calculated for the security of both men and horses.

On the 8th, I returned to camp, which had moved down and was now in a fertile bottom fifteen miles below the fort ...

On the 25th, I departed, with some others, to meet with St. Louis Company who were daily expected ...[4]

Fort Laramie. 1867, by A. J. Miller, Public Archives of Canada, C-426.

Joe Meek's biographer leaves, as usual, some exaggerated stories concerning the rabid wolves and has the noted artist, Alfred Jacob Miller, accompanying Sir. William Drummond Stewart to the 1833 Rendezvous. Miller did not come to the mountains until 1837. Also, Meek reported that William Sublette was present at the rendezvous while he was actually several hundred miles away on the upper Missouri. However, the description by Meek to Mrs. Victor of the rendezvous and its activities is certainly of value.

... returning as usual to the annual rendezvous, which was appointed this summer to meet on Green River. Here were the Rocky Mountain and American Companies; the St. Louis Company, under Capt. Wm. Sublette and his friend Campbell; the usual camp of Indian allies; and, a few miles distant, that of Captain Bonneville. In addition to all these, was a small company belonging to Capt. Stuart, an Englishman of noble family, who was traveling in the far west only to gratify his own love of wild adventure, and admiration of all that is grand and

*magnificent in nature. With him was an artist named Miller,
and several servants; but he usually traveled in company with
one or another of the fur companies; thus enjoying their
protection, and at the same time gaining a knowledge of the
habit of mountain life.*

*The rendezvous, at this time, furnished him a striking
example of some of the ways of mountain-men, least to their
honorable fame; and we fear we must confess that our friend Joe
Meek, who had been gathering laurels as a valiant hunter and
trapper during the three or four years of his apprenticeship, was
also becoming fitted, by frequent practice to graduate in some of
the vices of camp life, especially the one of conviviality during
rendezvous. Had he not given his permission, we should not
perhaps have said what he says of himself, that he was at times
often very "powerful drunk."*

*During the indulgence of these excesses, while at this
rendezvous, there occurred one of those incidents of wilderness
life which make the blood creep with horror. Twelve of the men*

were bitten by a mad wolf, which hung about the camp for two or three nights. Two of these were seized with madness in camp, sometime afterwards, and ran off into the mountains, where they perished. One was attacked by the paroxysm while on a hunt; when, throwing himself off his horse, he struggled and foamed at the mouth, gnashing his teeth, and barking like a wolf. Yet he retained consciousness enough to warn away his companions, who hastened in search of assistance; but when they returned he was nowhere to be found. It was thought that he was seen a day or two afterwards, but no one could come up with him, and of course, he too, perished. Another died on his journey to St. Louis; and several died at different times within the next two years.

At the time, however, immediately following the visit of the wolf to camps, Captain Stuart was admonishing Meek on the folly of his ways, telling him that the wolf might easily have bitten him, he was so drunk.

"It would have killed him, sure, if it hadn't cured him!" said Meek, alluding to the belief that alcohol is a remedy for the poison of hydrophobia.[5]

Zenas Leonard who was present at the rendezvous, records the following:

... arrived at the camp of Bowville, which at this time consisted of 195 men, together with a small company belonging to Mackenzie (American Fur Company) from the Missouri river, of 60 men. We were well received by these men, most of whom had been in the woods for several years, and experienced many hardships and privations, similar to what we had suffered. They seemed to sympathize with us about our loss, and all appeared anxious that we should turn in with them and restore our lost fortunes. After we had become thoroughly rested from the fatigue of our long tramp to this post, most of our men hired in different ways with this company. These men had been engaged in trapping in the vicinity of this rendezvous for a long time, and had nearly all the beaver, and were thinking about moving to some other section of the country.[6]

One of the most valuable descriptions of the rendezvous which gives excellent information on the location, activities, and, in particular, the rabid wolves was recorded by Charles Larpenteur:

As near as I can remember we reached the rendezvous on Green river on the 8th of July. There were still some of Capt.

91

Bonneville's men in a small stockade. He had come up the year previous (1832). Thus ended our journey so far.

  The day after we reached the rendezvous Mr. Campbell, with ten men, started to raise a beaver cache at a place called by the French Trou a' Pierre, which means Peter's hole. As I was sick, Mr. Campbell left me in camp, and placed Mr. Fitzpatrick in charge during his absence, telling the latter to take good care of me, and if the man Redman, whom he left as a clerk, did not answer, to try me. In a short time a tent was rigged up into a kind of saloon, and such drinking, yelling and shooting as went on I, of course, never heard before. Mr. Redman, among the rest, finally got so drunk that Mr. Fitzpatrick could do nothing with him, and there was not a sober man to be found in camp but myself. So Mr. Fitzpatrick asked me if I would try my hand at clerking. I remarked that I was willing to do my best, and at it I went. For several days nothing but whisky was sold, at $5 a pint. There were great quarrels and fights outside, but I must say the men were very civil to me. Mr. Fitzpatrick was delighted, and wondered to me why Mr. Campbell had not mentioned me for clerk in the first instance instead of that drunken Redman. After seven or eight days Mr. Campbell returned with ten packs of beaver. A few days afterward the rumor was circulated in camp that he was about to sell out their interest in the mountains to Fitzpatrick, Edmund Christy, Fraep, and Gervais. In the meantime sprees abated, and the trappers commenced to buy their little outfits, consisting of blankets, scarlet shirts, tobacco, and some few trinkets to trade with the Snake Indians, during which transactions I officiated as clerk.

The rumors at last became verified; the sales were effected, but things went on as usual until Mr. Campbell sent for me one morning. On entering his tent I was presented with a good cup of coffee and a large-sized biscuit; this was a great treat, for I believe that it was the first coffee I had drunk since I left Lexington. Then he remarked, "Charles, I suppose you have heard that I sold out our interest in the mountains; but I have reserved all your mess, ten mules, and the cattle (we had four cows and two bulls, intended for the Yellowstone). I have 30 packs of beaver, which Fitz is to assist me with as far as the Bighorn river, where I intend to make skin boats and take my beaver down to the mouth of the Yellowstone. There I expect to meet Sublette, who is to take the packs on to St. Louis. You are one of the ten men whom I have reserved, but Fitz would like much to have you remain with him, and I leave you the choice, to stay with him or come with me." My reply was, "Mr. Campbell, I have engaged to you, you have treated me like a gentleman, and I wish to follow you wherever you go." Upon which he said, "Very well, very well," with a kind smile; "go to your mess." On returning, my messmates asked me what was the result of my visit to the boss; and on being informed, a great shout of joy was the answer. The beaver was all packed and pressed ready for the march; so the next day the order came to catch up the animals, receive our packs, and move camp. This was not our final departure; it was merely to get a fresh grazing ground for the mules and horses.

A day or so later we learned that a mad wolf had got into Mr. Fontenelle's camp about five miles from us, and had bitten some of his men and horses. My messmates, who were old hands, had heard of the like before, when men had gone mad. It was very warm, toward the latter end of July; we were in the habit of sleeping in the open air, and never took the trouble to put up the tent, except in bad weather; but when evening came the boys set up the tent. Some of the other messes asked, "What is that for?" The reply was "Oh, mad wolf come— he bite me." When the time came to retire the pack saddles were brought up to barricade the entrance of our tent, the only one up in camp, excepting that of the boss. After all hands had retired nothing

93

*was heard in the camp except, now and then, the cry of "All's
well," and some loud snoring, till the sudden cry of, "Oh, I'm
bitten!" - then immediately another, and another. Three of our
men were bitten that night, all of them in the face. One poor
fellow, by the name of George Holmes, was badly bitten on the
right ear and face. All hands got up with their guns in pursuit
of the animal, but he made his escape. When daylight came men
were mounted to go in search, but nothing could be seen of him.
It was then thought that he had gone and was not likely to
return, and no further precaution was taken than the night
before. But it seems that Mr. Wolf, who was thought far away,
had hidden near camp; for about midnight the cry of "mad
wolf" was heard again. This time the animal was among the
cattle and bit our largest bull, which went mad afterward on the
Bighorn, where we made the boats. The wolf could have been
shot, but orders were not to shoot in camp, for fear of accidently
killing some one, and so Mr. Wolf again escaped. But we learned
afterward that he had been killed by some of Mr. Fontenelle's
men.*

*As well as I can remember it was the first week in August
when we were ordered to take final leave for the Horn. Our
party was then much reduced; the members of the new company
remained on Green river with the intention, according to
custom, to set out through the mountains so soon as trapping
time commenced.* [7]

On July 18th Nathaniel Wyeth wrote a letter to Mr. F.
Ermatinger of the Hudson's Bay Company from Green River.
Wyeth was not too impressed with the caliber of mountainmen
gathered at the rendezvous, referring to them as *"a great majority
of scoundrels."* He was, however, very impressed with the
efficiency and discipline of Robert Campbell's operations and the
American Fur Company officials.

Green River July 18th 1833

Mr. F. Ermatinger

> *Dear Sir   I arrived here on the 16th 9 days from your
camp Saw no Indians but saw the bones of Mr. More killed by
the Blkfeet last year and buried them. He was one of my men
who left me in Pier(r)es Hole last year. A Mr Nudd was also
killed by them. All the rest arrived well in the States. I found
here about 250 whites. A list of the Cos. and their Beaver which
I have seen I subjoin. I should have been proud of my
countrymen if you could have seen the American Fur Co. or the*

party of Mr. S. Campbell. For efficiency of goods, men, animals and arms, I do not believe the fur business has afforded a better example or discipline. I have sold my animals and shall make a boat and float down the Yellowstone and Missouri and see what the world is made of there. Mr. Wm Sublette and Mr. Campbell have come up the Missouri and established a trading fort at each location of the posts of the Am. Fur Co. with a view to a strong opposition. Good luck to their quarrels. I have got letters from the States ... About 25 American have been killed during the last year. A Snake village is here with us. I find Bonnevilles connections are responsible. (A statement that he has a draft from B. for horses follows but is crossed out.) he being very short of them. He lost one entire part among the Crows that is the Horses and of course all the beavers. A party under Bridger and Frapp also lost their horses by the Aricarees, also Harris party lost theirs by the same Inds. who have taken a permanent residence on the Platte and left the Missouri which is the reason I go by the last named river. Harris party did not interfere with any of my plans south of Snake River.

In my opinion you would have been Robbed of your goods and Bever if you had come here altho it is the west side of the mts. for Green River emtys into the head of the Gulph of California. I give you this as an honest opinion which you can communicate to the co. There is here a great majority of Scoundrels. I should much doubt the personal safety of any one from your side of the house.

My Respects to Mr. Payette and believe me yr. sincere friend

Nathl J. Wyeth

Drips and Fontenelle arrd July 8th 160 men and a good supply of animals. Obtained 51 packs of 100 lbs. ea Beaver.

Rocky Mtn. Fur Co. 55 packs 55 men well supplied one part not in Beaver sent home by Mr. Campbell.

Mess. Bonneville & Co. 22½ packs. Few goods few horses and poor Capt. Cerry goes home B. remains.

Harris party now in hand 7 packs Beaver and are on foot.[8]

From the records that have been left by those present at the rendezvous, it appears that there was present between 250-300 whites with an encampment of Indians, the Shoshones being the most numerous Sir William Drummond Stewart recorded,

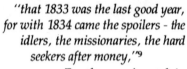

"that 1833 was the last good year, for with 1834 came the spoilers - the idlers, the missionaries, the hard seekers after money,"[9]

For the year's catch in beaver, the American Fur Company had 51 packs; the Rocky Mountain Fur Company 62 packs; Campbell, representing the St. Louis Fur Company, 30 packs; and Bonneville, 22½ packs. Bonneville's catch, which represented one year's work and heavy financial output, was very disappointing. In desperation he offered $1,000 for trappers at the rendezvous to work for him in the coming year. At the close of the summer activities Joseph Walker, with a detachment of approximately 40 men, was sent by Bonneville to California. George Nidever records:

> *In the spring, there were a large number of trappers gathered at the rendezvous in Green River valley and among them Capt. Walker and Company, bound for California. We joined him, making a party in all of 36. Upon the breaking up of the rendezvous we started southward ...*[10]

This expedition in search of beaver was Bonneville's last desperate attempt to make his time spent in the mountains profitable. It, however, failed.

Approximately 165 packs of beaver at 100 pounds per pack left the rendezvous enroute to St. Louis in the possession of the different companies. The 16,500 pounds of beaver valued at $60,000 represented a good year but distributed between four companies made the profits marginal.

Another event that took place at the Green River Rendezvous was the formation of a new company called the Rocky Mountain Fur Company and Christy. As previously mentioned, Edmund Christy had traveled to the mountains with Campbell. The new company was organized on July 20, 1833, and was to operate one year. Christy invested $6,607.82½ into the company. He was to be paid in beaver at the rendezvous at $3.25 per pound. The five original partners were not slow to accept a new partner, particularly one with ready cash. At the close of the rendezvous, Christy took 25 men and set out to trap the Snake River country. There is very little information on this company and Edmund Christy.

Even though the year's work had produced 62 packs of fur for the Rocky Mountain Fur Company, valued at $21,000 in St. Louis, the company was heavily in debt to Sublette and Campbell. After paying 50¢ per pound for the transportation charges to St. Louis the furs were worth $18,000 to the company. When the company was through paying the $5,000 they owed William Sublette plus the $15,000 for supplies, they were in debt over $1,000. They still owed their own 55 men for the year's work. It is conservative to put the total indebtedness of the Rocky Mountain Fur Company at $15,000 which was drawing interest at 6-8%. Sublette and Campbell had a death grip on the Rocky Mountain Fur Company, one which Fitzpatrick and his associates would soon try to break in a secret agreement with Nathaniel Wyeth.

The rendezvous broke up on July 24, 1833. Fitzpatrick and Milton Sublette left with Campbell. Accompanying them was Wyeth and Sir William Drummond Stewart. They traveled north to where the Wind River becomes the Bighorn River, at present day Thermopolis.

Here they constructed bull boats to transport the furs to the Missouri River. The reason for taking the river route back to St. Louis was two-fold. First, Campbell, was to meet William Sublette on the upper Missouri and, second, the Arikaras were raiding travelers along the Platte. M. S. Cerre, who was taking Bonneville's furs east also took the water route back to St. Louis. However, Etienne Provost, in charge of the American Fur Company's furs, took the Platte route and was successful in arriving at Fort Pierre without any trouble with the Arikaras.

On August 14, 1833, on the Bighorn River prior to departure, Fitzpatrick and Milton Sublette entered into a contract with Wyeth to bring supplies to the 1834 Rendezvous by July 1, 1834. Wyeth was to be paid the price of the supplies plus $3,521 at the rendezvous. The contract was conditional upon the company staying in business until the next summer and Wyeth being able to find financial backers in the east. Each party put up a $500 bond which would be forfeited if the conditions were not kept. The contract specified that the supplies would not cost more than $3,000 nor weigh over 8,000 pounds. The debt to Wyeth was to be paid in beaver at $4.00 per pound. The company gave Christy a much better deal on the price of the beaver than they were giving Wyeth. Wyeth figured he could bring $3,000 worth of supplies to the rendezvous from Vancouver for $4,554; the same would cost $11,382 from St. Louis. If Wyeth's figures are correct, the cost to the company would be $6,521. But the same amount of supplies would cost $15,000 from Sublette and Campbell, so here was the chance to break the stranglehold that Sublette and Campbell had on the company. The problem was how to keep the agreement a secret.

With the completion of the bull boats, Milton Sublette and Wyeth accompanied Campbell to the mouth of the Yellowstone River. Fitzpatrick did not accompany his partner but turned east with 30 men for the fall hunt and to show Sir William Drummond Stewart the land of "Absaroka."During the trip Fitzpatrick was robbed of everything he had by the Crow Indians. He finally regained some of his personal effects but lost all the furs. The furs eventually found their way into the hands of the American Fur Company. Fitzpatrick with just cause, blamed the American Fur Company for the robbery and the loss of the furs.

Campbell met William Sublette at the mouth of the Yellowstone where they started construction of Fort William three miles below Fort Union, which was owned by American Fur Company. Campbell was left in charge of the building and William Sublette took the furs down river to St. Louis. During the fall and winter of 1833 Kenneth McKenzie, in command of the American Fur Company forts on the upper Missouri, financially destroyed the St. Louis Fur Company by giving exhorbitant prices ($12) for beaver. Sublette and Campbell could not compete with this price. The American Fur Company, with their money and experience, won the competition. Sublette and Campbell decided that they would try to get out before they lost everything. Campbell remained on the river to try to make some kind of deal with McKenzie, while Sublette went to New York to talk business with the owners.

Even though McKenzie was destroying the opposition, the American Fur Company was worried. John Jacob Astor was retiring and the American Fur Company was going to lose his backing plus his political influence. Added to this was the threat of Ashley's influence in behalf of Sublette and Campbell, since Ashley was now a senator from Missouri. Also, the American Fur Company was in trouble with the government over a still being operated at Fort Union. With this uncertainty on the part of the American Fur Company, William Sublette, in February, 1834, was able to sell out all of his and Campbell's interest on the river at a good price and obtain an agreement from the American Fur Company that they would stay out of the mountains the ensuing year, 1835. Sublette had worked a miracle.

Thus at the end of 1833, the American Fur Company had taken another step closer in controlling the western fur trade. However, Sublette and Campbell were now free to put all of their attention and efforts to the fur trade in the mountains which at that time was being threatened by Wyeth. A letter written in October, 1833, at Hams Fork by Fitzpatrick to Milton Sublette reveals Fitzpatrick's great concern on the possible repercussions over the company's agreement with Wyeth. It would appear that Fitzpatrick was having second thoughts. Thus, the stage was set for the showdown at the 1834 Rendezvous.

A

B

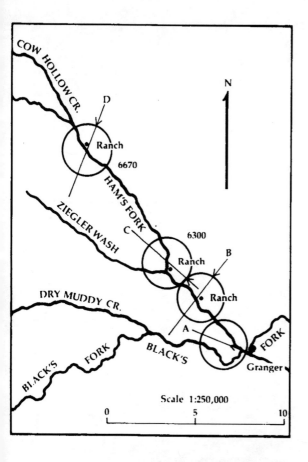

HAM'S FORK RENDEZVOUS
1834

There were four different rendezvous on Ham's Fork. Picture A is taken looking west at the junction of Black's (left) and Ham's (right) Fork. This was the rendevous site of the American Fur Company. Picture B is taken looking southwest. Ham's Fork is in the background at the base of the bluffs. The river flows from the extreme right to the extreme left of the picture. This was the first location of the Rocky Mountain Fur Company and Nathaniel Wyeth on Ham's Fork. Picture C is taken looking northwest. Ham's Fork can be seen in the background with the banks of the river covered with heavy brush. This site was the second site of the Rocky Mountain Fur Company, a few miles upstream from their first site (B) and 8 miles from the junction of Ham's and Black's Fork (A). Picture D is taken looking southwest. The banks of Ham's Fork can be seen covered with brush. This site was Nathaniel Wyeth's second location when he moved upstream 10 miles from site (B). The Ham's Fork River valley in these areas are only fertile close to the river. Consequently, the rendezvous locations were spread out along the river for some distance. Plus, it forced the companies to move the rendezvous sites upstream for better pasture. Today there are hay ranches located at the three rendezvous sites on Ham's Fork (B), (C), (D).

C

D

HAM'S FORK RENDEZVOUS
1834

Several important things happened in the east during the winter and spring of 1833-1834 that had a great impact on the upcoming rendezvous. As mentioned earlier, William Sublette had performed a miracle in selling his and Campbell's holdings on the upper Missouri to the American Fur Company. Also, during the winter, the leadership of the American Fur Company changed when John Jacob Astor ended his career with the company by going into retirement and selling his holdings of the western department to Pratte, Chouteau and Company of St. Louis. In January Milton Sublette met Wyeth in Boston and, after Wyeth had secured backing from Henry Hall and Mess. Tucker and Williams, they traveled to New York, Philadelphia and Baltimore to obtain supplies for the 1834 Rendezvous. Wyeth also bought supplies to be shipped around the Horn to Vancouver. The ship was then supposed to take a cargo of salmon back to New York. But, as fate had planned for Wyeth, the ship was struck by lightning and detained and consequently missed the salmon season.

When William Sublette returned to St. Louis after his settlement with the American Fur Company, he met Campbell and first became aware of the Rocky Mountain Fur Company and Christy's agreement with Wyeth. Moses Harris, Sublette's old traveling partner, had arrived in St. Louis from the mountains, accompanied by Ben Harrison, who brought with him at least two letters from Thomas Fitzpatrick. One was for William Ashley asking him for some Government pressure to be put on the American Fur Company since he was still fuming over the loss of his company's furs to the AFC. The contents of the other letter written to Milton Sublette contained information pertaining to the Fitzpatrick-Wyeth agreement and was given to Sublette's brother, William. The agreement of the Rocky Mountain Fur Company and Christy was, therefore, no longer a secret. William Sublette was now alerted to the attempt of that company to break his and Campbell's control over them. Wyeth reveals in his writings that he blamed Harrison for opening Fitzpatrick's letter and giving its contents to Sublette.

With this new information, William Sublette realized that many of the agreements and guide lines that he had made with the American Fur Company in February would now be jeopardized if Wyeth succeeded in getting supplies to the 1834 Rendezvous before his and Campbell's supply train got there. Sublette had told the American Fur Company that the Rocky Mountain Fur Company and Christy was ready to fold and part of their deal was based upon that happening. Wyeth was getting in the way. Furthermore, it did not sit well with William Sublette that his own brother was part of this new problem. William told Milton that if he tried to leave St. Louis, he would not honor certain drafts being held by Campbell and him. However, Wyeth loaned Milton $500 to pay William the debt. William had left New York thinking that he had the mountain fur trade to himself and Campbell, since the American Fur Company had promised to stay out of the mountains for the year of 1835. Now, however, the race to the rendezvous was on.

Wyeth left Independence on April 28, 1834, seven days before Sublette. Accompanying him was Joseph Thing, a Boston sea captain who was second in command. The rest of the group consisted of Milton Sublette, Jason Lee, a Methodist minister, and his four companions, and two naturalists, Thomas Nutall and Kirk Townsend, plus 75 other men and 250 horses. Milton Sublette was forced to return to the settlement on May 8th because of trouble with his leg. The diseased leg would cause his death on April 5, 1837, after an unsuccessful amputation.

William Sublette did not get away from Independence until May 5th. He was accompanied by William Anderson, who left one of the most important diaries of western travel. Sublette had under his command 37 men and 95 horses. Also leaving Missouri for the rendezvous was Michael S. Cerre with supplies for Bonneville and Fontenelle and with supplies for the American Fur Company. The route to the rendezvous was up the Platte following the Sweetwater over South Pass and descending the Sandy to its mouth at Green River. In a letter to Milton Sublette,

Fitzpatrick told Milton not to go as high as Horse Creek, but to go to the mouth of the Sandy River. It did not take William Sublette long to catch Wyeth. On May 12th, after just one week on the trail, Sublette passed Wyeth during the night. When Sublette reached Laramie Creek, he left 14 men, including William Patton who was in charge of starting construction on Fort William. The fort was a product of the deal between Sublette and the American Fur Company. Sublette needed a supply base from which he could work his mountain fur trade. When Wyeth passed Laramie Creek just a few days later, he found the men busily engaged on the construction of the fort.

When Wyeth arrived at Independence Rock on June 9th, he wrote Fitzpatrick a letter asking him not to trade with Sublette and informing him that Milton had returned to St. Louis because of his leg. He told Fitzpatrick that he would arrive at the rendezvous no later than July 1st. While enroute to the rendezvous, Jason Lee described an event that gives some insight to the callousness of most mountainmen. While hunting buffalo with one of the mountainmen, Lee and Townsend learned the meaning of "mountainmen cider." Townsend recorded:

> ... with his knife opened the body, so as to expose to view the
> great stomach, and still crawling and twisting entrails ... we
> saw out hunter plunge his knife into the distended paunch,
> from which gushed the green and gelatinous juices, and then
> insinuate his pan into the opening, and by depressing its edge,
> strain off the water which was mingled with its contents.[1]

The two easterners were still a little too "greenhornish" to try the western beverage. However, Townsend, being thirsty, was persuaded to drink some blood directly from the heart of the dead animal.

Sublette reached the Green River at the mouth of the Sandy River on June 13th. On the 15th he made contact with Fitzpatrick who was encamped about 12 miles upstream on the Green River. Sublette moved his camp on June 18th to Fitzpatrick's encampment. They decided, because of the need of better pasture, that the rendezvous would be held on Ham's Fork, a branch of Black's Fork of Green River. Sublette and Fitzpatrick's combined parties moved to Ham's Fork on June 19th.

Wyeth, desperately trying to catch Sublette and to find Fitzpatrick, left his camp, which was located about 25 miles up the Sandy River from its confluence with the Green River, on the evening of June 17th. He arrived at the Green on the 18th and went to the junction of Green and Sandy Rivers. Finding no one there, he turned and went upstream 12 miles where he found the encampment of Fitzpatrick and his rival, Sublette. Wyeth indicates in his journal:

> ... and much to my astonishment the goods which I had contracted to bring up to the Rocky Mountain Fur Co. were refused by those honorable gentlemen.[2]

The race was over. Sublette had been victorious again in winning the race to supply the summer rendezvous.

The rest of Wyeth's party arrived on the Green River on June 19th and camped one mile upstream from the junction of the Green and Sandy Rivers. Since Fitzpatrick and Sublette had moved to Ham's Fork, it became necessary for Wyeth to follow them. Wyeth then returned to his own camp, arriving about noon on June 19th. Under the date of June 20th, Wyeth leaves in his journal the directions that he took to the rendezvous on Ham's Fork:

> ... Made W.S.W. 8 miles then S. by E. 15 miles to Ham's Fork Fork running S.E. and a small stream.[3]

Wyeth's directions are in error. It is apparent that Wyeth meant S. by W. 15 miles instead of S. by E. 15 miles. Cyrus Shepard, one of Jason Lee's group, recorded the following regarding the directions taken from Wyeth's camp on the Green River and the distance traveled to the Ham's Fork Rendezvous.

> ... Traveled across the prairie in a Southwesterly direction for Ham's Fork, expected distance ten or twelve miles it however proved to be at least twenty five - and both men and animals were nearly exhausted when we arrived at said fork. This fork is the place selected for rendezvous this season for the companies in the mountains. Made our encampment about two miles below the general rendezvous.[4]

Jason Lee recorded the following pertaining to their location:

> ... we call this rendezvous or the place where all the companies in the Mountains or in this section of them have fixed upon to meet for the transaction of business. Some of the companies have not come in yet most of them are a mile above us on the same creek.[5]

Fitzpatrick and Sublette's first encampment on Ham's Fork

was approximately five miles from the confluence of Black's Fork and Ham's Fork. According to Lee and Shepard, they encamped about one to two miles down stream from Fitzpatrick.

At this point we must stop and examine Wyeth's dilemma in hearing that his agreement with Fitzpatrick was broken. From the rendezvous on Ham's Fork Wyeth wrote several letters to friends and business partners in the east. In examining three of these letters, we can recapture Wyeth's feelings on that occasion. The first letter written to Milton Sublette on July 1st contained the following:

... I arrived at Rendezvous at the mouth of Sandy on the 17th June. Fitzpatrick refused to receive the goods he paid however, the forfeit and the cash advance I made to you this however is no satisfaction to me. I do not accuse you or him of any intention of injuring me in this manner when you made the contract but I think he has been bribed to sacrifice my interests by better offers from your brother. Now Milton, business is closed between us,

but you will find that you have only bound yourself over to receive your supplies at such price as may be inflicted and that all you will ever make in the country will go to pay for your goods, you will be kept as you have been a mere slave to catch Beaver for others.

I sincerly wish you well and believe had you been here these things would not have been done. I hope that your leg is better and that you will yet be able to go whole footed in all respects.[6]

The second letter, also dated July 1st, was written to Mess. Tucker and Williams.

Gent. I arrived here on the 17th inst. and Wm Sublette arrived two days before me. This he was enabled to do by leaving one half of his goods and horses on the route, which of course I could not do. On arrival the Rocky Mountain Fur Co. refused to receive the goods alledging that they were unable to continue business longer, and that they had dissolved, but offered to pay the advances made to M.G. Sublette and the Forfeit. These terms I have been obliged to accept altho they would not even pay the interest on cash advances for there is no Law here. I have also sold a few goods at low prices. The proceeds of the Forfeit &c and Sales after deducting a small amt. for payment of wages of men who have gone home, from this place, I have forwarded to Mess. Von Phull & McGill of Saint Louis subject to your order, in one draft four months from date July 1st 1834 for $864.12½ and for $1002.81 same date 12 months both by Fitzpatric Sublette & Bridger, accepted by Sublette & Campbell of St. Louis.

In addition to not fulfilling their agreement with me every exertion is made to debauch my men in which they have had some success, but I have hired enough of theirs to make up, and do not fear falling short of troops. These circumstances induce me to quit their neighborhood as soon as possible.

I shall proceed about 150 miles west of this and establish a fort in order to make sales of the goods which remain on my hands. I have sent out messengers to the Pawnacks, Shoshonees, Snakes, Nez Perces and Flatheads to make robes and come and trade them at this Post. I am under the impression that these Indians will make a good quantity of Robes whenever they find they can sell them and I believe the Transportation will not be too expensive for the value of the article besides which

I have no doubt that tolerable good returns of Beaver may be made at this post. I propose to establish it on a river called Portneuf on Snake or Lewis River.

I feel much disappointed that the contract was not complied with. Had M.G. Sublette been able to come I think it would have been. I much fear that the gentlemen at home will get discouraged if no returns are made the first year. I shall do the best I can but cannot now promise anything immediate ...

Bonneville & Co. I have not seen, but he is not far from me on my proposed route. I fear that he has done nothing of consequence. I shall endeavour to take home his Beaver what there is of it if I can get an adequate price. I think his concern is finished ...

I have now with me 126 horses and mules in good order and 41 persons all told that are in the employ, and can hire as many more as I want. The amount due for wages is trifling. Almost all the men take up as fast as they earn, and would faster if I would let them, in goods at about 500 per ct. on the original cost. Our expenses after this year will be very small, and I have strong hopes as ever of success notwithstanding appearances so far.[7]

At Bear River on July 5th, Wyeth wrote his friend Ermatinger of Hudson's Bay Company and repeated his earlier statement:

I have again to repeat to you the advise which I before gave to you not to come with a small party to the Am. Rendezvous. There are here a collection of Scoundrels.[8]

As Wyeth mentions in his letters, he was paid the $500 that the Rocky Mountain Fur Company and Christy forfeited for not keeping their agreement and he was also reimbursed the $500 Wyeth had lent Milton in St. Louis to pay off his brother. Wyeth left the rendezvous on July 2nd and on August 6th, 1834, established Fort Hall, named after Henry Hall, one of his backers, near the junction of the Portneuf and Snake Rivers. In 1836 Wyeth sold out to the Hudson's Bay Company.

On June 20th the Rocky Mountain Fur Company and Christy was dissolved. Henry Fraeb was the first to sell out. He received 40 horses, 40 traps, 8 guns and $1,000 worth of merchandise. Jean B. Gervais was next to sell, acquiring 20 horses, 30 beaver pelts and $500 worth of merchandise. A public notice was issued:

Whereas a dissolution of partnership having taken place by mutual consent between Thos Fitzpatrick, Milton G. Sublette, John Baptiste Gervais and James Bridger members of the Rocky Mountain Fur Company all persons having demands against said company are requested to come forward and receive payment, those indebted to said firm are desired to call and make immediate payment as they are anxious to close the business of the concern.

Wm L Sublette for   *Thos Fitzpatrick*
Bridger & Fitzpatrick   *M G Sublette*
                       Henry Fraeb
                       J B Gervais
                       his
                       James X Bridger
                       mark[9]

With the dissolvement of the Rocky Mountain Fur Company and Christy, Fitzpatrick organized a new company calling it the Fitzpatrick, Sublette and Bridger Company. This company was so short lived that it was only a company on paper.

The Public are hereby notified that the business will in future be conducted by Thos Fitzpatric, Milton G. Sublette & James Bridger under the style & firm of Fitzpatrick, Sublette and Bridger.

Wm Sublette   *Thos Fitzpatrick*
                M G Sublette
                his
                James X Bridger
                mark[10]

It is interesting to note that Bridger and Milton Sublette were not even present at the dissolvement of the old company and the formation of the new one which bore their names. Bridger did not arrive at the rendezvous until June 25th and Milton was in St. Louis.

The exact date that Drips and Fontenelle arrived at the rendezvous is not certain, but they established their camp at the mouth of Ham's Fork. Fontenelle was successful in picking up some of the trappers from the old Rocky Mountain Fur Company. Wyeth also had no trouble acquiring men before he left the rendezvous on July 2nd.

Breaking up Camp at Sunrise. 1867, by A. J. Miller, Public Archives of Canada, C-427.

With the arrival of Bridger and his men on the 25th, Wyeth moved upstream 10 miles. Evidently he was anxious to put as many miles as possible between himself and his old partners. Wyeth recorded:

> Moved up the river N.W. 10 miles grass here pretty good but little timber and none but willows for the last 6 miles.[11]

Wyeth remained at this location until July 2nd. On the 28th of June, Fitzpatrick and Sublette and combined companies moved upstream for better pasture. Anderson writes: "We left our first lodgement on Ham's Fork and pitched our tents a few miles above on the same stream.[12] They remained there until Sublette had left for St. Louis, which, in effect, ended the rendezvous. On July 12th those still at the encampment moved upstream 15 to 20 miles.

Anderson's journal reveals that the June 28th encampment for Fitzpatrick and Sublette was 8 miles upstream from the mouth of Ham's Fork and the camp of the American Fur Company. Anderson recorded:

> Paid a visit to the American Fur Company about eight miles below at the junction of Hams Fork and Blacks Fork. This company is conducted by Dripps and Fontenelle. Rice pudding &c in the mountains were not unwelcome, but most unexpected rarities.[13]

Thus on June 28th there were still three camps along Ham's Fork. The American Fur Company was still at the mouth of Ham's Fork. Fitzpatrick and Sublettes' camp was 8 miles

111

upstream and Wyeth's camp was 14 miles upstream from the mouth of Ham's Fork. Jason Lee records in his journal that on July 2nd he traveled a few miles downstream to Sublette's camp. Lee wrote: *"This day sealed a long communication to Dr. Fisk and carried them down to Wm Sublett's camp."*[14]

Cyrus Shepard recorded about the visit:

> *Rode with J. Lee to Messers Sublette's & Fitzpatrick's camp a few miles down Creek, were politely received & took tea with Mr. S and returned to camp soon after Sun set.*[15]

Bonneville was not present at the 1834 Rendezvous but supplies were delivered to him on Bear River by Cerre. On July 9th, Fitzpatrick paid William Sublette $1,258.66 plus interest for the note of 1833 plus $10,183 for the 1834 supplies. Also on July 9th, Edmund Christy gave a note valued at $2,355 due him by Fitzpatrick which they could not pay. The note was to be paid in full by 1836. Apparently, the new firm of Fitzpatrick, Sublette and Bridger was still unable to pay its debts and was heavily in debt to Sublette and Campbell. Very probably Sublette forced the dissolvement of the Rocky Mountain Fur Company and Christy since he was holding the debts of Christy and two fifths of the debts of Fraeb and Gervais. Consequently, Sublette had been able to keep his word to the American Fur Company that the Rocky Mountain Fur Company was going to fold. Sublette left the rendezvous on July 10th, 1834, accompanied by Christy and Cerre. Several journals contain excellent accounts of the activities of the 1834 Rendezvous.

Anderson recorded on June 26th: *"Nothing in the camps, now but drunken songs & brawls day or night ..."*[16] He also leaves an excellent description of the activities on July 4th:

> *Startled this morning by the loud, & quick rattle of fire arms, & the rapid irregular hooping, each man sprang to his gun and prepared for action. For a moment there was a most singular scene of hurry & confusion, & alarm, but lo! the magic words '4th of July' charmed all into order & security. Laughter & jesting succeeded to preparation or trepidation. This evening both camps are nearly deserted from vanity -- Mr. Fitzpatrick & Mr Sublette have gone, attended by the greater part of both parties, bearing two flags, to return a visit made us yesterday by the Ameri. Fur Comp. & to outbrag them, if practicable. Two race horses are taken down to sweat for their folly or convince where their arguments avail naught ...*[17]

There was some degree of law throughout the camps. Anderson recorded on July 8th: *"Rode down to Dripps camp to defend a murderer but conscience made a coward of him and he fled."*[18]

Captain Thing, traveling with Wyeth and second in command, recorded:

> *The mountain men are all assembled on this river this season for Rendezvous and as crazy a set of men as I ever saw, drinking is the order of the day and trade is then best effected as it seems, two or three glasses of grog is the best introduction to trade for that is the time men feel the richest and can buy all the world in thirty minutes, in particular if you will trust them.*[19]

Townsend's description of the rendezvous follows:

> *22d - We are now lying at the rendezvous. W. Sublette, Captains Cerre, Fitzpatrick, and other leaders, with their companies are encamped about a mile from us, on the same plain, and our own camp is crowded with a heterogeneous assemblage of visitors. The principal of these are Indians, of the Nez Perce, Bannock and Shoshone tribes, who come with the furs and peltries which they have been collecting at the risk of their lives during the last winter and spring, to trade for ammunition, trinkets, and "fire water." There is, in addition to these, a great variety of personages amongst us; most of them calling themselves white men, French-Canadians, half-breeds, &c., their color nearly as dark, and their manners wholly as wild, as the Indians with whom they constantly associate. These people, with their obstreperous mirth, their whooping, and howling, and quarrelling, added to the mounted Indians, who are constantly dashing into and through our camp, yelling like fiends, the barking and baying of savage wolf-dogs, and the incessant cracking of rifles and carbines, render our camp a perfect bedlam. A more unpleasant situation for an invalid could scarcely be conceived. I am confined closely to the tent with illness, and am compelled all day to listen to the hiccoughing jargon of drunken traders, the sacre and foutre of Frenchmen run wild, and the swearing and screaming of our own men, who are scarcely less savage than the rest, being heated by the detestable liquor which circulates freely among them.*
>
> *It is very much to be regretted that at times like the present, there should be a positive necessity to allow the men as much rum as they can drink, but this course has been*

sanctioned and practised by all leaders of parties who have hitherto visited these regions, and reform cannot be thought of now. The principal liquor in use here is alcohol diluted with water. It is sold to the men at three dollars the pint! Tobacco, of very inferior quality, such as could be purchased in Philadelpha at about ten cents per pound, here brings two dollars! and everything else in proportion. There is no coin in circulation, and these articles are therefore paid for by the independent mountain men, in beaver skins, buffalo robes, &c., and those who are hired to the companies, have them charged against their wages.

I was somewhat amused to-day by observing one of our newly hired men enter the tent, and order, with the air of a man who knew he would not be refused, twenty dollars worth of rum, and ten dollars worth of sugar, to treat two of his companions who were about leaving the rendezvous!

30th - Our camp here is a most lovely one in every respect, and as several days have elapsed since we came, and I am convalescent, I can roam about the country a little and enjoy it. The pasture is rich and very abundant, and it does our hearts good to witness the satisfaction and comfort of our poor jaded horses. Our tents are pitched in a pretty little valley or indentation in the plain, surrounded on all sides by low bluffs of yellow clay. Near us flows the clear deep water of the Siskadee, and beyond, on every side, is a wide and level prairie, interrupted only by some gigantic peaks of mountains and conical butes in the distance. The river, here, contains a great number of large trout, some grayling, and a small narrow-mouthed white fish, resembling a herring. They are all frequently taken with the hook, and, the trout particularly, afford excellent sport to the lovers of angling. Old Izaac Walton would be in his glory here, and the precautionary measures which he so strongly recommends in approaching a trout stream, he would not need to practise, as the fish is not shy, and bites quickly and eagerly at a grasshopper or minnow.

Buffalo, antelopes, and elk are abundant in the vicinity, and we are therefore living well. We have seen also another kind of game, a beautiful bird, the size of a half grown turkey, called the cock of the plains, (Tetrao urophasianus). We first met with this noble bird on the plains, about two days' journey east of Green river, in flocks or packs, of fifteen or twenty, and so exceedingly tame as to allow an approach to within a few feet, running before our horses like domestic fowls, and not unfrequently hopping under their bellies while the men amused themselves by striking out their feathers with their riding whips. When we first saw them, the temptation to shoot was irresistible; the guns were cracking all around us, and the poor grouse falling in every direction; but what was our disappointment, when, upon roasting them nicely before the fire we found them so strong and bitter as not to be eatable. From this time the cock of the plains was allowed to roam free and unmolested, and as he has failed to please our palates, we are content to admire the beauty of his plummage, and the grace and spirit of his attitudes.[20]

Osborne Russell, who had traveled with Wyeth to the mountains and continued on with him to the Snake River and assisted in the building of Fort Hall, writes:

The next day we arrived at a stream running (in) to the Platte called Sweet Water, this we ascended to a rocky mountainous country untill the 15th of June then left it and crossed the divide between waters of the Atlantic and Pacific Oceans: and encamped on Sandy Creek a branch running into Green River which flows into the Colorado of the West. The next day moved down Sandy NWN direction and arrived at Green river on the 18th of June. Here we found some white Hunters who informed us that the grand rendezvous of White and Indians would be on a small western branch of the River about 20 miles distant, in a South West direction. Next day June 20th we arrived at the destined place. Here we met with two companies of Trappers and Traders: One is a branch of the "American Fur Company," under the direction of Mess Dripps and Fonanell: the other is called the "Rocky Mountain Fur Company," The names of the partners are Thomas Fitzpatric, Milton Sublett and James Bridger. The two companies consist of about six hundred men, including men engaged in the service, White, Half Breed and Indian Fur Trappers. This stream is called Ham's fork of Green River. The face of the adjacent country is very mountainious and broken except in the small alluvial bottoms along the streams, it abounds with Buffaloe, Antelope, Elk and Bear, and some few Deer along the Rivers. Here Mr. Wyeth disposed of part of his loads to the Rocky Mountain Fur Company and on the 2d of July we renewed our march towards Columbia River.[21]

Philip Edwards, one of Jason Lee's party, wrote:

Here is the hardy mountain veteran who has ranged these wilds for more than thirty years. Pecuniary emolument was perhaps his first inducement, but now he is as poor as at first. Reckless of all provision for the future, his great solicitude is to fill up his mental insanity by animal gratification. Here is the man, now past the meridian of life, who has been in the country from his youth, whose connections and associations with the natives have identified his interests and habits with theirs.

To form an adequate conception of their apparel, you must see it. A suit of clothes is seldom washed or turned from the time it is first worn until it is laid aside. Caps and hats are made of beaver and otter skins, the skins of buffalo calves, &c. Some of these are fantastically ornamented with tails and horns. These ornaments may be badges of distinction, for aught that I

*know, but being a stranger in the country, I am not able to speak
decidedly. You will perhaps recollect to have seen in the "far
west" of our own United States, the buckskin hunting shirt
and leggins gracefully hung with fringes along the arms and
sides. But I am sure you have never seen the tasty fashion of
fringes carried to perfection. Here they are six or seven inches
long, and hung densely on every seam, I believe, both of the
hunting shirt and leggins. Indeed their weight is a great
burden. But it is perhaps adviseable, under existing
circumstances, that I should leave your imagination to supply
the picture ...*[22]

Jason Lee, writing to Dr. Fisk from the rendezvous on June
29th, indicates his feelings toward Wyeth and the mountainmen:

*I would not have it mentioned to his injury, but the Capt.
is a perfect infidel as it respects revealed religion. This I
mistrusted some time since, but recently, of his own accord, he
avowed his infidelity. You probibly remember what was said in
Boston concerning the roughness of the men, and the promise
he made of saving us as much as possible from being annoyed by
their profaneness; so far from fulfilling his promise, he indulges
freely in the habit himself, though he says he is ashamed of it,
not on moral principles, but on those of good breeding. Hence
you may judge what kind of society we have been obliged to
mingle with on our journey. But except that we have been
treated with the greatest respect both by the Capt. and men.*

*The Capt. I must say has acted the part of a Gentleman
towards us. He went to the place of Rendezvous and returned
before the company reached it. He came and informed me, that
he heard, that the Indians threatened to "give them
missionaries Hell," and that he heard some thing of the kind
himself, and advised us to say nothing to them on the subject of
religion, for it was not possible to do them any good, and be
careful not to give them the least reason, or excuse for abusing
us, and if we were molested, to be firm, and not show the least
symptoms of fear, adding that he did not want to get into a
scrape on our account, or any other, but in case of abuse to call
upon him, and rest assured that when men put themselves
under his protection that he would not forsake them in the hour
of danger. I replied that I feared no man, and as I intended to
treat every man respectfully I apprehended no danger when men
were sober, and when drunk, I would keep out of their way. As*

soon as we arrived, I went at once, to their Camp in Company with the Capt. and was never treated more kindly by any people in my life. The Gentlemen at the head of the companies, though they frankly profess their opposition to our enterprise, yet they deny having made any threats, (though their men may have made some), and declare that men of our profession are the last they would think of abusing. I bless God I know that no weapon formed against us can prosper without his permission.[23]

Another important event that took place at the rendezvous, which would have great impact on the forthcoming rendezvous, was that of the dissolvement of the Fitzpatrick, Sublette and Bridger Company and the formation of the Fontenelle and Fitzpatrick Company. On July 19th Anderson recorded in his journal the following:

Mr. Fitzpatrick & B visited the A.F.C.s camp, which has moved within 8 or 10 miles to transact some business which is as yet sub rosa.

July 20th our camps joined together for several days March, when there will probably be a general breaking up till winters cold shall drive them to their folds.[24]

During the meeting on July 19th the formation of the new company started to take shape. While the two camps were traveling together, the details and agreements were worked out between Fontenelle and Fitzpatrick. On August 1st Anderson recorded in his journal:

We have moved on to a little creek (Cottonwood Creek) about six miles from Horse Creek, in about twice the distance from the wind-river mountain whose sides are blanced with snow.[25]

On August 3rd, encamped at the same location as on August 1st, the final transaction took place creating the Fontenelle and Fitzpatrick Company. Anderson recorded under that date:

The arrangement some time contemplated between the two neighboring camps, has been this day effected. They are now una anima, uno corpore.[26]

Even though the name of the new company bore only the names of Fontenelle and Fitzpatrick, Milton Sublette, James Bridger, and Andrew Drips were part of the company. As mentioned earlier, William Sublette left the rendezvous on July 10th with forty packs of beaver valued at $12,250 in St. Louis. He

Pawnee Indians On the War-Path. 1867, by A. J. Miller, Public Archives of Canada, C-434.

traveled by the old route, stopping to see the progress of Fort William. Arriving in St. Louis in the latter part of August, he met Campbell who had returned from the upper Missouri where he had been finalizing the selling of their posts to the American Fur Company. Not all of the 40 packs that Sublette brought with him to St. Louis belonged to the now defunct company of Fitzpatrick, Sublette and Bridger. Therefore, not all of the $12,250 was theirs. In fact, after paying Sublette the 50¢ per pound transportation charge, the furs in St. Louis were valued at less than $10,000, certainly not enough to pay their debt to Sublette and Campbell. It is easy to see why the merger between Fitzpatrick and Fontenelle had taken place on August 3rd.

Later, on August 7th, Fitzpatrick and Fontenelle returned to St. Louis to make arrangements for supplies for the 1835 Rendezvous.

On September 14, 1834, Fontenelle wrote the following report to his backer, Pierre Chouteau, Jr., from Bellevue:

The heretofore arrangements between him (William Sublette) and Messrs. Fitzpatrick, Milton Sublette and others having expired last spring, they concluded not to have anything more to do with William Sublette and it will surprise me very much if he takes more than ten packs down next year. I have entered into a partnership with the others and the whole of the beaver caught by them is to be turned over to us by agreement made with them in concluding the arrangement.[27]

Fitzpatrick and Fontenelle were dependent on the American Fur Company for supplies. Their problem was that the AFC promised Sublette they would stay out of the mountains in 1835. During the winter and spring of 1834-35, arrangements were finally made between the American Fur Company and Fontenelle-Fitzpatrick and Sublette-Campbell. This Agreement would bring about the selling of Fort William by Sublette and Campbell to Fontenelle and Fitzpatrick in 1835. The contract entered into by Fontenelle and Fitzpatrick in purchasing the fort called for some percentage of the Fontenelle-Fitzpatrick operations in 1835 to go to Sublette and Campbell. Also the agreement would bring an end to the annual supply train to the rendezvous under the direction of William Sublette. William Sublette and Robert Campbell were looking at other financial activities. They wanted to put their efforts into real estate and mercantilism in Missouri.

Another unforeseen circumstance started to develop in 1835 that would rapidly bring a decline to and the eventual death of that unique happening in the Rocky Mountains, the summer rendezvous. This circumstance was the lack of demand for beaver pelts. For without a market, the pelts were worthless.

During the spring of 1835, Sublette and Campbell made arrangements to sell Fort William to the Fontenelle, Fitzpatrick and Company. On April 9th Campbell and Fitzpatrick left for Fort William to finalize the transaction. They arrived there sometime in May. Campbell spent a couple of weeks at the fort and, accompanied by Andrew Sublette and 12 other men, returned to St. Louis, taking with him several packs of buffalo robes. On June 27th Campbell met Fontenelle, who had left Bellevue on June 22nd on his way to the mountains with the supply train. Traveling with Fontenelle were Dr. Marcus Whitman and Samuel Parker plus 50-60 additional men, 6 wagons and about 200 horses. Whitman and Parker had been sent by the American Board of Commissioners of Foreign Missions to see if missionary work could be carried on with the Flathead and Nez Perce tribes.

Fontenelle arrived at Fort William on July 26th where the supplies were taken from the wagons and loaded onto mules. Whitman recorded: *"August 1st left the fort for rendezvous with pack animals only, the company having left their wagons at the fort."* Fontenelle remained at the fort while Fitzpatrick continued on with the supplies to the rendezvous. Fitzpatrick left Fort William on August 1st and arrived at the rendezvous on Green River and Horse Creek on August 12th. Whitman recorded:

12th. Arrived at rendezvous on Green River, a branch of the Colorado of the west. Most of the traders and trappers of the mountains are here and about two thousand Shoshoni or Snake Indians, and forty lodges of Flathead & Napiersas (Nez Perce) and a few Utaws.[1]

Parker wrote:

After stopping for the night upon New Fork, a branch of Green River we arose on the 12th at the first breaking of the day, and continued our forced march ... In the afternoon, we came to the Green River a branch of the Colorado, in the latitude 42°, where the caravan hold their rendezvous. This is in a widely extended valley, which is pleasant, with a soil sufficiently fertile for cultivation, if the climate was not so cold.

The American Fur Company have between two and three hundred men constantly in and about the mountains, engaged in trading, hunting and trapping. These all assemble at rendezvous upon the arrival of the caravan, bring in their furs, and take new supplies for the coming year, of clothing, ammunition, and goods for trade with the Indians. But few of these men ever return to their country and friends. Most of them are constantly in debt to the company, and are unwilling to return without a fortune, and year after year passes away, while they are hoping in vain for better success.[2]

The 1835 Rendezvous had attracted an extra large encampment of Indians and the Hudson's Bay Company. Osborne Russell recorded:

On the 10th of June a small party belonging to the Hudson's Bay Company arrived from Fort Vancouver on the Columbia River under the direction of Mr. F. Ermatinger accompanied by Capt. Wm. Stewart an English half pay Officer who had passed the winter at Vancouver and was on a tour of pleasure in the Rocky Mountains. On the 12th they left Fort Hall and started for the grand rendezvous on Green River.[3]

At the rendezvous Dr. Whitman removed from Jim Bridger an arrowhead that he had received three years earlier. Whitman wrote:

I extracted an arrow point from the back of James Bridger, one of the partners of the company which had been shot in by the Blackfeet Indians near three years previous; and one from another man which had been shot in by the same Indians about a year before. These Indians and whites or trappers often fight and both seem mutually to exult in each others destruction.[4]

Parker made reference in his journal to the operation:

While we continued in this place, Doct. Whitman was called to perform some very important surgical operations. He extracted an iron arrow, three inches long, from the back of Capt. Bridger, which was received in a skirmish three years before, with the Blackfeet Indians. It was a difficult operation the arrow was hooked at the point by striking a large bone, and a cartilaginous substance had grown around it. The doctor pursued the operation with great self possession and perseverance; and his patient manifested equal firmness. The Indians looked on meanwhile, with countenances indicating wonder, and in their own peculiar manner expressed great astonishment when it was extracted. The Doctor also extracted another arrow from the shoulder of one of the hunters, which had been there two years and a half.[5]

While at the rendezvous, Whitman and Parker discussed with the Flathead and Nez Perce leaders the idea of bringing to the Indians the teachings of Christianity and felt that they had found a *"promising field for missionary labor."*[6] In fact, Whitman was so impressed that he decided to return east and *"obtain associates to come out with him next year ... and establish a mission among these people, and by so doing, save at least a year, in bringing the gospel among them."*[7]

Another event took place at the rendezvous that bears repeating by way of Parker's journal:

A few days after our arrival at the place of rendezvous, and when all the mountain men had assembled another day of indulgence was granted to them, in which all restraint was laid aside. These days are the climax of the hunter's happiness. I will relate an occurance which took place near evening, as a specimen of mountain life. A hunter, who goes technically by the name of great bully of the mountains, mounted his horse with a loaded rifle, and challenged any Frenchman, American, Spaniard or Dutchman, to fight him in single combat. Kit Carson, an American told him if he wished to die, he would accept the challenge. Shunar defied him. C. mounted his horse, and with a loaded pistol, rushed into close contact, and both almost at the same instant fired. C's ball entered S's hand, came out at the wrist and passed through the arm above the elbow. Shunar's ball passed over the head of Carson; and while he went for another pistol, Shunar begged that his life might be spared. Such scenes, sometimes from passion, and sometimes for amusement, make the pastime of their wild and wandering life. They appear to have sought for a place where, as they would say, human nature is not oppressed by the tyranny of religion, and pleasure is not awed by the frown of virtue ... Their toils and privations are so great, that they more readily compensate themselves by plunging into such excesses, as in their mistaken judgement of things, seem most adapted to give them pleasure. They disdain the commonplace phrases of profanity which prevails among the unpious vulgar in civilized countries, and have many self-phrases, which they appear to have manufactured among themselves, and which, in their imprecations, they bring into almost every sentence and on all occasions. By varying the tones of their voices, they make them expressive of joy, hope, grief, and anger. In their broils themselves, which do not happen everyday, they would not be ungenerous. They would see 'fair play' and would 'spare the last eye'; and would not tolerate murder, unless drunkenness or great provocation could be pleaded in extenuation.

Their demoralizing influence with the Indians has been lamentable, and they have practiced impositions upon them, in all the ways that sinful propensities dictate. It is said they have sold packs of cards at high prices, calling them bibles; and have told them, if they should refuse to give white men wives, God would be angry with them and punish them eternally; and on almost any occasion when their wishes have been resisted, they have threatened them with the wrath of God. If these things are true in many instances, yet from personal observation, I should believe, their more common mode of accomplishing their wishes has been by flattery and presents; for the most of them squander away their wages in ornaments for their women and children.[8]

Carson leaves his own account of the duel:

There was a large Frenchman in the party of Captain Drips, an overbearing kind of man, and very strong. He made a practice of whipping every man that he was displeased with — and that was nearly all. One day after he had beaten two or three men, he said he had no trouble to flog Frenchmen, and as for Americans, he would take a switch and switch them. I did not like such talk from any man, so I told him that I was the worst American in camp. There were many who could thrash him but for the fact that they were afraid, and that if he used such expressions any more, I would rip his guts.

He said nothing but started for his rifle, mounted his horse, and made his appearance in front of the camp. As soon as I saw this, I mounted my horse also, seized the first weapon I could get hold of, which was a pistol, and galloped up to him and demanded if I was the one he intended to shoot. Our horses were touching. He said no, drawing his gun at the same time so he could have a fair shot at me. I was prepared and allowed him to draw his gun. We both fired at the same time, and all present said that but one report was heard. I shot him through the arm and his ball passed my head, cutting my hair and the powder burning my eye, the muzzle of his gun being near my head when he fired. During the remainder of our stay in camp we had no more bother with this French bully. [9]

With the close of the rendezvous, Parker intended to travel with Bridger to Pierre's Hole. From there Parker wanted to be guided by Indians to the Oregon Country. The rendezvous broke up on August 21st and Parker, accompanying Bridger and his 50 men, left in mid-day from the rendezvous enroute to the "Trois Tetons." Parker wrote:

> *August 21st commenced our journey in company with Capt. Bridger ... Went only about three miles from the place of rendezvous and encamped.* [10]

Historians and writers have disagreed over the exact location of the 1835 Rendezvous, with some feeling that the location was near the mouth of New Fork on the Green River. However, Parker's journal pinpoints the location. He states:

> *On the 22nd I parted with Doct. Whitman ... Today we traveled twenty miles, through somewhat barren country, and down several steep descents, and arrived at what is called Jackson's Hole, and encamped upon a small stream of water, one of the upper branches of the Columbia river.* [11]

As Parker's diary indicates, Bridger's party had traveled 23 miles from the rendezvous to reach Little Jackson Hole in Hoback Canyon. This places the location of the rendezvous near the confluences of Green River and Horse Creek and not at the 42° parallel which Parker had made reference to earlier in his journal. The site, therefore, was the same as the 1833 Rendezvous. The 24th was the Sabbath and the groups did not travel, but on the 25th Parker recorded: "*We traveled four hours on the 25th, to another branch of Lewis or Snake river, and encamped in a large pleasant valley, commonly called Jackson's large hole.*"[12]

An interesting incident took place in Little Jackson Hole on the Sabbath. Meek leaves the following information:

> *On the following day religion services were held in the Rocky Mountain camps. A scene more unusual could hardly have transpired than that of a company of trappers listening to the preaching of the word of God. Very little pious reverence marked the countenances of that wild and motley congregation. Curiosity, incredulity, sarcasm, or a mocking levity, were more*

plainly perceptible in the expression of the men's faces, than either devotion or the longing expectancy of men habitually deprived of what they once highly valued. The Indians alone showed by their eager listening that they desired to become acquainted with the mystery of the 'Unknown God.'

The Rev. Samuel Parker preached, and the men were as politely attentive as it was in their reckless natures to be, until, in the midst of the discourse, a band of buffalo appeared in the valley, when the congregation incontinently broke up, without staying for a benediction, and every man made haste after his horse, gun, and rope, leaving Mr. Parker to discourse to vacant ground.

The run was both exciting and successful. About twenty fine buffaloes were killed, and the choice pieces brough to camp, cooked and eaten, amidst the merriment mixed with something coarser, of the hunters. On this noisy rejoicing Mr. Parker looked with somber aspect: and following the dictates of his religious feeling, he rebuked the sabbath-breakers quite severely. Better for his influence among the men, if he had not done so, or had not eaten so heartily of the tenderloin afterwards, a circumstance which his irreverent critics did not fail to remark, to his prejudice; and upon the principle that the "partaker is as bad as the thief," they set down his lecture on sabbath-breaking as nothing better than pious humbug.

Dr. Marcus Whitman was another style of man. What ever he thought of the wild ways of the mountain-men he discreetly kept to himself, preferring to teach by example rather than precept; ...[13]

Fitzpatrick, accompanied by Whitman and 85 men including Gervais and Fraeb, did not leave Green River until August 27th. They arrived at Fort William where once again Fontenelle and Fitzpatrick exchanged jobs. Fontenelle continued on to the settlements with the furs which amounted to 120 packs of beaver and 80 packs of buffalo robes. Fitzpatrick remained at Fort William until January of 1836 at which time he traveled to St. Louis.

Prior to Fitzpatrick's return to St. Louis, D.D. Mitchell, representing the American Fur Company, arrived at Fort William with the intention of trying to purchase the fort. However, suitable agreement could not be reached.

When Fitzpatrick arrived in February, he found that Fontenelle had not been tending to the company's business but had been drinking heavily. William Sublette had been having a difficult time collecting the debts owed him by the Fontenelle, Fitzpatrick and Company. Even the American Fur Company was getting weary of Fontenelle and would no longer cover his debts. Apparently, Fitzpatrick, Milton Sublette and Bridger had jumped from the frying pan into the fire when they had joined forces with Fontenelle. Also during the winter of 1835-1836, William Sublette and Campbell had renewed their agreement with each other for another three years. The partnership was doing well financially. As to the location of the five partners during the winter of 1835-1836, the following information is available. Fontenelle, Milton Sublette and Fitzpatrick were in St. Louis. Fitzpatrick, of course, arrived there late in the season. Drips and Bridger were doing the hard work, winter quartering there in the mountains preparing for the spring trapping season. It is interesting to note that during the previous winter of 1834-1835 the same situation was found. Fontenelle, Sublette and Fitzpatrick were in St. Louis handling business matters while Drips and Bridger kept the company alive.

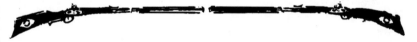

GREEN RIVER (SISKEEDEE-AGIE) RENDEZVOUS
1836

The supply train left Bellevue on May 14th for the 1836 Rendezvous under the direction of Thomas Fitzpatrick. Accompanying him was his partner, Milton Sublette, who was going to the mountains even though his leg had been amputated a few months earlier. Hugh Campbell, Robert Campbell's brother, had sent him a cork leg from the east which enabled him to get around fairly well. Also present once again was Sir William Drummond Stewart, but one person not present as the supply train left Bellevue was Lucien Fontenelle. Dr. Marcus Whitman made reference to the fact that Fontenelle was missing and that he had been replaced: *"Thomas Fitzpatrick, who had succeeded the deposed Lucien Fontenelle as the commander of the American Fur Company's 1836 caravan, gave Whitman the welcome which his predecessor had promised."*[1]

Dr. Whitman, writing from Vancouver on September 18, 1836, to the Reverend Samuel Parker, sheds some light on why Fontenelle was not present in Bellevue: *"Capt Fontenelle had become so intemperate that the Company had disposed of him."*[2] Apparently Lucien's drinking during the winter had cost him his job.

Dr. Whitman, who had gone west with Parker in 1835 and returned east that fall to get recruits, had arrived in Bellevue and asked Fitzpatrick to wait a few days before leaving for the rendezvous. Whitman had hurried to Bellevue ahead of his party which consisted of his bride, Narcissa Whitman, Reverend and Mrs. Henry Spaulding, and William H. Gray, hoping to make arrangements to travel to the rendezvous with the supply train. Fitzpatrick informed Whitman that he was not opposed to the missionaries traveling with the caravan but that he would not postpone his departure.

Whitman and his party would have to catch up. Whitman accepted that stipulation and his group was able to overtake Fitzpatrick at Loup Fork on May 24th.

The route of the supply train this year varied somewhat from earlier routes in that it traveled on the north side of the Platte River until it reached Fort William. Writing on June 4th near the forks of the Platte to family members in the east, Narcissa Whitman leaves an excellent description of the caravan.

> *The Fur Com. is large this year. We are really a moving village — nearly four hundred animals with ours, mostly mules and seventy men. The Fur Com. has seven wagons and one cart, drawn by six mules each, heavily loaded; the cart drawn by two mules carries a lame man, (Milton Sublette) one of the proprieters of the Com. We have two waggons in our com(pany). Mr. and Mrs. S. and Husband and myself ride in one, Mr. Gray and the baggage in the other. Our Indian boys drive the cows and Dulin the horses. Young Miles leads our forward horses, four in each team. Now E. (Edward) if you wish to see the camp in motion, look away ahead and see first the pilot and the Captain Fitzpatrick, just before him — next the pack animals, all mules loaded with great packs — soon after you will see the waggons and in the rear our company. We all cover quite a space. The pack mules always string along one after the other just like Indians.*

> *I wish I could describe to you how we live so that you can realize it. Our manner of living is far preferable to any in the States. I never was so contented and happy before. Neither have I enjoyed such health for years. In the morn as soon as the day breaks the first that we hear is the word — arise, arise. Then the mules set up such noise as you never heard which puts the whole camp in motion. We encamp in a large ring baggage and men, tents and waggons on the outside and all the animals, except the cows (which) are fastened to pickets, within the circle. This arrangement is to accomodate the guard who stand regularly every night and day, also when we are in motion, to protect our animals from the approach of the Indians who would steal them. As I said the mule's noise brings every man on his feet to loose them and turn them out to feed.*

> *Now H. (Harriet) & E. you must think it very hard to have to get up so early after sleeping on the soft ground. When you find it hard work to open your eyes at seven o'clock, just*

think of me, every morn at the word "Arise" we all spring. While the horses are feeding, we get our breakfast in a hurry and eat it. By this time, the word "Catch up, catch up," rings throu the camp for moving. We are ready to start usually at six — travel till eleven, encamp, rest and feed, start again about two — travel until six or before if we come to a good tavern — then encamp for the night ...

Our table is the ground, our tablecloth is an Indian rubber cloth used when it rains as a cloak; our dishes are made of tin — basins for tea cups, iron spoons and plates, each of us, and several pans for milk and to put our meat in when we wish to set it upon the table—each one carries his own knife in his scabboard and it is always ready for use. When the table things (are) spread, after making our forks of sticks and helping ourselves to chairs, we gather around the table. Husband always provides my seat and in a way that you would laugh to see us. It is the fashion of all this country to imitate the Turks.

Mr. Dunbar and Allis have supped with us and they do the same. We take a blanket and lay down by the table and those whose joints will let them follow the fashion. Others take out some of the baggage (I suppose you know that there is no (stone) in this country. Not a stone have I seen of any size on the prairie.) For my part I fix myself as comfortably as I can, sometimes on a blanket, sometimes on a box, just as it is convenient. Let me assure you of this, we relish our food none the less for sitting on the ground while eating. We have tea and a plenty of milk which is a luxury in this country. Our milk has assisted us very much in making our bread since we have been journeying. While the fur company has felt the want of food, our milk has been of great service to us, but was considerable work to supply ten persons with bread three times a day. We are done using it now. What little flour we have left we shall preserve for thickening our broth, which is excellent. I never saw anything like buffalo meat to satisfy hunger. We do not want any thing else with it. I have eaten three meals of it and it relishes well. Supper and breakfast we eat in our tent. We do not pitch it at noon. Have worship immediately after sup & breakfast.[3]

The supply train arrived at Fort William about June 18th. Also ariving at Fort William on June 20th was Joshua Pilcher, who was there representing Pratte, Chouteau and Company trying to buy out the owners of the fort. He had come over from Fort Pierre on the upper Missouri. Fort William had become very competitive, drawing considerable Indian trade away from some of the American Fur Company posts. In writing to some of the men at Fort Pierre, Pilcher shows his concern regarding the success of Fontenelle, Fitzpatrick and Company at Fort William.

> *To the Gentlemen of Fort Pierre ... it depends on the arrangements I make west of the mountains, Should I not compromise with those fools you will have opposition heavy.*[4]

Evidently Pilcher was planning to accompany the supply train to the rendezvous and to accomplish somehow his assignment of purchasing the company. He explains why in a letter written to Pierre Chouteau on June 21st from Fort William:

> *In the afternoon of yesterday I reached this post and found Mr. Fitzpatrick and all hands still here, though they arrived some ten days ago — for reasons I inquire not — everything I see and hear admonished me to move with caution and prudence ... The party for the mountains is about to move not however without leaving a large outfit for this post for the Indian trade ... The miserable animals with which I left the Missouri have nearly given out; and as I find an apparent reluctance to furnish others here, I am obliged to continue my route with them; but now that I am with the party I feel no uneasiness; for it is very certain that I never lose sight of them horses or **no horses until I put a period to this business.***[5]

Meek's memories of the caravan when he first encountered it on the Sweetwater River on July 4th would indicate that most of the wagons had been left at Fort William, for he states:

> *The caravan on leaving the settlements had consisted of nineteen laden carts, each drawn by two mules driven tandem, and on a slight wagon, belonging to the American Company; two wagons with two mules to each, belonging to Capt. Stuart; and one light two-horse wagon, and one four-horse freight wagon, belonging to the missionaries. However, all the wagons had been left behind at Fort Laramie, except those of the missionaries, and one of Capt. Stuart's; so that the three that remained in the train when it reached the Sweetwater were alone in the enjoyment of the Nez Perces' curiosity concerning them; a curiosity which they divided between them and the domesticated cows and calves belonging to the missionaries; another proof, as they considered it, of the superior power of the*

white man's God, who could give to the whites the ability to tame their wild animals to their uses.[6]

At Independence Rock Fitzpatrick had a message sent ahead to the rendezvous site on Green River that supplies were enroute and would arrive soon. Upon receiving the message of the approaching caravan, some of the trappers and Indians decided to ride out and meet them. As Meek tells it:

> *... trappers prepared to give them a characteristic greeting. To prevent mistakes in recognizing them, a white flag was hoisted on one of their guns, and the word was given to start. Then over the brow of a hill they made their appearance, riding with that made speed only an Indian or a trapper can ride, yelling, whooping, dashing forward with frantic and threatening gestures; their dress, noises, and motions, all so completely savage that the white men could not have been distinguished from the red.*
>
> *The first effect of their onset was what they probably intended. The uninitiated travelers, including the*

missionaries, believing they were about to be attacked by Indians, prepared for defence, nor could be persuaded that the preparation was unnecessary until the guide pointed out to them the white flag in advance. At the assurance that the flag betokened friends, apprehension was changed to curiosity and intense interst. Every movement of the wild brigade became fascinating. On they came, riding faster and faster, yelling louder and louder, and gesticulating more and more madly, until, as they met and passed the caravan, they discharged their guns in one volley over the heads of the company, as a last finishing feu-de-joie; and suddenly wheeling rode back to the front as wildly as they had come. Nor could this first brief display content the crazy cavalcade. After reaching the front, they rode back and forth, and around and around the caravan, which had returned their salute, showing off their feats of horsemanship, and the knowing tricks of their horses together; hardly stopping to exchange questions and answers but seeming really intoxicated with delight at the meeting. What strange emotions filled the breasts of the lady missionaries, when they beheld among whom their lot was cast, may now be faintly outlined by a vivid imagination, but have never been, perhaps never could be put into words ...

When the trappers and Nez Perces had slaked their thirst for excitement by a few hours' travel in company with the Fur Company's and Missionary's caravan, they gave at length a parting display of horsemanship, and dashed off on the return trail to carry to camp the earliest news.[7]

William Gray also leaves a description of the welcome:

From Rock Independence information was sent forward into the mountains of the arrival of the caravan, and about the time and place they expected to reach the rendezvous. This information reached not only the American trapper and hunter in the mountains, but the Snake, Bannock, Nez Perce' and Flathead tribes, and the traders of the Hudson's Bay Company. Two days before we arrived at our rendezvous, some two hours before we reached camp, the whole caravan was alarmed by the arrival of some ten Indians and four or five white men, whose dress and appearance could scarcely be distinguished from that of the Indians. As they came in sight over the hills, they all gave a yell, such as hunters and Indians only can give; whiz, whiz, came their balls over our heads, and on they came, in less time than it will take you to read this account. The alarm was but for a moment; our guide had seen a white cloth on one of their guns, and said, 'don't be alarmed, they are friends,' and sure enough, in a moment there they were. It was difficult to tell which was the most crazy, the horse or the rider; such hopping, hooting, running, jumping, yelling, jumping sage brush, whirling around, for they could not stop to reload their guns, but all of us as they came on gave them a salute from ours, as they passed to the rear of our line and back again, hardly stopping to give the hand to any one. On to camp we went.[8]

The caravan arrived at the rendezvous on July 6th. The rendezvous was once again located at Horse Creek and Green River in the vicinity of Fort Bonneville. Kit Carson recorded: *"We reached the rendezvous at the mouth of Horse Creek on Green River ... we remained here about twenty days ..."*[11] Osborne Russell who had been traveling to the rendezvous with a large encampment of Indians leaves the following information:

The whole camp of Indians and whites left Bear river and travelled to Ham's fork, excepting Mr Dripps and a small party who went round to Blacks fork of Green river to get some furs and other articles deposited there in the ground. After reaching Ham's fork the Indians concluded to separate in different directions as we were in too large a body and had too many horses to thrive long together. They were instructed to be at the mouth of horse creek on Green River about the 1st day of July as we expected supplies from the U S about that time. We laid about on the branches of Green river until the 28th of June when we arrived at the destined place of Rendezvous. On the 1st of July Mr. Wyeth arrived from the mouth of the Columbia on his way to the U S with a small party of men 3d (6th) The outfit arrived from St. Louis consisting of 40 men having 20 horse carts drawn by mules and loaded with supplies for the ensueing year. They were accompanied by Dr Marcus Whitman and lady Mr H H Spaulding and lady and Mr. W H Gray Presbyterian missionaries on their way to the Columbia to establish a mission among the Indians in that quarter. The two ladies were gazed upon with wonder and astonishment by the rude Savages they being the first white women ever seen by these Indians and the first that had ever penetrated into these wild and rocky regions. We remained at the rendezvous until the 16 of July and then began to branch off into parties for the fall hunt in different directions.[10]

Meek describes the rendezvous as follows, recalling the welcome given to the missionaries and the members of the supply train by the Indians:

It was then that Indian finery was in requisition! Then the Indian women combed and braided their long black hair, tying the plaits with gay-colored ribbons, and the Indian braves tied anew their streaming scalplocks, sticking them full of flaunting eagle's plumes, and not despising a bit of ribbon either. Paint was in demand both for the rider and his horse. Gay blankets, red and blue, buckskin fringed shirts, worked with beads and porcupine quills, and handsomely embroidered mocassins, were eagerly sought after. Guns were cleaned and burnished, and drums and fifes put in tune.

After a day of toilsome preparation all was ready for the grand reception in the camp of the Nez Perces. Word was at length given that the caravan was in sight. There was a rush for horses, and in a few moments the Indians were mounted and in line, ready to charge on the advancing caravan. When the command of the chiefs was given to start, a simultaneous chorus of yells and whoops burst forth, accompanied by the deafening din of the wardrum, the discharge of fire-arms, and the clatter of the whole cavalcade, which was at once in a mad gallop toward the on-coming train. Nor did the yelling, whooping, drumming, and firing cease until within a few yards of the train.

All this demoniac hub-bub was highly complimentary toward those for whom it was intended; but an unfortunate ignorance of Indian customs caused the missionaries to fail in appreciating the honor intended them. Instead of trying to reciprocate the noise by an attempt at imitating it, the missionary camp was alarmed at the first burst and at once began to drive in their cattle and prepare for an attack. As the missionary party was in the rear of the train they succeeded in getting together their loose stock before the Nez Perces had an opportunity of making themselves known, so that the leaders of the Fur Company, and Captain Stuart, had the pleasure of a hearty laugh at their expense, for the fright they had received.

A general shaking of hands followed the abatement of the first surprise, the Indian women saluting Mrs. Whitman and Mrs. Spalding with a kiss, and the missionaries were escorted to their camping ground near the Nez Perce encampment. Here the whole village again formed in line, and a more formal introduction of the missionaries took place, after which they were permitted to go into camp.

When the intention of the Indians became known, Dr. Whitman, who was the leader of the missionary party, was boyishly delighted with the reception which had been given him. His frank, hearty, hopeful nature augured much good from the enthusiasm of the Indians. If his estimation of the native virtues of the savages was much too high, he suffered with those whom he caused to suffer for his belief, in the years which followed. Peace to the ashes of a good man! And honor to his associates, whose hearts were in the cause they had undertaken of Christianizing the Indians. Two of them still live—one of whom, Mr. Spalding, has conscientiously labored and deeply suffered for the faith. Mr. Gray, who was an unmarried man, returned the following year to the States, for a wife, and settled for a time among the Indians, but finally abandoned the missionary service, and removed to the Wallamet valley. These five persons constituted the entire force of teachers who could be induced at that time to devote their lives to the instruction of the savages in the neighborhood of the Rocky Mountains.

The trappers, and gentlemen of the Fur Company, and Captain Stuart, had been passive but interested spectators of the scene between the Indians and the missionaries. When the excitement had somewhat subsided, and the various camps had become settled in their places, the tents of the white ladies were beseiged with visitors, both civilized and savage. These ladies, who were making an endeavor to acquire a knowledge of the Nez Perce tongue in order to commence their instructions in the language of the natives, could have made very little progress, had their purpose been less strong than it was. Mrs. Spalding perhaps succeeded better than Mrs. Whitman in the difficult study of the Indian dialect. She seemed to attract the natives about her by the ease and kindness of her manner, especially the native women, who, seeing she was an invalid, clung to her rather than to her more lofty and self-asserting associate.

On the contrary, the leaders of the American Fur Company, Captain Wyeth and Captain Stuart, paid Mrs. Whitman the most marked and courteous attentions. She shone the bright particular star of that Rocky Mountain encampment, softening the hearts and the manners of all who came within her *womanly influence. Not a gentleman among them but felt her silent command upon him to be his better self while she remained in his vicinity; not a trapper or camp-keeper but respected the presence of womanhood and piety. But while the leaders paid court to her, the bashful trappers contented themselves with promenading before her tent. Should they succeed in catching her eye, they never failed to touch their beaver-skin caps in their most studiously graceful manner, though that Should prove so dubious as to bring a mischievous smile to the blue eyes of the observant lady.*

But our friend Joe Meek did not belong by nature to the bashful brigade. He was not content with disporting himself in his best trapper's toggery in front of a lady's tent. He became a not infrequent visitor, and amused Mrs. Whitman with the best of his mountain adventures, related in his soft, slow, yet smooth and firm utterance, and with many a merry twinkle of his mirthful dark eyes. In more serious moments he spoke to her of the future, and of his determination, sometime, to 'settle down.' When she inquired if he had fixed upon any spot which in his imagination he could regard as 'home' he replied that he could not content himself to return to civilized life, but thought that when he gave up 'bar fighting and Injun fighting' he would go down to the Wallamet Valley and see what sort of life he could make of it there. How he lived up to this determination will be seen hereafter.

The missionaries remained at the rendezvous long enough to recruit their own strength and that of their stock, and to restore to something like health the invalid Mrs. Spalding, who, on changing her diet to dried meat, which the resident partners were able to supply her, commenced rapidly to improve. Letters were written and given to Capt. Wyeth to carry home to the States. The Captain had completed his sale of Fort Hall and the goods it contained to the Hudson's Bay Company only a short time previous, and was now about to abandon the effort to estabish any enterprise either on the Columbia or in the Rocky Mountains. He had, however, executed his threat of the year previous, and punished the bad faith of the Rocky Mountain Company by placing them in direct competition with the Hudson's Bay Company.[11]

William Gray leaves a detailed description of the location and population of the rendezvous and their activities:

In two days' easy travel we arrived at the great American rendezvous, held in an extensive valley in the forks formed by Horse Creek and Green River, on account of the abundance of wood, grass, and water all through the valley. Each party selected their own camp grounds, guarding their own animals and goods, as each felt or anticipated the danger he might be exposed to at the time. We will pass through the city of about fifteen hundred inhabitants — composed of all classes and conditions of men, and on this occasion two classes of women, — starting from a square log pen 18 by 18, with no doors, except two logs that had been cut so as to leave a space about four feet from the ground two feet wide and six feet long, designed for an entrance, as also a place to hand out goods and take in furs. It was covered with poles, brush on top of the poles; in case of rain, which we had twice during our stay at the rendezvous, the goods were covered with canvas, or tents thrown over them. Lumber being scarce in that vicinity, floors, doors, as well as sash and glass, were dispensed with. The spaces between the logs were sufficient to admit all the light requisite to do business in this primitive store. At a little distance from the store were the camps of the fur company, in which might be seen the pack-saddles and equipage of the mules, in piles to suit the taste and disposition of the men having them in charge. The trading-hut was a little distance from the main branch of Green River, so situated that the company's mules and horses could all be driven between the store and the river, the tents and men on either side, the store in front, forming a camp that could be defended against an attack of Indians, in case they should attempt any thing of the kind. Green River, at the point where our city in the mountains is situated, is running from the west due east. West of the fur company's camp or store were most of the camps of the hunters and trappers; east of it, close to the river, was the missionary camp, while to the south, from one to three miles distant along Horse Creek, from its junction with Green River, where the Snake and Bannock Indians were camped, to six miles up that stream, were the camps of the Flatheads and Nez Perces. All these tribes were at peace that year, and met at the American rendezvous. The Indian camps were so arranged in the bends of the creek that they could defend themselves and their horses in case of any attack from the neighboring tribes, and also guard their horses while feeding in the day-time. The whole city was a military camp; every little camp had its own guards to protect its occupants and property from being stolen by its neighbor. The arrow or the ball decided any dispute that might occur. The only law known for horse-stealing was death to the thief, if the owner or the guard could kill him in the act. If he succeeded in escaping, the only remedy for the man who lost his horse was to buy, or steal another and take his chances in escaping the arrow or ball of the owner or guard. It was quite fashionable in this city for all to go well armed, as the best and quickest shot gained the case in dispute. Of the number assembled, there must have been not far from one hundred Americans,—hunters and trappers; about fifty French, belonging principally to the caravan; some five traders; about twenty citizens, or outsiders, including the mission party. The Snakes and Bannocks mustered about one hundred and fifty warriors; the Nez Perces and Flatheads, about two hundred. By arrangement among themselves they got up a grand display for the benefit of their white visitors, which came off some six days after our American caravan had arrived at the rendezvous.

The procession commenced at the east or lower end of the plain in the vicinity of the Snake and Bannock camps. The Nez Perces and Flatheads, passing from their camps down the Horse Creek, joined the Snake and Bannock warriors, all dressed and painted in their gayest uniforms, each having a company of warriors in war garb, that is, naked, except a single cloth, and painted, carrying their war weapons, bearing their war emblems and Indian implements of music, such as skins drawn over hoops with rattles and trinkets to make a noise. From the fact that no scalps were borne in the procession, I concluded this must be entirely a peace performance, and gotten up for the occasion. When the cavalcade, amounting to full five (some said six) hundred Indian warriors (though I noticed quite a number of native belles covered with beads), commenced coming up through the plain in sight of our camps, those of us who were not informed as to the object or design of this demonstration began to look at our weapons and calculate on a desperate fight. Captain Stewart, our English nobleman, and Major Pilcher waiting on the mission ladies and politely informed them of the object of the display; they assured them there would be no danger or harm, and remained at their tents while the cavalcade passed. Mrs. Whitman's health was such that she could witness most of the display. Mrs. Spalding was quite feeble, and kept her tent most of the time. All passed off quietly, excepting the hooting and yelling of the Indians appropriate to the occasion. [12]

Nathaniel Wyeth, having sold Fort Hall to the Hudson's Bay Company and on his way east, was present at the rendezvous. Gray notes that Wyeth was at the rendezvous and introduced two Hudson's Bay men who had arrived there on July 12th. The missionaries felt that the arrival of the Hudson's Bay men and their subsequent permission to travel with them back to Walla Walla was an answer to their prayers. For they had been scheduled to travel there with the Nez Perce and Flatheads on their return home from the rendezvous and this trip would have taken many more weeks.

Gray also leaves the descriptions of eight mountainmen in his journal, including those of the prestigious Jim Bridger and Joe Meek. He wrote the following concerning this reckless breed of men:

These men had all abandoned civilization and home for the wild hunter life in the midst of the mountains. They had enjoyed its wild sports, felt its fearful dangers and sufferings, and become, most of them, connected with native women— a large proportion of them with the Nez Perce and Flathead tribes. Their family, at least, could be benefited by education, and taught the benefits of civilization and Christianity. The men had expressed kind wishes, good feelings, and treated them kindly; why should they not include this class of men and their families in their efforts to benefit the Indians in valleys of the Columbia River. [13]

The rendezvous of 1836 was the setting for the final triumph of the American Fur Company. Pilcher had been true to his word, and Fontenelle, Fitzpatrick and Company had sold out their holdings including Fort William to Pratte, Chouteau and Company. The papers containing this agreement have, to this date, not been found, however.

With the breakup of the rendezvous, the missionaries started for Walla Walla on July 18th with the Hudson's Bay caravan under the direction of John McLeod and Thomas McKay. Gray's journal contains an interesting entry concerning the feelings between the Hudson's Bay men and the American trappers.

There appeared a mutual dislike, a sort of hatred between them. This chief trader of the Hudson's Bay Company, in the conversations had with him, informed the mission party that it was not the wish of the company to encourage any of these mountain hunters and trappers to go to the Columbia River to settle, or to have any thing to do with them, assigning as a reason that they would cause trouble and difficulties with the Indians. He also gave them to understand that should they need manual labor, or men to assist them in putting up their houses and making their improvements, the company would prefer to furnish it, to encouraging these men in going into the country. This intimation was distinctly conveyed to the party, with the advise and intimations received from Captain Wyeth, who had seen and understood all the policy of the Hudson's Bay Company, and had been compelled to sell his improvements at Fort Hall to this same McLeod, and his goods designed for the trade to D. McLaughlin, soon after their arrival in the country. These facts and statements, with the decided manner of Mr.

McLeod, compelled the mission party to defer any effort for these mountain men, but subsequently they advised the sending of a man to travel with their camps. [14]

The American Fur Company, as of mid-summer 1836, had gained complete control of the American fur trade but certainly did not have the field to itself. Certainly, the feelings demonstrated by the Hudson's Bay men and the American trappers indicate that a keen rivalry existed not only between the two companies but between the two countries. In addition to the fur trade rivalry, the control of the Oregon country was of major importance to both countries.

The missionary's freight wagon was left at the rendezvous, but Dr. Whitman insisted on taking the light wagon with him. At Fort Hall the wagon was converted into a cart which was used until their arrival at Fort Boise where it was abandoned.

Fitzpatrick and Milton Sublette left the rendezvous and took the furs back to Fort William. Milton remained at the fort, which was now under the ownership of Pratte, Chouteau and Company, while Fitzpatrick continued on to the settlements with the furs. Milton died at the fort on April 1, 1837. There seems to have been hard feelings between him and Fitzpatrick at the time of his death as shown in a letter written by Milton to the company.

With the arrival of the caravan in Bellevue came the end of an era. The golden era of the fur trade days was gone. The rivalry between American companies was a thing of the past.

The major problem that faced Pratte, Chouteau and Company regarding the fur trade during the winter of 1836-1837 was the popularity of the silk hat that was destroying the value of and demand for beaver pelts. Added to this problem was the ever-increasing decline of beaver and the threat of the Hudson's Bay Company.

The untamed wilderness domain that the mountainmen had known and loved would never be the same now that each year more missionaries and settlers would come west. The control of the mountains was slipping from the mountainmen even now and would eventually collapse entirely to the westward movement.

GREEN RIVER (SISKEEDEE-AGIE) RENDEZVOUS
1837

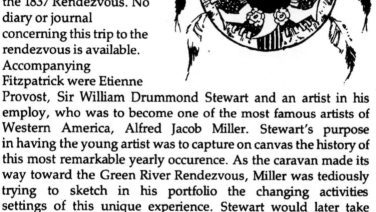

The supply train under the direction of Thomas Fitzpatrick and numbering 30 wagons and two carts left Newport or Independence enroute to the 1837 Rendezvous. No diary or journal concerning this trip to the rendezvous is available. Accompanying Fitzpatrick were Etienne Provost, Sir William Drummond Stewart and an artist in his employ, who was to become one of the most famous artists of Western America, Alfred Jacob Miller. Stewart's purpose in having the young artist was to capture on canvas the history of this most remarkable yearly occurence. As the caravan made its way toward the Green River Rendezvous, Miller was tediously trying to sketch in his portfolio the changing activities settings of this unique experience. Stewart would later take Miller to Scotland where he would commission him to paint large murals based upon his field sketches.

During the sixteen-year history of the rendezvous, neither mountainman, traveler, missionary, nor visitor left a more detailed description of this wilderness experience than did Alfred Miller. The following comments which accompanied his sketches help tell the story of the rendezvous caravan as it traveled westward:

BREAKING UP CAMP AT SUNRISE

At four o'clock in the morning, it is the duty of the last men on guard to loosen the horses from their pickets, in order to range and feed. At daylight, everybody is up; — our provisors are busy with preparations for breakfast; — tents and lodges are collapsed, suddenly thrown down, wrapped up, and bundled into the wagons.

If the sun is 20 minutes above the horizon when our breakfast is finished, we conceive he has a reproachful look. By this time the horses are driven in, and each man hurries after his own, saddles or harnesses him, and the train puts itself enroute.

At this period, one of the strongest contrasts presents itself, and illustrates in a striking manner the difference between the white and red man.

While all is activity and bustle with the Anglo-Saxon as if he feared that the Rocky Mountains would not wait for him, the Indian lingers to the last moment around the camp fire, — he neither enters into or sympathizes with our diligence, and seems to regret that stern necessity forces him to accept our company for his convoy.[1]

NOON-DAY REST

Every day at 12 o'clock the caravan halts, the horses are permitted to rest and feed, men receive their dinner, and then take a Siesta. The time however to me was too valuable to indulge in the luxury, — so immediately after the halt, I would mount the wagon, get out my portfolio, and go to work. Our Captain, who took great interest in this matter, came up to me one day while so engaged, & said 'you should sketch this and that thing' and so on. 'well!' I answered, 'if I had half a dozen pair of hands it should have been done!'

Capt: 'That would be a great misfortune.'

'Why?'

Capt: 'It would be very expensive in the matter of kid gloves ...'

... a guard is stationed of course, on the bluffs to prevent a surprise, and also to look after the horses, for, 'Some must watch while others sleep. Thus runs the world away.'[2]

CROSSING THE RIVER
TRAPPER TRYING ITS DEPTH &C.

The Caravan having reached the banks of the river, the first thing to be ascertained is whether the wagons and charettes can cross without resort to boats, or damage to the goods with which they are laden.

A trusty and experienced man is now selected whose business it is to cross the river and try its depths, and then return by a different route, looking out the shallowest parts and marking them in his mind's eye as a trail for the company ...

When he has reached the Caravan finding the river fordable, the whole body is put in motion (single file) with the guide at their head, and in this manner they make their way safely to the opposite bank.[3]

THREATENED ATTACK
APPROACH OF A LARGE BODY OF INDIANS

On this eventful morning our caravan, pursuing as usual the even tenor of its way, we descried one of our hunters returning to the camp at full gallop. His speech was to the purpose, "Injins all about—that will be some raising of h'ar—as sure as shootin." On his heels followed others confirming this. At this juncture, it would have been a good study (if the matter had not been so serious) to watch the countenances of the different men. The staid indifference of the old trappers ready for any emergency, the greenhorns (braggarts of the camp fire) pale about the gills and quite chopfallen. No boasting now! Monsieur Proveau, subleader, with a corpus round as a porpoise, revolving in his mind what was to be done. A problem! ...

All of us were more or less uncomfortable decidedly, and as sensitive about our scalps as a Chinese concerning his pig-tail que. We were not kept long in suspense. A cloud of dust soon divulging a piratical horde of wretches, painted without regard to harmony of color, coming down on us at top speed,—armed to the teeth, and when they reached us, they commenced riding around in a menacing manner.

We stopped the camp and held a parley. Their argument was capital. They were on their own grounds, and we were "interlopers" — winding up with a demand for black-mail on the instant ...

The great point was to get the chiefs and leaders to smoking as soon as possible so as to gain diplomatic time ... At last we got the chiefs seated in the council circle, and the pipe circulating, each taking a few whiffs. The first two with much ceremony, and muttering to the sun for the Great Spirit, and the next to the earth. The upshot was that we had to blackmail them extensively. —Cloth, blankets, guns, tobacco & knives were accordingly hauled out of the wagons and given to them.

After losing the day, and taking leave of our most unwelcome guests, we asked them which way they were going? They pointed to about South-West — Well ours was North East, and we absolutely started in that direction, resolving to turn on the right course, as soon as we were ready.[4]

PRAIRIE SCENE: MIRAGE

The caravan is proceeding at its usual steady pace, both men and horses suffering for want of water — the day is hot and oppressive. Suddenly in the distance, an extensive Lake looms up, - delightful to the eye, the surface reflecting islands, and trees on its borders; — but what is the matter with the horses? they neither raise their ears, quicken their motion, or snort, as is their wont on such occasions.

Poor brutes! — well do they know that there is no water for them. It is the mirage, an optical delusion; the deception is so perfect that you can scarcely credit your sense. On the priarie is ... a man dis-mounted, he is, doomed for a certain time to walk ... has been caught asleep on his guard, and this the penalty for a week. In the army, they ornament one ancle with a chain and ball, and by way of variety sometimes mount him astride of a hot brass cannon, under a mid-summer's sun. The punishment is probably not too great, when we consider the consequences that might follow the neglect.[5]

OUR CAMP

About half an hour before the halt for evening, scouts are sent out in advance of the main body, in order to reconnoitre and select a spot combining the requisites for an encampment; — as the wagons and charettes approach the location, they take a circuitous course, and by the time the last vehicle has reached the ground, the Caravan has formed a circumference of 5 or 600 feet; — the horses and mules are now unharnessed, and loosed to feed, leaving the vehicles at a distance of some 30 feet apart, forming a species of barricade; towards sundown the horses are driven in and picketed ...

Most extensive cookery ensues, and the prairie forms the only table available for the viands.

The teamsters find sleeping departments under the wagons, with sweet soft grass to lie on; — they have also a serenade provided for them, but it is chaunted by the wolves, who set up a hideous concert at times; — the former however are quite accustomed to this, and it does not affect their sleep in the least.[6]

PICKETING HORSES

It is near sunset and the whole camp is very busy, the horses and mules have been driven in, and each man runs toward them as they come, secures his own horse, catches him by the lariat (a rope trailing on the ground from his neck), and leads him to a good bed of grass, where a picket is driven, and here he is secured for the night, (We asked permission to purchase an exemption from this service, — but it was not granted — "breach of discipline, favortism &c." in short, reasons were as plentiful as blackberries why it should not be done, so we had to attend to this duty during the whole journey.) the lariat permitting him to graze to the extent of a circle 25 feet in diameter, and all this is eaten down pretty close by morning. The grass is quite sufficient without any other provender to keep the animals in good condition, if the work given them to do is not too heavy, or if they are not compelled to make forced marches.

The selection of the Camp is of so much importance that scouts are sent out previous to the half of the Caravan, whose duty it is to select sites combining above all things the two great requisites, an abundance of both water & grass.[7]

CAMP FIRE, PREPARING THE EVENING MEAL

A Trapper is ... preparing that most glorious of all mountain morsels, "a hump rib" for supper.

He is spitting it with a stick, the lower end of which is stuck in the ground near the fire, inclined inwards.

The fire is often made from the bois de Vache, but as we had the best of all sauces, viz: most ungovernable appetites, and most impatient dispositions for this same roasting operating, the circumstance did not affect us in the least. 'We found hunger so troublesome that it was quite a common thing to rise again at midnight and roast more meat, if we had any.

The guard for the first watch of the night is seated to the left. His duty expires at 12 o'clock when he is relieved by another, who continues the guard until 5 o'clock, A.M., when the horses are unloosed to feed preparatory to starting.

Breakfast is ready at sunrise, and when finished the tents are struck, luggage packed, horses caught up, and another day's journey commenced.[8]

Lucien Fontenelle was in command of Fort William when the caravan arrived in June. Since the 1836 Rendezvous, when Fontenelle had been left behind and Pratte, Chouteau and Company had deposed him because of his drinking, the veteran of the mountains had in some way induced the company to give him another chance. At Fort William the wagons were left behind and the supplies loaded into carts. Miller leaves an excellent description of the Fort and some impressions of Fontenelle.

> ... *situated about 800 miles West of St. Louis, is a quadrangular form, with bastions at the diagonal corners to sweep the fronts in case of attack; over the ground entrance is a large block house, or tower, in which is placed a cannon. The interior is possibly 150 feet square, a range of houses built against the palisades entirely surround it, each apartment having a door and window overlooking the interior court. Tribes of Indians encamp here 3 or 4 times a year, bringing with them peltries to be traded or exchanged for dry-goods, tobacco, vermillion, brass, and diluted alcohol. Fontenel was in command of the fort, and received us with kindness and hospitality. We noticed around his apartment some large first-class engravings, from which we drew conclusions most favorable to Mr. F.*
>
> *This gentleman afterwards accompanied us to the Rocky Mountains, where he distinguished himself for speed of foot in running from a grizzly bear; he having no gun with him at the time.*[9]

The caravan left Fort William on June 27th with 45 men and 20 carts and arrived at the rendezvous on July 18th. Osborne Russell had arrived at Green River at the rendezvous on June 10th in preparation for the rendezvous. He wrote:

> ... *10th. Travelled west to the Main river about 25 mls and struck the river about 12 mls below the mouth of horse creek. Here we found the hunting Parties all assembled waiting for the arrival of Supplies from the States. Here presented what might be termed a mixed multitude. The whites were chiefly Americans and Canadian French with some Dutch, Scotch, Irish, English, halfbreed, and full blood Indians, of nearly every tribe in the Rocky Mountains. Some were gambling at Cards some playing the Indian game of hand and others horse racing while here and there could be seen small groups collected under shady trees relating the events of the past year all in good Spirits and health for Sickness is a Stranger seldom met with in these regions. Sheep Elk Deer Buffaloe and Bear Skins mostly supply*

the Mountaineers with clothing bedding and lodges while the meat of the same animals supplies them with food. They have not the misfortune to get any of the luxuries from the civilized world but once a year and then in such small quantities that they last but a few days. We had not remained in this quiet manner long before something new arose for our amusement The Bonnak Indians had for several years lived with the whites on terms partly hostile frequently stealing horses and traps and in one instance killed two White Trappers. They had taken some horses and traps from a party of French trappers who were hunting Bear river in April last, and they were now impudent enough to come with the village of 60 lodges and encamp within 3 mls of us in order to trade with the whites as usual still having the stolen property in their possession and refusing to give it up. On the 15 of June 4 or 5 whites and two Nez Percey Indians went to their village and took the stolen horses (whilst the men were out hunting buffaloe) and returned with them to our camp. About 3 o'clk PM of the same day 30 Bonnaks came riding at full gallop up to the Camp — armed with their war weapons. They rode into the midst and demanded the horses, which the Nez Percey had taken, saying they did not wish to fight with the whites. But the Nez Percey who were only Six in number gave the horses to the whites for protection which we were bound to do as they were numbered among our Trappers and far from their own tribe. Some of the Bonnacks on seeing this started to leave the Camp one of them as he passed me observed that he did not come to fight Whites but another a fierce looking Savage who still stopped behind called out to the others saying "we came to get horses or blood and let us do it." I was standing near the Speaker and understood what he said I immediately gave the whites warning to be in readiness for an attack nearly all the men in camp were under arms Mr. Bridger was holding one of the stolen horses by the bridle when one of the Bonnaks rushed thro. the crowd seized the bridle and attempted to drag it from Mr Bridger by force without heeding the cocked rifles that surrounded him any more than if they had been so many reeds in the hands of Children. He was a brave Indian but his bravery proved fatal to himself, for the moment he seized the bridle two rifle balls whistled thro. his body. The others wheeled to run but 12 of them were shot from their horses before they were out of the reach of Rifles. We then mounted horses and pursued them destroyed and plundered their village and followed and fought

151

them three days when they begged us to let them go and promised to be good Indians in future. We granted their request and returned to our Camp satisfied that the best way to negotiate and settle disputes with hostile Indians is with the rifle; for that is the only pen that can write a treaty which they will not forget. Two days after we left them three white trappers ignorant of what had taken place went into their village and were treated in the most friendly manner The Indians said however they had been fighting with the Blackfeet. July 5th a party arrrived from the States with supplies The cavalcade consisting of 45 men and 20 Carts drawn by Mules under the direction of Mr. Thomas Fitzpatrick accompanied by Capt. Wm Stewart on another tour to the Rocky Mountains. Joy now beamed in every countenance. Some received letters from their friends and relations Some received the public papers and news of the day others consoled themselves with the idea of getting a blanket a Cotton shirt or a few pints of Coffee and sugar to sweeten it just by way of a treat gratis that is to say by paying 2,000 percent on the first cost by the way of accomodation for instance Sugar 4$ per pint Coffee the same Blankets 20$ each Tobacco 2$ pr pound alcohol 4$ per pint and Common Cotton Shirts 5$ each etc And in return paid 4 or 5$ pr pound for Beaver. In a few days the bustle began to subside, the furs were done up in packs ready for transportation to the States and parties were formed for hunting the ensuing year One party consisting of 110 men were destined for the Blackfoot Country under the direction of L B Fontanelle as commander and James Bridger Pilot.

I started with five others to hunt the head waters of the Yellowstone Missouri and Big horn rivers a portion of country I was particularly fond of hunting On the 20th of July we left the Rendezvous and travelled up Green River about 10 mls. 21st We travelled up green river till noon when we discovered a trail of 8 or 10 Blackfeet and a Buffaloe fresh killed and butchered with the meat tied up in small bundles on the ground which they had left on seeing us approach and run into the bushes, we supposing them to be a small scouting party tied their bundles of meat on to our saddles and still kept on our route but had not gone far before we discovered them secreted among some willows growing a long a branch which crossed our trail I was ahead leading the party when I discovered them we stopped and one of my comrades whose name was (William) Allen began to arrange the load on his pack mule in the meantime I reined my horse to the left and rode onto a small hillock near by and casting a glance towards the bushes which were about 150 yds distant I saw two guns pointed at me I instantly wheeled my horse but to no purpose the two balls struck him one in the loins and the other in the shoulder which dropped him under me the Indians at the Same time jumped out of the bushes 60 or 70 in number and ran toward us shooting and yelling I jumped on a horse behind one of my comrades and we scampered away towards the rendezvous where we arrived at dark. 25th The parties started and we travelled with Mr. Fontanelle's party up Green River 10 mls intending to keep in their company 5 or 6 days and then branch off to our first intended route 26th we travelled 20 mls NW across a low range of hills and encamped in a valley lying on a branch of Lewis fork called "Jackson's Little Hole."[10]

Robert Newell, also arriving on June 10th, left the following information:

We proceeded up green river to the mouth of hors creek whare all hunters were wating on the arival of the supplies from St Louis we arived there on the 10th of June I engaged to Drips & fontinelle for one year for the perpose to trade with the crow indians I left with a small party of crows and 2 white men on the 22d of July from green river at the mouth of horse creek ...[11]

William Gray, traveling east to find a wife and recruit more missionaries for the Oregon Country, arrived at the rendezvous site on July 2nd, with some Nez Perce and Flathead companions. Upon his arrival, he mentions that Drips was already camped on Horse Creek waiting for the supply train. Gray leaves a splendid account of events prior to the arrival of the caravan on July 18th and activities surrounding the rendezvous until his departure on July 25th.

July 2nd, Sabbath, This morning moved camp about nine, and proceeded over about twelve miles on to Green River and camped near the mouth of Horse Creek on an island. The camp of Mr. Drips is a short distance from us on Horse Creek. Mr. McLeod said to me this morning, after I remarked to him "Had I known yesterday that you were going to move camp today, I should have gone over yesterday." He said to me, "There is no Sabbath in this country." — which is truly the case — No Sabbath. No Sabbaths dawn here to give rest to the body and food to the mind; desolation and profanity is inscribed on all that pertains to man, as if all who had reached these heights had already attained the final consummation of every Earthly *object, and once here, they have no fears in relation to this world or the next. They seem to have cast off all fears of both God and man.*

July 3rd Today we have remained in camp. I called on Mr. Drips this morning to see if I could make arrangements to leave soon for the States. He thinks not. Soon after I returned to our camp, about twenty-five of the Delaware Indians came to our camp, by permission, to have a scalp dance, which differs from the Flat Head's materially. The men are mostly naked, all holding some implements of war. Their dance consists in jumping first on one then on the other foot, and passing and repassing each other in every direction, and going and jumping round in the ring. Their musical instrument, which is the same as the Flat Head's, is so managed as to change the time, beating slow, then quick with a double beat; at every change of their music, they give the yell and jump in a different position, placing their bodies in a different position, erect, stooping forward, and on both sides stooping down as if to look through the bushes, or the ring for their enemies, and stepping from one side or the other, keeping time with their music, and yelling at intervals, and firing their guns; their scalps, perhaps three whole ones, were cut into nine or ten pieces, pretending to be as many scalps, all strung on one pole. Their dance continued for about four hours, when they all retired ...

July 5th ... Mr. Harris called on me this afternoon. He thinks there is prospect of my leaving soon after the Company arrive from St. Louis.

July 6th. In camp all day. This evening my Flat Heads came over to my camp. One of them says he will go with me to the States. Today I was told, in conversation with Messrs. McLeod, McKay, Walker, and McLane, that Indian women are a lawful commerce among the men that resort to these mountains from the States and elsewhere. They named to me a man by the name of Dr. Newell, as he is called, who won a woman on a wager. On hearing his old Flat Head wife was coming with McLeod's party, he said he must get rid of the woman. Accordingly, he went and sold her to her previous owner for One Hundred Dollars. A second individual, they tell me, lost his wife on a wager. A few days after, he won a horse and bought his wife back again. The buying and selling of Indian women is a common occurance at this Rendezvous, especially among those having a white face. The principal White trader from the East of the Mountains, I am told, has taken three wives. He tells the Indians to take as many as they can—thus setting at defiance every principle of right, justice and humanity, and law of God and man ...

July 10th. In camp. I have commenced a letter today to Dr. Whitman. This afternoon Mr. McLeod tells me we are to move camp on the morrow. Some few "Snakes" arrived at Mr. Drip's camp on ... They have a scalp dance today.

July 11th. This morning we broke camp and moved up to the old camp at which we rendezvoused last year, expecting the company from St. Louis soon ...

July 12th. This morning a man by the name of Mr. Forsythe has offered to assist me in taking down our horses for the use of one to ride and carry his supplies going down. I have accepted his offer. Captain Thing has arrived from Fort Hall. This evening I have heard the report of several guns, at or near Mr. Drip's camp, and from their noise, and yelling of persons about, I should think they were mad or intoxicated with liquors. I have also heard in a loud voice the dying words of the Saviour on the Cross repeated, followed by a loud laugh. No tongue can tell the extent that blasphemy is carried at this place. There seems to be no thought of God but to blaspheme his name ...

July 18th. Tuesday. The Company from St. Louis have arrived. A young man by the name of Mr. Ewing has called upon me. Capt. Stewart and others are with the Company; also a Mr. Miller, etc. They have been since the 27th of June, coming from Fort William, on Laramie's Fork ... Mr. Miller, who is a portrait painter, called at tea or supper ...

July 19th. This morning I learned that the Company would probably remain at this place till the 5th or 10th of August, to get through with their business. I have concluded to proceed as soon as possible ... I rode up to Mr. McLeod's camp to let him know my determination. On returning, the Snakes passed the camp in their usual manner of arriving at this Rendezvous. They were all mounted on their best war horses, about two hundred and fifty. They proceded upon the gallop, singing, yelling, and firing their arms, some naked, some dressed in various ways to suit their fancy ...

July 25th, Tuesday ... We are to leave this morning after breakfast. At eight we were on our way ...[12]

Alfred Miller was busy at the rendezvous, sketching and painting different scenes of interest. One of the first sketches Miller did after arriving at the rendezvous was a witness of the parade provided by the Snake Indians to honor the arrival of the caravan. Miller wrote concerning this sketch:

> ... an Indian procession took place while we sojourned at the
> great rendezvous on Green River, in Oregon. Here we
> encamped for a month in the midst of upwards of two thousand
> Snake Indians, who were friendly and hospitable. The cavalcade
> was projected in honor of our Leader's arrival amongst them,
> and was extremely unique and interesting. The Indian chief,
> Ma-wo-ma, rode in front, while the main body followed
> without any military order or platooning. Some of the dresses
> worn were magnificent, and although vermillion was worth
> four dollars per oz., a lavish use of that article was exhibited
> on their bodies and faces. The Snakes in comparison with other
> tribes may be considered in affluent circumstances, — they have
> a large supply of fine horses and live in a district abounding
> with game, — have the finest lodges we saw, — and impressed
> us more than any other tribe with their courteous and friendly
> manners.[13]

Miller made a series of sketches of the rendezvous and left
written descriptions of them. Some of the most striking follow:

LARGE ENCAMPMENT Nr THE CUT ROCKS

At certain specified times during the year, the American
Fur Company appoint a "Rendezvous" at particular localities
(selecting the most available spots) for the purpose of trading
with Indians and Trappers, and here they congregate from all
quarters. The first day is devoted to "High Jinks," a species of
Saturnalia in which feasting, drinking, and gambling form
prominent parts.

Sometimes an Indian becomes so excited with "Fire
Water" that he commences "running a muck" — he is pursued,
thrown or knocked down, and secured, in order to keep him from
mischief. "Affairs of honor" now and then are adjusted between
rival Trappers — one of the parties, of course, receiving a
complete drubbing; — all caused evidently from mixing too
much Alcohol with their water. Night closes this scene of
revelry and confusion. The following days exhibit the strongest
contrast to this. The Fur Company's great tent is raised; — the
Indians erect their picturesque white lodges; — The
accumulated furs of the hunting season are brought forth, and
the Company's tent is a beseiged and busy place. Now the
women come in for their share of ornaments and finery, being,
as Tony Lumpkin expresses it, "in a con-cat-enation
accordingly." The free trapper most especially bestowing

presents on his favorite regardless of expense. [14]

SCENE AT "RENDEZVOUS"

A large body of Indians, Traders, and Trappers are here congregated, and the view seen from a bluff is pleasing and animated.

In the middle distance a race is being run, the horses in all cases running in a direct line and never in a circle as with us. The bets pending on the result are extraordinary in character and diversity, and the Indians are passionately fond of this species of gambling. If an Indian happens to lose all, he will stake the dress he wears against 3 or 4 ounces of vermillion (worth here about $4 per oz.), and if you win can demand it at once, leaving him almost in the condition of Adam before the fall. The Company's tent is besieged on such occasions. No matter who lose, they are sure to win.

Ball playing with bandys and other games are largely indulged in, and the Company make it a point to encourage the Indians in these sports to divert their minds from mischief. White Lodges ranging from 12 to 16 ft. in height are scattered at random over the plain and reach almost to the foot of the distant mountains. [15]

RENDEZVOUS

The scene represented is the broad prairie; the whole plain is dotted with lodges and tents, with groups of Indians surrounding them;— In the river near the foreground Indians are bathing; to the left rises a bluff overlooking the plain whereon are stationed some Braves and Indian women. In the midst of them is Capt. Bridger in a full suit of steel armor. This gentleman was a famous mountain man, and we venture to say that no one has travelled here within the last 30 years without seeing or hearing of him. The suit of armor was imported from England and presented to Capt. B. by our commander;—it was a fac-simile of that worn by the English life-guards, and created a sensation when worn by him on stated occasions. [16]

INDIAN COUNCIL

We had several opportunities while encamped at the Rendezvous on Green River (where some 3,000 Indians were met together) of attending their Councils.

Old men generally officiated as speakers, while before them sat the sages and warriors, generally in squatting positions, interspersed with chiefs on horse-back, every one as rigid as the statue of the Commendatore in "Don Giovanni."

157

Each had his turn to harangue amid the most profound silence; and such sentences as were translated to me were short, pithy apothegms, mixed up with considerable boasting. "Their enemies were cowards — serpents with forked tongues (parliamentary for liars), cheats, &c. With a compliment to their own nation, — their wish to be at peace, and to bury the hatchet, one orator would conclude, and the next take the parole.[17]

ENCAMPMENT

The sketch represents an encampment of Shoshonee Indians, near Green River, Oregon. On the elevated ground, or bluff, are a group of Indians in painted robes. On the plain below they are preparing jerked meat, this is performed by cutting it up into thin slices and laying it on frame work, composed of crotched sticks supporting poles; — under these a suppressed fire is built, so as to smoke and dry it at the same time.

Before we started from St. Louis we became acquainted with Capt. Sublette, who was then a substantial merchant in that city. He had been one of the pioneers to the "Far West" and almost the first thing he did was to hand us a piece of this prepared meat so as to give us a foretaste of mountain life. He told us that every season he caused a bale of meat to be brought down to him which lasted 6 or 8 months.

The Indians and Trappers, after having prepared it properly, fold it in smoked buckskin and stow it away either for Winter consumption, or as a provision in making journeys where game is scarce.[18]

One of Miller's paintings entitled "The Trapper's Bride" depicts a trapper taking a wife, or purchasing one. Here is his description:

The prices varying in accordance with circumstances. He (the trapper) is seated with his friend, to the left of the sketch, his hand extended to his promised wife, supported by her father and accompanied by a chief, who holds the calumet, an article indispensable in all grand ceremonies. The price of acquisition, in this case, was $600 paid for in the legal tender of this region: Vis: Guns, $100 each, Blankets $40 each, Red Flannel $20 pr. yard, Alcohol $64 pr Gal., Tobacco, Beads &c. at corresponding rates.

A Free Trapper (white or half-breed), being ton or upper circle, is a most desirable match, but it is conceded that he is a

158

ruined man after such an investment, the lady running into unheard of extravagencies. She wants a dress, horse, gorgeous saddle, trappings, and the deuce knows what beside. For this the poor devil trapper sells himself, body and soul, to the Fur Company for a number of years. He traps beaver, hunts the Buffalo and bear, Elk &c. The furs and robes of which the Company credit to his account.[19]

Also present at the rendezvous were the representatives of Hudson's Bay Company. Both McLeod and McKay, who had escorted the missionaries to Walla Walla at the close of the 1836 Rendezvous, were present. Captain Thing, Wyeth's companion in 1834, and who was now in command of Fort Hall for the Hudson's Bay Company, arrived at the rendezvous on July 12th.

As the rendezvous drew to a close and the trappers were preparing to leave for the fall hunt, Miller was there to make sketches and written comments. The following two excerpts describe the preparation for departure:

Trappers are divided into three classes, — the hired, the free, and the trapper "on his own hook." After the Saturnalia which continues for 3 days at the rendezvous where they take their fill of eating & drinking, they then commence seriously their preparation for departure. On starting for the hunt the trapper fits himself out with full equipment. In addition to his animals he procures 5 or 6 traps (usually carried in a trap-sack), ammunition, a few pounds of tobacco, a supply of moccasins, a wallet called a "possible sack," gun, bowie knife, and sometimes a tomahawk

Caravan "En Route." 1867, by A. J. Miller, Public Archives of Canada, C-417.

Over his left shoulder and under his right arm hung his buffalo powderhorn, a bullet pouch in which he carries balls, flint, and steel, with other knick-knacks.

Bound round his waist is a belt, in which is stuck his knife in a sheath of buffalo hide, made fast to the belt by a chain or guard of some kind, and on his breast a pipe holder, usually a gage d'amour in the shape of a heart, worked in porcupine quills by some dusky charmer. Encircled with danger, they wander far and near in pursuit of "sign" of beaver. Ever on the alert, a turned leaf, grass pressed down, or the uneasiness of his animals, are signs palpable to him of proximity to an Indian foe, and places him on his guard.[20]

TRAPPING BEAVER

In hunting the beaver two or more trappers are usually in company. On reaching a creek or stream, their first attention is given to "sign." If they discover a tree prostrate, it is carefully examined to ascertain if it is the work of Beaver, and if thrown for the purpose of damming the stream. Foot prints of the animal on the mud or sand are carefully searched for, and if fresh, they then prepare to set their traps. One of these is baited with "medicine" — hidden under water, and attached to a pole driven firmly on or near the bank. A "float-stick" is made fast to the trap, so that if the Beaver should carry it away, the stick remains on the surface of the water and points out its position.

With all the caution the poor trappers take, they cannot always escape the Lynx eyes of the Indians. The dreadful war whoop, with bullets and arrows about their ears, are the first intimations of danger. They are destroyed in this way from time to time, until by a mere chance their bones are found bleaching on the borders of some stream where they have hunted.[21]

It is not certain when the rendezvous officially broke-up, but it is possible the rendezvous did last until August 5 or 10th as Gray suggested in his journal of July 19th. In any case, Fitzpatrick and Drips took the furs back to St. Louis only to find that the financial panic of 1837 had affected those in the fur trade. The price of beaver was down considerably.

Winter quarters for the mountainmen was located on Powder River. Very few Indians camped with the trappers this year. In fact, only a few had been seen during the fall hunt. The mountainmen attributed this separation to the smallpox epidemic on the upper Missouri during 1837.

Fontenelle, who had accompanied the caravan to the mountains and had remained in the mountains in charge of a trapping detachment, went to Fort William for supplies during the winter. He was told by Mr. Woods, the chief trader, that business at the fort was slow. The new trading posts on the North and South Platte were taking away much of the Indian trade. Newell, who was at winter quarters on Powder River, recorded:

> *I found our camp all well. Mr. fontinielle had gone with 25 men to the north fork of the platte for suplies but has not yet returned. Our camp went through the blackfoot country last fall without Seeing any indians we suppose many of them have died with the Small pox.*

> *We are now on powder river waiting for Mr fontinelle our camp is eighty strong Cold wether and the 22d of January 1838 ... 4th of March A tremendious Storm we have lost Several horses and mules by hard weather this winter ... our time is principally Spent in peeling cotton wood bark for our horses as that is their principal food on the north fork of the platte times is hard about five trading houses to eight hundred lodges of Soux ... times is getting hard all over this part and low all peltries are on the decline.*[22]

As the supply train left Westport, a familiar face was missing from among its ranks. Thomas Fitzpatrick, who had for years been involved in the rendezvous caravans, was not going to the mountains. Andrew Drips was in charge and accompanying him was August Johann Sutter, who would later build Fort Sutter and become a legend in his own time. A large group of missionaries, including William H. Gray, Elkanah Walker, Cushing Eells, Asa B. Smith and their wives, were also along this year. Cornelius Rogers was traveling with the missionaries as an assistant. As usual, Sir William Drummond Stewart was making the trip, but this would be his last visit to the mountains before returning to Scotland and his inheritance.

By 1838 Pierre Chouteau had gained control of Pratte, Chouteau and Company and had changed the name to Pierre Chouteau, Jr. and Company. It was, however, still commonplace to refer to the Chouteau Company as the American Fur Company. According to Cornelius Rogers, the supply train, including the missionaries, consisted of *"75 men and 150 horses and mules."*[1] Cushing Eells described the caravan as follows:

> *When the caravan was in motion, the guide mounted on a large and distinguishably white mule led the way, those acting in part as scouts were in advance or not according to circumstances. Next to the guide was the wagon of Capt. Stewart with four mules attached thereto. The owner of this outfit was an English Gent. traveling for pleasure, then followed the cart of Capt. Drips hauled by three mules harnessed in single file. Said Gent. was viceregent of the Fur Co.*
>
> *Next in order was a train of 2 doz. or less carts carrying*

the goods of the F. Co. To each cart two mules were attached, one before the other. Then came the one-horse wagon and loaded pack animals of the mission band, with their drivers.[2]

The supply train arrived at Fort William on May 30th. Through the diaries that were kept by the missionaries, the reader is given an excellent look at the activities surrounding the 1838 Rendezvous. Cornelius Rogers, Mary Richardson Walker, Cushing Eells and his wife, Myra Fairbanks Eells, Asa B. Smith and his wife, Sarah Gilbert White Smith, all kept excellent diaries and wrote very informative letters while traveling to Oregon. The following narratives are taken from the diaries of five of the missionaries concerning the layover at Fort William.

ASA B. SMITH

30th. Travelled 5 miles this morning & reached Laramy's fort, where we expect to rest a little before we go any farther. This is the 38th day since we set out from Westport & have travelled every day. Our animals as well as ourselves are much fatigued & need rest. For several days past, we have lived entirely on meat. Today we allowed ourselves a little hard bread with our dinner. We find it rather trying to be deprived of vegetable food, but most of us seem to bear it without material injury tho' some of our company suffer much in consequence of not having different food. The fort where we now are is on Laramy's fork, a branch of the Platte, which we forded without difficulty. Soon after we arrived here it commenced raining & now I have a little leisure to sit down in my tent & rest.

31st. Did not move camp, but remained to rest our animals &c. Did but little except cook & eat. Cut our buffalo meat up fine like sausage meat & cooked it, which answered well for a change. All the variety we have is in the different manner of cooking.

June 1st. Did not move camp, but remained still on the ground & rested what we could. The day hung rather heavily & we began to feel like moving again. Had a call from some of the squaws, the wives of the men at the fort. Most of them had children. Fontanelle's wife was over & his son, a bright lad of about 12 years came with her. It is much in fashion for these mountaineers to have wives.

2nd. Set out this morning ...[3]

MYRA F. EELLS

30th. Wednesday. Last night a number of Indian women came to see us. They were neatly dressed and ornamented with beads. Suppose they are wives of white men at the fort and in the mountains. Moved camp at 6, rode 2 hours, crossed Larimie's Fork and came to Fort William, 5 miles. Sell Mr. Walker's horse to Capt. Fontinelle for 40 dollars. Three Indian women, wives of capts. Drips, Fontinelle and Wood, with their children call on us. The children are quite white and can read a little.

31st. Thursday. The ladies engaged in washing, mending, etc. Our husbands making repairs and arrangements for the remainder of the journey. Give the wagon to Capts. D. & F. They, with Mr. Wood, take tea with us.

June 1st. Friday. Attend to writing. Indian women and children continually calling on us. The company give us a horse. Mr. Gray takes one he left here a year ago.

2d. Saturday. Leave here this morning, ride into the Fort. It is a large, hewed log building with an opening in the center. Partitions for various objects. It compares well with the walls of the Conn. State Prison. A fort in this country is a place built to accomodate the Company as they go and come from the Mts. to trade with the Indians for firs. Start at 7, ride 5½ hours — 12 miles. Encamped in the open prairie at a clear spring at the foot of the Black Hills. Left four of our cattle because their feet were so sore they could not travel. Hope to get them at some future day. Mr. Walker and Rogers drive the cattle. Mr. (Gray) drives mules with Mr. S. and E. ... Some of the Mts. appear to be above the clouds.[4]

MARY R. WALKER

30th. Wednesday. Cross Laramey Fork. Just as we got our tents pitched it commenced raining. Cleared off in the afternoon. Mrs. Smith & Gray washed. I mended Mr. W's coat & marked blankets. In the evening received a visit from the wife of a fur trapper.

31st. Thursday. Washed for myself & Mr. Rogers. Took me most of the forenoon. Almost blistered my arms. Not much fatigued, much less than if I had been riding. To dine with us had Mr. Clark, son of the Clark who accompanied Lewis. He & his brother are travelling in the company thro from St. Louis. In the afternoon arranged my trunks, &c.

164

June 1st. Friday. Ripped & dyed my pongee dress. Made sundry repairs, &c. Recd. visits from squaws.

2d. Saturday. Left Fort Williams or Larimier. Capt. Fontenelle & son, several squaws & children joined the Company. The fort is constructed of hewn timbers set in the ground. We rode into it. Inside were several big buildings, most of them without glass. The halfbreed children look as likely as any. Capt. Drips takes his Indian wife along.[5]

SARAH G.W. SMITH

30th. Wed. Since I last wrote we have travelled 250 miles over an uninhabited wilderness. Have been following the Platte & have today crossed Laramie fork & are encamped near the fort. There are no Indians here, they have all gone to fight with the Pawnees. We are among the Sioux. We see some females probably the wives of white men. Last eve we received a call from one of the wives of some trader. Her attendant said she had never seen a white woman & had come 3 miles to see us. She was dressed in fine style. Perhaps her dress cost 100 dollars. It was trimmed in beads & other ornaments throughout & beads of a costly kind about her neck. Her dress was mountain sheepskin, white & soft as kid. I wish you could have seen her. I certainly never saw so much ornament but it all showed the barrenness of her mind. It is said these trappers take great pleasure in dressing their Indians brides but care not for their minds. Some of our company will take wives from here to go with them to the mountains. Capt. Dripps has two. The country over which we have passed since the 20th is very interesting ...

31st. Thursday. Have been much engaged today, washing & repairing my clothes, found it very pleasant to rest a day or rather change exercise for I have labored as hard today as on any day. We prepared a dinner & invited some of the company to dine with us. We shall remain here some days.

June 1st. Much engaged repairing our clothing. Received a call from some Indian females, wives of Capt. Dripps & Fontenelle, also a son of Fontenelle, a fine lad of 12 years. They wished to have us sing, & so we sang, Yes, my Native Land, I love thee. It is interesting to converse with these people & also to learn some of their superstitious notions. In passing through the buffalo country we have often seen buffalo heads lying with the faces toward the east. The Indians believe if they face the sun's rising, buffalo will rise, if toward the sun's going down, buffalo will go down. We often see several placed in a circle, around these Indians meet, sing, smoke the pipe & pray to the great Spirit that buffalo may increase. One thing is interesting. When they have been on a hunting expedition & been successful, they will build a fire & bake the best pieces of meat they have & offer it as a sacrifice to the great Spirit.

June 2nd. Sat. Moved camp today & were very glad. Had remained quiet as long as could enjoy it.[6]

CORNELIUS ROGERS

About 250 or 300 miles above the main forks of the Platte, a stream called Lorimer's Fork enters that river from the south. Here is a station of the American Fur Company, called Fort William. There are also two other stations near, belonging to other traders. This is in the Sioux country. Here the Black Hills commence, and extend west nearly to Wind River Mountains, and north to the Missouri. They are a range of low, broken hills, covered with scattering pitch pines, of a small size. These give them the black appearance from which they derive their name.

The fort mentioned is a stockaded enclosure of about 200 feet square, with buildings on the inside around the square, leaving the middle an open space for work. A few men are left here to trade with the Indians, and take care of the furs. We left the fort on the 2d ...[7]

It is interesting to note that the fort was still referred to as Fort William by Mrs. Eells and Cornelius Rogers. Mrs. Walker referred to it as *"Fort Williams or Larimier."* Asa Smith called it *"Laramy's fort."* Apparently by 1838 the owners, occupants and those traveling past the fort were having a hard time in settling on a name for it.

The missionaries left their wagon at the fort and some of their cattle because of their deplorable condition. However, they purchased two horses to help take up the slack of leaving the wagon. As mentioned in the writings of the missionaries, Lucien Fontenelle and family, who were at the fort when the caravan arrived, continued on with the supply train to the rendezvous. Also one of Drip's Indian wives was waiting at the fort for her husband and continued on with him.

The caravan arrived at the rendezvous on June 23rd. From the diaries of the missionaries the location and activities of the rendezvous are very easily identified. Asa Smith recorded:

Thursday 21st. Travelled about 12 miles & reached a river which is called Popiasia (Popo Agie) *on which we encamped. The place of rendezvous is to be on the opposite bank, but the river is now too high to be forded.*

Fri. 22. Today we are happy to rest from our travelling, but is rather tedious to remain in our tents without any chair. Obliged to sit or lie down upon the ground. It is hard to get accustomed to this kind of life. I feel anxious to have a house to live in & some of the conveniences of civilized life, but this I cannot expect for months to come & then but little.

Sat. 23d. Forded the Popiasia & encamped near the place of rendezvous on the bank of the Big Horn (Wind River) near its junction with the Popiasia. Here we find a good supply of timber and grass for the horses. This is to be our home for perhaps 3 or 4 weeks.

Sab. 24th. Today we have had two sermons read. In the morning a few of the company attended. The men who come into the mountains are such as care for none of these things. We have however been treated by them with much kindness & attention. I find them generous hearted men who are ready to render assistance when needed. They are much like the sailors in this respect. The Lord has been very merciful to us, bringing us along thus far on our journey. We have now travelled about 1,100 miles since we left Westport.

Mon. 25th. Built a pen for our horses to secure them nights so as not to have a guard. This we built with trees &

brush, something like what is called slash fence at the east.

Tuesday, 26th. Had a long ride after the cattle. They went away yesterday & we set out this morning after them & did not return with them till about 2 p.m. It was a long & tedious ride & I found myself very much fatigued.

Sat. 30th. Time begins to drag heavily here. Do little but lounge about. No ambition to undertake any thing. If I begin to read, I am so sleepy I can do nothing. This is owing to our diet. Go to the camp frequently. Have distributed several Bibles & testaments among the men. They were rec'd very kindly.

July 1. Sab. Preached this morning from the text "God is love." Had several men from the camp to hear me. They listened with attention but there is little hope of benefitting them. This has seemed something like the Sab. & I feel that it has been a blessing to me. It is ruinous to live without sabbaths as we have.

Mon. 2nd. Guarded the horses all day. This we do in turn each one day.

Tuesday. 3d. Considerable carousing in camp today. It seemed to be a preparation for the 4 of July. The company have a plenty of alcohol & it is used quite freely here at the rendezvous.

Wed. 4th. This has been a high day here. The day was celebrated much as in the States by the baser sorts. The alcohol has been freely used & many were thoroughly drunk.

Thurs. 5th. Today Bridger arrived with his company consisting of about 100 men, about 60 squaws & a multitude of half breed children. For it is the custom in this country for white men to take unto themselves wives from among the natives. Their arrival was attended with the firing of guns & noisy shouts. A party came & saluted us soon after their arrival with singing, accompanied by the Indian drum & dancing around a scalp, firing of guns, etc. They were mostly half breeds. They were all on horseback & managed their horses with great skill. This evening a company came on foot & entertained us with music & dancing.

Fri. 6th. This morning rec'd a visit from a company of half breeds, squaws & children, & were entertained by them with a scalp dance. This is a very common amusement among the Indians. The weather has been exceedingly warm for a few days past & we find it very uncomfortable remaining here. The insects are very troublesome.

Sat. 7th. Began to make preparations for setting out on our journey from this place.

Sab. 8th. This morning a Kayuse came to our camp & inquired for Mr. Gray. He was from Wallawalla with a party with Mr. Ermatinger of the Hudson's Bay Company at their head. Come on to meet us. This was good news to us. We learned that supplies were sent on for us, so that we shall soon be where we can have a little more vegetable food.

Monday 9th. Spent the day in writing letters to send back by the company & in preparation for our journey. Rev. Mr. Lee, one of the Methodist missionaires beyond the Mountains, is with us on his return to the States. He appears to be a very fine man & has given us much information respecting missionary labors among the Indians. It is good to meet a missionary brother here in the wilderness ...

Thursday 12th. Set out from the Rendezvous.[8]

In writing to Reverend Greene from the rendezvous on July 10th, Asa Smith informs the Secretary of the American Board of Foreign Ministers that there was a lot of friction and unhappiness among the missionaries. This letter was delivered to Greene by Jason Lee, who arrived at the rendezvous with Ermatinger, traveling east to recruit more people to the missionary program in Oregon.

Sarah Smith wrote the following in her journal:

21st. Thurs… Travelled today over mountains and awful ravines, so steep that the horse could hardly carry me. It seemed many times as if I should fall over his head. Many places were frightful. We ascended one mountain & road along on its summit some distance where we had an extensive view of the surrounding landscape, which was most splendid. What fartherest met our view were the lofty snow capped mountains of the Wind river stretching along from north to south, a great distance below them numerous bluffs & plains. Here & there clusters of beautiful trees cloathed with green the Popesia (river) flowing in beautiful meanderings through the valley …

22nd. (June) Friday. Find it very pleasant to rest today. Have been sewing this afternoon. Mrs. S. & myself took a short walk in the grove & it being very cold, Mr. S. built a fire & we sat by it some time, read our Bible & held a season of prayer together. We find it good to get away alone & pray. Retirement is what we most need & for that we have little opportunity. O I long for some little spot we can call our home & live as we please. We still love Mr. and Mrs. Walker & are happy in their society. Still love retirement. But that in our present situation we can not have. We shall know how to prize it when we can enjoy it.

June 23. Sat. Spent part of the day washing clothes. In the afternoon crossed the Popesia by fording. Crossed in two places, the river being separated by an island. Are encamped on the bank of the Big Horn. (Wind River) Mr. S. has built a little house by putting down poles & fastening the oilcloth & blankets to them. It is a little larger than the tent because it is the same size at the top as at the bottom or on the ground. Here we keep all our baggage & have things convenient & pretty. Mr. & Mrs. Walker are also more comfortable.

24. Sab. Have had worship today in the open air, under the shade of some large trees. Some of the company met with us. Brother Walker led the services this morning, Brother Eells this afternoon. Were happy to enjoy such a privilege in this wilderness.

25th Mon. Have been sewing today. It is very warm & we are much troubled with mosquitoes. Saturday night we had a rice pudding, except for that we have had nothing but buffalo for a long time and I should love a crust of brown bread even if it was very poor. It being so warm, we feel the need of vegetable food more than we did. We did not take sufficient supply of flour and rice and what we have we dare not eat. For Mr. Gray is often telling us we shall starve & starve to death unless we use the most rigid economy. Dear friends when you sit at your table loaded with the good bread, vegetables & other luxuries, will you not think of those who are deprived of them? Will you not think of the missionary who has left them all for the cause of Christ & who is looking to your charity for a bare support?

June 26. Tues. Am quite alone today. Mr. S. with others have gone after the cows which have strayed away. Have been reading & writing this morning. The other ladies are washing. No gentleman at home but Mr. Gray. We are camped a little distance from the company to be freed from their noise. I have been thinking of home this morning & how you look there. I can see every one of you. Mother is flying about preparing something good for dinner, Father and brother are making hay. Dear little Roxanna is in school & all things going on pleasantly. Perhaps some one may be thinking of Sarah and wishing to hear where & how she is. Little Charlie is in school too. I hope he is a good boy & will make a missionary.

27th. Wed. Spent the day sewing, Am making a gingham sunbonnet which I had not time to make before I left the States. This afternoon Mr. S. & I have been berrying, picked more than a quart of wild currants. They are green but may be good cooked.

28th. Thurs. Spent the day writing & sewing. To prevent our being idle, we have taken in a little sewing for the company. Have four calico dresses to make for some hunters & it is some work to make one being much ruffled. We feel under obligation to the company for their kindness to us & are happy to confer a favor on them. Mr. S. has had some opportunity to furnish a little medicine for them and has also given some Bibles which were kindly received. Have had a visit this afternoon from 6 Indian females.

29th. Friday. This morning spent several hours washing flannels. Was not near as tired as I used to be at home. Think the journey has increased my strength much. This afternoon ventured to make a rice pudding, thought it very nice without eggs and very little sugar.

30th. Sat. Spent the morning sewing on the hunter's dress & this afternoon made a couple of pies, chopped the meat with a butcher knife on the back of a cottonwood tree which Mr. S. peeled off. Rolled the crust with a crooked stick in a hollow bark, baked them in the tin baker out of doors in the wind but they were good & we had a good supper.

July 1st. Sab. This is communion Sabbath in Brookfield but not in the mountains. Mr. S. preached this morning, Brother Walker this afternoon.

July 2nd. Mon. This is monthly concert day. I trust the Christians in Brookfield will not forget those who have gone out from them & to whom they have pledged their prayers. Surely they cannot if they love the cause of Christ as they ought. Have today finished the hunter's dress.

3rd. Tues. Been assisting Mrs. Walker finish her dress today. Been feasting on dry buffalo. It is very good, better than you would expect. This is what we shall use upon the plains where there is no game.

4th Wed. independence day. I suppose you are having some celebrations in New England. I spent the morning washing & made biscuit pudding for dinner. Received a call from an Indian with nothing on but a buffalo hide. It is very warm and I am sitting under a tree.

5th. Thurs. Mr. S. & myself have taken a pleasure ride this morning of some miles, breakfasted at 10. Received a salute from some of Bridger's party who have just arrived. This company consists of about 100 men & perhaps 60 Indian females & a great number of half breed children. Their arrival was attended with firing of guns & noisy shouts. Thought perhaps that we would be interested, therefore came & saluted us with firing, drumming, singing & dancing. Their appearance was rude & savage, were painted in a most hideous manner. One carried a scalp of the Black foot in his hand. It is dreadful to hear how the whites treat the Indians. Bridger's party have just been among the Black Foot tribe. This tribe have long been a terror to neighboring tribes & to the whites, but now their number is much reduced by the smallpox & it is still raging. The Indians made no attack on B's party but this party attacked them & shot 15 of them dead without excuse but to please their wicked passions. Thus sending 15 souls to eternity & to the bar of God unprepared. A man told me of it who had a part in the horrid scene. Said that one they shot and wounded but not killed. Said that this Indian grasped the limb of a white man who stood near & made signs begging that his life might be spared while others dragged him away & cut his body in pieces regardless of his groans & entreaties. This fellow semed to exult in it.

6th. Friday. Received a call this morning from a company of Indian females, half-breeds & children, who gave us a salute of music accompanied with the scalp dance. This is a favorite amusement with them. Their singing is little more than a yell & dance a hop.

7th Sat. Have been writing most of the day. Nothing of interest has taken place. Very windy & our little house suffers some.

8th. Sunday. Today a company from Fort Hall has arrived with Mr. Ermatinger at their head. Rev. Mr. Lee is in company with them on his way to the States. He is one of the Methodist missionaries from west of the Mountains. This arrival fills our hearts with joy. This company will go with us through the most dangerous part of the country. We were intending to move camp on Tuesday next, but were feeling anxious for our safety. Supplies have been sent us from Mr. Spalding of flour, rice, Indian meal &c.

9th. Mond. Have done quite a washing & baked a rice pudding for dinner. Mr. Lee dined with us.

10th. Tues. Had a call from a poor drunken creature who professes great attachment to Mr. Smith. Presented me with a butcher knife & a large red feather. Must receive them or offend him.

11th. Wed. Been making preparations to leave here tomorrow. Had a rice pudding for dinner.

12th. Thurs. Travelled 20 miles ...[9]

Cushing Eells wrote:

The goods of the F Co. shipped from St. L consisted largely of clothing, blankets, tobacco, whiskey or rum. Said articles were sold at fabulous prices. The strong drink was $30 per gal. High prices did not restrain (men) from its use, so long as it was obtainable.[10]

Myra Eells' diary contains the following:

21st. Thursday. Move camp at 6 ... encamp on the Popuasua (Popo Agie) 12 miles. The water so high we can not cross the river, or we should be at the (rendezvous) which is on the opposite side. A shower.

22nd. (June, 1838) Wash, mend & read a little. A shower at noon. Coffee, sugar and tea, two dolls, per pint; blankets from 15 to 16 dollars apiece; pipe, one doll, tobacco from 5 to 6 dollars per lb.; a shirt, 5 dollars.

23d. Saturday. The water so low it is thought we may ford the river. Mr. Gray and Eells go to find a fording place. Succeeded, though the water is high. All are busy getting the baggage across, which must be put on the tallest horses. This done, the horses taken back, we mount them and follow our husbands in deep water, but in 20 minutes were all across safe, though some of us have wet feet, but this is nothing new in this country. Encamped in a grove of cottonwood trees near the Wind River. Here we expect to spend a few days, but know not how many. Hear nothing from Mr. Spaulding or Dr. Whitman or the Indians who were to meet us here.

24th. Sabbath. To-day for the first time since we left Westport, we have a Sabbath of rest. Mr. Walker preached in the forenoon from 2d Peter 3:7. Mr. Eells preached in the afternoon from Ps. 66:13. Trust it has been a profitable day to us all. Hope some good may result from the sermons of this day. Some eight or ten men came from the company to attend our worship.

25th. Monday. The gentlemen, except Mr. Eells, who is on horse guard, engaged in making a pen for the animals at night. Mr. (Joseph) Walker, an American trader in the mountains, comes to our camp with a large company, perhaps 200 or 300 hundred horses.

26th. Tuesday. Our cattle could not be found last night; Mr. W. and S. go to look for them. Mr. Eells guards the horses. Mr. G. making a report to the A. Board. Mr. R(ogers) goes hunting buffalo. About one o'clock Mr. W., S. & S(tevens) return with the cattle - find them on the trail towards Walla Walla, at least 12 miles, walking on as regularly as though they were driven. Heat oppressive in the middle of the day.

27th. Wednesday. I repair my dress, which is about worn out. Mr. Gray attends to baking. Mr. Rogers returns from buffalo hunting, kills two. I cut and help make a gown for Mrs. Craig.

28th. Thursday. High winds. Mr. G. and his wife, Mr. E. and myself take a ride up the river. More timber than we have seen since we left Fort William ... Mr. Eells commences writing letters.

29th. Friday. Mrs. Drips, Walker and Robinson call on us. Wish me to cut a dress for Mrs. R. I cut out a gown for Mr. Clark.

30th Saturday. The calico these garments are made of costs 2 dollars a yard, and is of ordinary quality.

July 1st. Sabbath. Worship in the open air under the cottonwood trees. Mr. Smith preaches in the morning, Mr. Walker in the afternoon, 50 or 60 men come from the other camp. Feel that we have been fed with spiritual food to-day.

2d. Monday. All in camp, hear nothing from any to escort us over the mountains ... Anxiously wait for the time when we shall get to our fields of labor.

3d. Tuesday. Four Indian women called to see us last evening. Mrs. Gray and I make a rice pudding. An old Indian comes and seats himself at the door of our tent but (we) can not understand him at all. He then goes to Mr. Walker's tent and tries to talk, but can not be understood. Mr. Richardson and Stevens go hunting buffalo.

4th. Wednesday. No church bells, no beating of drums or roaring of cannons to remind us of our blood-bought liberty. How different one year ago. Then I attended a meeting for Sabbath school children. Here Capts. Drips, Walker and Robbins take dinner with us. Major Harris comes to us again. Says that nine days out of eleven it rained and snowed constantly since he left us. He said that the snow was 12 or 14 inches deep in the mountains. The men do business about camp and guard horses. Mr. Gray and Mr. Eells finish the report to the A. Board. Heat oppressive in the middle of the day.

5th. Thursday. Last night were troubled exceedingly by the noise of some drunken men. About one was awakened by the barking of dogs, soon we heard a rush of drunken men coming directly towards our tent. Mr. Eells got up immediately and went to the door of the tent in a moment. Four men came swearing and blaspheming, inquiring for Mr. Gray. Asked if Mr. Richardson was at home. Mr. Eells answered their inquiries and said little else. They said they wished to settle accounts with Mr. Gray, then they should be off. They said they did (not) come to do us harm, had they attempted it, the dog would have torn them to pieces. They then began singing. Asked Mr. Eells to sing with them. He told them he did not know their tunes. They asked if they disturbed him by keeping him up. He made no reply. They said silence gave consent and went away ... giving us no more trouble, only that we were constantly in fear lest they would come back again.

All this while, Mr. G. and myself were making preparations for our escape, while Mr. Gray was loading Mr. E's gun, his own being lent.

Capt. Bridger's company comes in about 10 o'clock, with drums and firing - an apology for a scalp dance. After they had given Capt. Drip's company a shout, 15 or 20 mountain men and Indians came to our tent with drumming, firing and dancing. If I might make the comparison, I should say that they looked like the emissaries of the Devil worshipping their own master. They had the scalp of a Blackfoot Indian, which they carried for a color, all rejoicing in the fate of the Blackfoot in consequence of the small-pox. The dog being frightened took the trail across the river and howled so that we knew him and called him back When he came he went to each tent to see if we were all safe, then appeared quiet. Thermometer, 90 degrees.

6th. Friday. Last night twelve white men came, dressed and painted Indian style, and gave us a dance. No pen can describe the horrible scene they presented. Could not imaging that white men, brought up in a civilized land, can appear to so much imitate the Devil. Thermometer, 100 degrees. Cut two dresses for children. About noon, the white men and Indians gave us another dance. All writing.

7th. Saturday. Finish our letters, prepare for the Sabbath ... Hear nothing from Mr. Spaulding.

8th. Sabbath. Prepare for public services. An express comes from Dr. Whitman, Mr. E(rmatinger) and one Indian for a guide on the opposite side of the river to escort us over the mountains. Say that we have 4 fresh horses and provisions at Fort Hall, sent us by Mr. Spaulding and Dr. Whitman ... Mr. Lee, a Methodist missionary on the Columbia, Mr. Edwards and Mr. Ewen came here with him and are going to the States, which gives a safe conveyance for our letters. No public exercises to-day.

9th. Monday. All writing. Messrs. Lee, Edwards and Ewen call on us. Mr. Edwards has been an associate in missionary labor with Mr. Lee, who is on his way to the States for a reinforcement to that Mission. Mr. Ewen has been over the mountains for his health. Thermometer, ninety.

10th. Tuesday. Heat oppressive. Capt. Bridger and Mr. Newell dine with us. Two years ago Dr. Whitman took an Indian spear (out) of Capt. Bridger's back that had been there three years.

Wednesday. Make arrangements for the remainder of the journey. The gentlemen tell us we have not begun to see danger and hardship in travelling.

12th. Thursday. About 20 men to go over the mountains (i.e., to Walla Walla) *Bid farewell to our new-formed acquaintances ...*[11]

Mary Walker stated:

21st. Thursday. Have reached the place near where they rendezvous. Encamped on the South W. side of the Popeasia. Have plenty of wood, water, grass, greens and thickets. Know not how long we may be detained here. Health good. The animals are in better order, most of them than when we started.

22nd. (June, 1838). Busy repairing. Concluding whether we had better cross Popeasia. Mr. & Mrs. S. went out and were gone several hours, so husband came & made me quite a pleasant visit.

23d. Saturday. About noon took a sudden start & crossed the river without the least difficulty. Mr. S. is going to construct a lodge, so we shall (have) our tent to ourselves. Our situation is delightful. In a little grove of cotton wood, consisting of some 20 trees, in the forks of the Popeasia & Wind Rivers. Husband looks more happy than I have seen him in a long time.

Stampede by Blackfeet Indians. 1867, by A. J. Miller, Public Archives of Canada, C-435.

24th. Sabbath. Mr. S. has gone to living by himself. Query, does not the course he is pursuing cost him some misgivings? It will be pleasant not to hear so much fault finding ... Mr. Walker preached on the a.m. on judgment, sitting in the open air in the shade of our beautiful grove. He had 18 hearers, We enjoyed the meeting much. In the afternoon Mr. Eells preached. Had only our family ... Read "Saints Rest" between & after meetings. Husband seems to like to stay in the tent now. We all put on our Sunday dresses & acted as much like Sabbath at home as we could. I think I am rather happy.

25th. Monday. Spent most of the day talking & dividing things with Mrs. S.

26th. Tuesday. The cattle strayed ... Think I enjoy myself, quite as happy as Mrs. S. for she has seemed to cry half of the time, but I have not once since she left. Think I have (not) refrained as long before since we left Westport.

27th. Wednesday. Gray & Robertson came to get their dresses cut. Mrs. Gray baked mince pies; the day before yesterday she fried cakes. This morning Mr. W. almost got out of patience with G.

28th. Thursday. Mr. Walker traded for a pony & paid 80 dollars in goods for one that in the States would not be worth 20. Tent in a clutter all day.

30th. Saturday. Baked pudding, sewed on a hunting dress, weather warm. Health good. Mosquitoes plenty.

July 1st. Sabbath. Public exercises at half past ten ... I judge as many as 40 persons from the camp, many of (whom) could not understand what was said but they enjoyed the singing ... The day has been so warm, I feel languid enough.

4th. Wednesday. Rode out in the morning ... Had baked pudding & greens for dinner. Washed a few things, made a few repairs. A fine day, hope friends at home have had some what of a good time. I do want to hear from (them) very much. Could be quite content if I could hear, but not to see nor hear, it seems too bad.

5th. Thursday. Last night disturbed by drunkards. Rose early and washed. A large company arrived under command of Capt. Bridger, some of them came to salute us. One man carried the scalp of a Blackfoot. The musick consisted of ten horns, accompanied by the inarticulate sound of the voice. They hollered, danced, fired (guns) & acted as strangely as they could.

6th. Friday. Some of the squaws came to get dresses cut. We were again saluted by a company on foot. The same musick, scalp, etc. Their faces were painted. White men acted like Indians. It is said that many of the white men in the Mts. try to act as much like Indians as they can & would be glad if they really were so. Several squaws were here who united in the dance. They were warmly clad, (though) the weather was excessively hot. For several nights the noise in the camp has continued nearly all night. Some of the Capts. & I suppose many of the men are drunk nearly all the time.

7th. Saturday. Baked some pies in the morning. Finished putting together my riding dress.

8th. Sabbath. The day has been to us a day of rejoicing. A company of 14 from Hudson Bay Co. arrived. Among them were Rev. Jason Lee, from the Methodist Mission, on his way to the States & several boys who are going to be educated. They came to Green River, expecting to find the rendezvous there. But on reaching (that place) found no signs. The country full of buffalow. But in an old trading house, they found a line, "Come on to the Popeasia; plenty of whiskey & white women." They accordingly came and on the fourth day found us.

Monday 9, Tues 10, Wed. 11. Wrote one big letter to all the folks and one small one to sisters. Forgot to tell them how little Indian children ride & how the mothers do. How much the way is shortened by the company of plants & minerals; was sorry not to be able to write more. [12]

Kit Carson stated that he "started to find the main camp which was on a tributary of Green River. We remained with the main party till July, and then went into rendezvous on the Popoachi, a tributary of Wind River. About the twentieth of August we started ..."[13]

Robert Newell, who had spent the winter in the mountains, started for what he believed to be the rendezvous site at Green River and found only buffalo. He wrote:

Left the party and went in search of the St. Louis outfit I went down green river at the mouth of horse creek I found whare Some of that party had been that day in two days after I found them on a fork of green river they informed me the St Louis party was on their way to wind river whare they intended to hold rendezvous I returned to our camp and found them on the head of green river we changed our Course went on to the head of wind river from thare down to the fork of po po isha whare we found Mr. Drips with our Supplies Commenced Sales and men who had been in the Company a long time commenced leaving owing to the company being So hard Some run off Stole horses

*traps and other articles of value After a long and tedious time we
left for hunting.*[14]

According to Newell, the company men were apparently
being very hard nosed in regards to business at the rendezvous.
Prices were extremely high and some trappers were slipping
away from the rendezvous because they could not pay the
company their debts. Credit was a thing of the past. Newell
implies that in desperation for supplies some trappers were even
stealing from their supplier. From Newell's account it is apparent
that the yearly rendezvous was in trouble and very possibly
would not be held again. John McLoughlin, writing his superiors
in October, 1838, refers to the information given him by Francis
Ermatinger, who *"made a visit to the American rendezvous chiefly for
the purpose of gathering information."*[15] McLoughlin continues:

> *The annual supply caravan from St. Louis, consisted of
> 25 Waggons under a strong escort of men, and the collective
> hunts and trade of the American Company for the year ending
> June 1838, was little over 2000 Beaver and Otter skins. The
> complement of men employed, in their country service, though
> now greatly reduced in number exceeds 125, of different classes,
> some at fixed wages, and others, receiving five Dollars p. lb. for
> the Beaver skins they collect. Their trade, cannot certainly
> support such expensive machinery, and we are almost induced
> to believe, the reports in circulation, that a great portion of their
> debts, are cleared off by cards and alcohol. They are striving to
> reduce the price of Beaver to three dollars p. pound, but there is
> no certainty of the point being carried, as the attempt produced
> an alarming excitment among their men. Many even of the best
> Trappers, would have entered our service, had we been desirous
> of such acquisition; but their overtures were declined, as it is
> clearly to our interest to push up the price of goods, on the
> American side of the frontiers.*[16]

If Ermatinger's claim that the trappers brought in only 2,000
pelts this year was accurate, then the beaver trade indeed was in
trouble. His further claim that only 125 trappers were present
adds additional support to this premise. Apparently many men
had left the mountains because of ever increasing problems. The
five dollars per pound prize for beaver that he mentions was an
exorbitant price to pay for beaver in the mountains. The high
cost, no doubt, was brought about by the Hudson's Bay
Company's competition at Fort Hall. It would be interesting to

know how many American trappers' pelts found their way to
Fort Hall and not to the rendezvous. Here may be the answer as
to why only 2,000 pelts were taken back to St. Louis. The
American Company was being forced to be competitive in what
they paid for beaver, but Chouteau felt that they could not
continue to pay $5.00. Newell mentioned that before the
rendezvous was over the company was already trying to get the
price down to $3.00. The Hudson's Bay Company felt that the
Chouteau Company would destroy itself by charging exorbitant
prices for goods at the rendezvous and forcing them to pay high
prices for beaver pelts to stay competitive would be a final blow.
In a letter written by Cornelius Rogers dated July 3, 1838, *"Camp
of the American Fur Company, in rendezvous, eastern base of Wind
River Mountains and junction of Popo Agie and Wind River,"*[17] the
young man makes the following prediction about the Hudson's
Bay Company and the American rivalry in the mountains:

> *This is a term used to designate the place where all the
> trappers meet at this season of the year to bring in their furs, and
> obtain their future supplies. At the appointed time, they meet at
> some point most convenient for all. None are excluded: - free
> traders, hired men, &c., all come in, and procure their supply of
> clothes, ammunition, &c. Rendezvous generally last 20 or 30
> days, and the whole time is spent in drinking, gambling horse-
> racing, quarrelling, fighting &c. Alcohol is the only liquor
> brought here, and is sold at $4 a pint. Some men will spend a
> thousand dollars in a day or two, and very few have any part of
> their year's wages left when rendezvous breaks up.*

> *Our company are encamped about 300 yards from the
> main camp; so we are a little out of their noise, but they come
> down nearly every day to give us an Indian dance. They always
> treat us with kindness; but they wish to give us a specimen of
> mountain life. When the time for separation comes, it becomes
> each one to look well to his effects; for he is in danger of being
> stripped of everything he possesses.*

> *The American Fur Company must soon abandon the
> mountains. The trade is unprofitable, and the men are becoming
> dissatisfied; besides, the Hudson's Bay Company will break
> down all opposition. Their resources are boundless, and they
> stop at no expense. They are now establishing posts through all
> the country which is accessible west of the mountains; and they
> sell their goods for less than one-fourth the price charged by the*

other company. What their intentions in regard to the possession of this country are, I cannot tell. One of their officers, with some men, arrived here yesterday. He came to meet and assist us on to Fort Hall, which is about 15 days' ride, with pack animals, from this place. Mr. Spaulding also will meet us on the way. Mr. Spaulding and Dr. Whitman, it is said, are well and doing well.

There are no Indians except a few trappers of the Shawnees and Delawares. There are a few lodges of the Snakes around the point of the mountain; but they will not come here. There are two classes of the Snake nation. One is the Shoshonies, or those who have horses. They are friendly but have some of the roving savage disposition. The others are called Diggers, from the fact that they live principally upon roots. They inhabit the mountains, seldom venturing to the plains, and are harmless inoffensive people. [18]

Osborne Russell, traveling to what he thought was the annual rendezvous on Green River, was surprised to find no one there. He recorded the following:

July 1st we travelled down this stream to the plains and steered our course NE towards "horse creek" where we expected to find the Rendezvous. The next day we arrived at the place but instead of finding the Camp we found a large band of buffaloe near the appointed place of meeting. We rode up to an old log building which was formerly used as a store house during the Rendezvous where I discovered a piece of paper fastened upon the wall which informed me that we should find the Whites at the forks of Wind River. This was unwelcome news to us as our animals were very much jaded ... There we found Mr. Dripps from St Louis with 20 horse carts loaded with Supplies and again met Capt. Stewart likewise several Missionaries with their families on their way to the Columbia river. On the 8th Mr. F. Ermatinger arrived with a small part from the Columbia accompanied by the Rev. Jason Lee who was on his way to the U S On the 20 of July the meeting broke up and the parties again dispersed for the fall hunt ... During our Stay at the Rendezvous it was rumored among the men that the Company intended to bring no more supplies to the Rocky Mountains and discontinue all further operations. This caused a great deal of discontent among the Trappers and numbers ... [19]

When Newell arrived at the Green River site in late June, he made no mention of a note. He was informed of the location of the rendezvous from other trappers who had been at the Green River site a few days before his arrival and were now two days travel down Green River. The trappers who informed Newell had apparently not left a note at the site to publicly announce the new location. However, when Russell arrived at Green River on July 1st, he found a note on the old building. Who left it? Was it Newell? Newell was a free trapper and not a company man. He had no loyalties to Chouteau or Hudson's Bay. The Ermatinger party as well as both Newell's and Russell's parties went to the Green River site expecting to find trapper and the caravan. At some point from the close of the 1837 Rendezvous and the spring of 1838, the word was out that the rendevzous was to be on the Green River. Why then was the location in question? It was no secret that the company was not happy having the Hudson's Bay men attend the American rendezvous for when they assembled together a great deal of friction was the inevitable result. This was pointed out in 1836 by Narcissa Whitman as she witnessed the two rival companies camped together at the rendezvous. Consequently, the following information taken from a letter written by Elkanah Walker in October, 1838, regarding the 1838 Rendezvous is not surprising. Walker wrote: *"its (rendezvous) place being kept a secret, it was expected that the H.B.C. would not find it."*[20]

Cushing Eells also mentioned the secrecy of the rendezvous location. *"In 1838 a change of location was made. The point chosen was the Popiasua (Popo Agie) or Wind River ... The object was secrecy, and thereby to prevent the H B Co. from interferring in their trade."*[21]

On another occasion Eells recorded:

Some one who was somewhat friendly to the missionaries, either Dr. Robert Newell, an independent trapper, or a half breed named Black Harris, who had learned of the rendezvous of the American Fur Company, had with charcoal written on the old storehouse door, come to Poposua on Wind river and you will find plenty trade, whiskey, and white women. The words white women told them what was meant, and Mr. Ermatinger went immediately there arriving only four days, before the company was ready to start on their return to the States.[22]

Mrs. Victor, in her reminiscences of Joel Meek, stated that the *"American Fur Company had changed the location of the rendezvous because it had become vexed at the Hudson's Bay Company. The location on Wind River was much more inconvenient to the H.B. Co. than on Green.*"[23]

So whoever it was that left the note scribbled on the old building had let the cat out of the bag and all concerned groups eventually found the rendezvous. And even if the company men were not happy to see the arrival of Ermatinger's party, the missionaries were.

The old building referred to by Russell could possibly be Fort Bonneville. However, Aubrey L. Haines, editor of Osborne Russell's journal, states in his work that it was not Bonneville's Fort. This statement is based on the book **Altowan** written by Sir William Drummond Stewart who implies that the fort was in ruin. The fort was standing in 1836 for the missionaries used it as living quarters. Yet the following evidence needs to be considered. Russell refers to the old building where he found the note as *"formerly used as a store house during the Rendezvous."*[24] Eells refers to the note written *"On the old storehouse door."*[25] The only storehouse ever mentioned in any journal or diary at the Green River rendezvous site was Fort Bonneville. Whether the old building was Fort Bonneville or not cannot be definitely ascertained at this writing. Hopefully some diary will be found that will answer the question.

The Hudson's Bay men, once again escorting the missionaries to Walla Walla, left the rendezvous on July 12th. It is not certain when the summer gathering broke up nor who took the furs back to the settlement. However, Drips remained in the mountains with Bridger as his guide. Both Provost and Fontenelle were in the settlements in the fall of 1838 and very possibly could have been the leaders of the returning caravan that fall.

At the close of 1838 there were two questions that had to be answered regarding the American fur trade. First, the mountainmen were faced with the question as to whether there would be a rendezvous in 1839 at which they could obtain supplies. And second, Pierre Chouteau was asking himself if it was worth his time and effort to take supplies to the mountains in the spring.

GREEN RIVER (SISKEEDEE-AGIE) RENDEZVOUS
1839

By the spring of 1839 Pierre Chouteau had made his decision to send a caravan to the mountains. The caravan that left Westport on May 4th under the direction of Moses Harris was very small compared to those of earlier years. Accompanying the supply train was Dr. Frederick A. Wislizenus, a German physician, whose journal is the only detailed account of the 1839 caravan and rendezvous.

He leaves the following information concerning the caravan:

> *Our caravan was small.*
> *It consisted of only twenty-seven persons. Nine of them were in the service of the Fur Company of St. Louis (Chouteau, Pratte, & Co.), and were to bring the merchandise to the yearly rendezvous on the Green River. Their leader was Mr. Harris, a mountaineer without special education, but with five sound sences, that he well knew how to use. All the rest joined the expedition as individuals. Among them were three missionaries, two of them accompanied by their wives, whom a christian zeal for converting the heathen urged to the Columbia ... The majority of the party were Americans; the rest consisted of French Canadians, a few Germans, and a Dane. The Fur Company transported its goods on two-wheeled carts, of which there were four, each drawn by two mules, and loaded with 800 to 900 pounds. The rest put their packs on mules or horses, of which there were fifty to sixty in the caravan.*[1]

The missionary couples mentioned by Wislizenus were Reverend and Mrs. John S. Griffith and Mr. and Mrs. Asahel Munger.

The caravan arrived at the fort on Laramie Creek on June 14th. Apparently there was no question in Wislizenus' mind about calling the Fort Laramie. He recorded the following about his stay there at the fort:

> The next morning (June 14th), we left camp in good humor, for the crotchety master of human crotchets, I mean the weather, smiled on us; and the vicinity of Fort Laramie, but sixteen miles distant, promised us a speedy meeting with human beings. Before we reached the fort, we encountered the first "pale faces" we had seen since our departure from Missouri. They were French Canadians, clad half Indian fashion in leather, and scurrying along on their ponies, bedight with bells and gay ribbons, as if intent to storm some battery. Old acquaintances greeted each other, question piled on question; and each briefly told, in Canadian patios, the adventures he had been through. Meanwhile we came in view of the fort.

> At a distance it resembles a great blockhouse; and lies in a narrow valley, enclosed by grassy hills, near by the left bank of the Laramie, which empties into the North Platte about a mile below. Toward the west a fine background is formed by the Black Hills a dark chain of mountains covered with ever green trees. We crossed the Laramie toward noon, and encamped outside the fort. The fort itself first attracted my attention. It lies on a slight elevation, and is built in a rectangle of about eighty by a hundred feet. The outside is made of cottonwood logs, about fifteen feet high, hewed off, and wedged closely together. On three sides there are little towers on the wall that seem designed for watch and defense. In the middle a strong gate, built of blocks, constitutes the entrance. Within, little buildings with flat roofs are plastered all around against the wall, like swallows' nests. One is the store house; another the smithy; the others are dwellings not unlike monks' cells. A special portion of the court yard is occupied by the so-called horse-pen, in which the horses are confined at night. The middle space is free, with a tall tree in it, on which the flag is raised on occasions of state. The whole garrison of the fort consists of only five men; four Frenchmen and a German. Some of them were married to Indian women, whose cleanliness and neat attire formed an agreeable contrast to the daughters of the wilderness whom we had hitherto seen. In this connection, let me call attention to a mistaken idea often entertained as to these forts. They are often thought of as military forts, occupied by regular troops, and

under military rule, whereas they are mere trading forts, built by single trading companies, and occupied by a handful of hired men to have a safe point for storing their goods, from which barter may be carried on with the Indians. Such forts exist on both sides of the Rocky Mountains, established by American and English companies; but nowhere is there a military fort erected by government of either country. The simple construction, as above described, protects them adequately against any attack on the part of the Indians. Out of abundant caution some of them have a little cannon on the wall. As far as I know, there is no fort on the North Platte save Fort Laramie; but several American trading companies have built forts along the South Platte, the Arkansas, the Green River, and the Missouri. Beyond the Rocky Mountains are only English forts.

Fort Laramie was built in 1835 by Robert Campbell, and was then called Fort William. Later it passed into other control, and was rechristened Fort Laramie after one Laramie, who was killed here by the Indians. The custom of perpetuating the memory of departed friends by transferring their names to the place where they fell, is so habitual in the Rocky Mountains, and the occasions giving rise to it are unfortunately so frequent, that at least half the names owe their origin to such events. The fort is at present in possession of Piggit, Pagin and Jaudron. In many respects it has a very favorable location. There is sufficient wood in the vicinity and good pasture. A few days' journey further there is abundance of buffalo and other game, and the Platte from this point is navigable for small boats; at least Campbell has already gone down from here to the Missouri in buffalo boats. Then, too, it is a very suitable center for trade with important Indian tribes, especially the Sioux and Crows ...

As we stayed there the rest of the day, several races took place between our horses and those of the fort; and of course there was betting and swapping of horses. I swapped my horse, which was somewhat run down by the journey and thin, for a swift, well fed Indian horse trained to hunt buffalo. The Indian horses are said to have come originally from Mexico. They are of a small breed, and seldom can be called handsome; but they are very swift and hardy, and as they know no food save grass, are much more suitable for such a journey than American horses, which usually grow lean on mere grass. Still American horses,

187

because they are larger and handsomer, are much sought after by whites and Indians, and, when once they are acclimated, are superior.[2]

The caravan left Fort Laramie on June 15th, having only rested one day. Apparently when the caravan left Westport in May, the exact location of the rendezvous was not known. Wislizenus' journal suggests that Harris knew the rendezvous was not on the Popo Agie as in 1838. However, he was not certain as to where on Green River it was to be located since, at the close of the 1838 Rendezvous, the trappers were not even sure that there would be a supply train in 1839. In fact, some trappers, such as Osborne Russell, were not present at the rendezvous simply because they were not aware that it was taking place. On New Fork, according to Wislizenus, Harris sent out men to find the rendezvous site. They returned with Andrew Drips and Joseph Walker who notified Harris that the rendezvous was once again at the junction of Horse Creek and Green River. Wislizenus, who arrived at the rendezvous on July 5th and remained there until July 10th, recorded the following about the 1839 Rendezvous:

> *Our next objective point was the upper Green River valley, which is thrust like a bay of prairie between the main chain of the Rockies and the projecting Wind River Mountains. Our direction was northeast. The road thither leads over sandy hills and plateaus. The Wind River Mountains lay to our right, permitting a closer view of the precipitous, weather-beaten granite formations cut by deep ravines. As intervening bulwark, there were foothills, dark with evergreens, but void of snow. To our left new snow peaks come into view, the Grand River Mountains. We crossed several streams, first the Little Sandy and the Big Sandy, then the New Fork; all having their sources in the Wind River Mountains and flowing into the Green River. The water is clear and cool, the river bed pebbly. The shores are usually fringed with willows. In these little rivers there are, furthermore, denizens characteristic of western waters. For, while the Platte has few fish, and little beside catfish are found in the other streams, many trout are found on this side. On the second day we found traces of whites and Indians, that had journeyed ahead of us through this region a short time before, probably to the rendezvous, which takes place yearly about this time in he neighborhood of the Green River. As our destination was the same, though our leader did not*

know precisely what place had been chosen for it this year, some of our men were sent out for information. They returned the next day while we were camping on the New Fork, with two agents of the fur company, Trips (Drips) and Walker. These agents were accompanied by their Indian wives and a lot of dogs. The two squaws, quite passable as to their features, appeared in highest state. Their red blankets, with the silk kerchiefs on their heads, and their gaudy embroideries, gave them quite an Oriental appearance. Like themselves, their horses were bedight with embroideries, beads, corals, ribbons and little bells. The bells were hung about in such number that when riding in their neighborhood, one might think one's self in the midst of Turkish music. The squaws, however, behaved most properly. They took care of the horses, pitched a tent, and were alert for every word of their wedded lords. From the agents we learned that this year's meeting place had been fixed on the right bank of the Green River at the angle formed by its junction with Horse Creek. We were now about a day's journey from the place. Starting off in company in the afternoon, we covered, at a more rapid pace than usual, about twelve miles, and then camped on a branch of the New Fork, whose shores were framed with fine pines. It was the Fourth of July, the great holiday of the United States. Our camp, however, presented its humdrum daily appearance. We stretched out around the fires, smoked and, in expectation of what the morrow would bring, went quietly asleep. The next morning we started early, and reached toward noon the Green River, so long desired. The Green River (Colorado of the West) rises in the northwestern slope of the Wind River Mountains, flows in southwestern direction, and empties into the Gulf of California. Where we first saw it, it is a clear, rippling streamlet, abounding in trout; neither very broad, nor very deep; but later on it becomes a broad, rushing stream. Its navigation is said to present enormous difficulties. We crossed the river, and were then in the acute angle formed by it and Horse Creek (a brook coming from the northwest and emptying here into the Green River). The space between is level; the ground a loamy sand. The camping place was about two miles above the Horse Creek, along the right bank of the Green River. The plain between the two streams is here about three miles broad. The rendezvous has repeatedly been held here. According to observations formerly made, the place is in longitude 107 degrees 12 minutes west, and between 44 and 45 degrees north latitude. (42° - 43°) So we were about four degrees north of St. Louis. The journey which we had made from the border of Missouri, according to our rough calculations, was near 1,200 miles.

We reached the camping place. What first struck our eye was several long rows of Indian tents (lodges), extending along the Green River for at least a mile. Indians and whites were mingled here in varied groups. Of the Indians there had come chiefly Snakes, Flatheads and Nez-perces, peaceful tribes, living beyond the Rocky Mountains. Of whites the agents of the different trading companies and a quantity of trappers had found their way here, visiting this fair of the wilderness to buy and to sell, to renew old contacts and to make new ones, to make arrangements for future meetings, to meet old friends, to tell of adventures they had been through, and to spend for once a jolly day. These trappers, the "Knights without fear and without reproach," are such a peculiar set of people that it is necessary to say a little about them. The name in itself indicates their occupation. They either receive their outfit, consisting of horses, beaver traps, a gun, powder and lead, from trading companies, and trap for small wages, or else they act on their own account, and are then called freemen. The latter is more often the case. In small parties they roam through all the mountain passes. No rock is too steep for them; no stream too swift. Withal, they are in constant danger from hostile Indians, whose delight it is to ambush such small parties, and plunder them, and scalp them. Such victims fall every year. One of our fellow travelers, who had gone to the mountains for the first time nine years ago with about one hundred men, estimated that by this time half the number had fallen victims to the tomahawks of the Indians. But this daily danger seems to exercise a magic attraction over most of them. Only with reluctance does a trapper abandon his dangerous craft; and a sort of serious home-sickness seizes him when he retires from his mountain life to civilization. In manners and customs, the trappers have borrowed much from the Indians. Many of them, too, have taken Indian women as wives. Their dress is generally of leather. The hair of the head is usually allowed to grow long. In place of money, they use beaver skins, for which they can satisfy all their needs at the forts by way of trade. A pound of beaver skins is usually paid for with four dollars worth of goods; but the goods themselves are sold at enormous prices, so-called mountain prices. A pint of meal, for instance, costs from half a dollar to a dollar; a pint of coffee-beans, cocoa beans or sugar, two dollars each; a pint of diluted alcohol (the only spiritous liqour to be had), four dollars; a piece of chewing tobacco of the commonest sort, which is usually smoked, Indian fashion, mixed with herbs, one to two dollars. Guns and ammunition, bear traps, blankets, kerchiefs, and gaudy finery for the squaws, are also sold at enormous profit. At the yearly rendezvous the trappers seek to indemnify themselves for the sufferings and privations of a year spent in the wilderness. With their hairy bank notes, the beaver skins, they can obtain all the luxuries of the mountains, and live for a few days like lords. Coffee and chocolate is cooked; the pipe is kept aglow day and night; the spirits circulate; and whatever is not spent in such ways the squaws coax out of them, or else it is squandered at cards. Formerly single trappers on such occasions have often wasted a thousand dollars. But the days of their glory seem to be past, for constant hunting has very much reduced the number of beavers. This diminution in the beaver catch made itself noticeable at this year's rendezvous in the quieter behavior of the trappers. There was little drinking of spirits, and almost no gambling. Another decade perhaps and the original trapper will have disappeared from the mountains.

The Indians who had come to the meeting were no less interesting than the trappers. There must have been some thousands of them. Their tents are made of buffalo hides, tanned on both sides and sewed together, stretched in cone shaped over a dozen poles, that are leaned against each other, their tops crossing. In front and on top this leather can be thrown back, to form door and chimney. The tents are about twelve feet high and twenty feet in circumference at the ground and give sufficient protection in any kind of weather. I visited many tents, partly out of curiosity, partly to barter for trifles, and sought to make myself intelligible in the language of signs as far as possible. An army of Indian dogs very much resembling the wolf, usually beset the entrance. From some tents comes the sound of music. A virtuoso beats a sort of kettle drum with bells around with all his might, and the chorus accompanies him with strange monotone untrained sounds that showed strong tendency to the

191

minor chords. A similar heart-rending song drew me to a troop of squaws that were engrossed in the game of "the hand," so popular with the Indians. Some small object, a bit of wood, for instance, is passed from hand to hand among the players seated in a circle; and it is some one's part to guess in whose hands the object is. During the game the chorus steadily sings some song as monotonous as those to which bears dance. But the real object is to gamble in this way for some designated prize. It is a game of hazard. In this case, for example, a pile of beads and corals, which lay in the midst of the circle, was the object in question. Men and women are so carried away by the game, that they often spend a whole day and night at it. Other groups of whites and Indians were engaged in barter. The Indians had for the trade chiefly tanned skins, moccasins, thongs of buffalo leather or braided buffalo hair, and fresh or dried buffalo meat. They have no beaver skins. The articles that attracted them most in exchange were powder and lead, knives, tobacco, cinnabar, gaily colored kerchiefs, pocket mirrors and all sorts of ornaments. Before the Indian begins to trade he demands sight of everything that may be offered by the other party to the trade. If there is something there that attracts him, he, too, will produce his wares, but discovers very quickly how much or how little they are coveted. If he himself is not willed to dispose of some particular thing, he obstinately adheres to his refusal, though ten times the value be offered him. The peltry bought from the Indians must be carefully beaten and aired, at peril of having objectionable troops billeted on you. The Indians, accustomed to every kind of uncleanliness, seem to have a special predilection for a certain kind of domestic animal, and even to consider it a delicacy. So, for instance, I have repeatedly seen an old granddam summering before the tent with her gray-haired spouse, and busily picking the "heavy cavalry" from his head. But the fingers that deftly caught the prisoner with equal deftness carried him to the mouth, where the unhappy creature was buried alive. Chacun a son gout!

The rendezvous usually lasts a week. Then the different parties move off to their destinations and the plain that today resounded wth barbarous music, that was thronged with people of both races, with horses and dogs, returns to its old quiet, interrupted only now and then by the muffled roar of the buffalo and the howl of the wolf.[3]

Kit Carson, trapping the head waters of the Missouri in the spring of 1839, stated ... *"We commenced our hunt trapping of the tributaries of the Missouri to the head of Lewis Fork, and then started for the rendezvous on Green River, near the mouth of Horse Creek. There we remained until August ..."*[4] According to Carson, the rendezvous ended sometime in August. No details were given by the journalists as to how many furs were taken back to St. Louis, but according Wislizenus' statement, *"this dimunition in the beaver catch,"*[5] should imply that it was small.

Wislizenus notes that Ermatinger had traveled over from Fort Hall with 14 men and was present at the rendezvous. Hudson's Bay Company was still keeping the pressure on the American Company. Wislizenus accompanied some of Ermatinger's men who were enroute to California when he left the rendezvous on July 10th.

Robert Newell, who was present at the rendezvous, indicates that he returned to Fort Hall with Ermatinger, leaving the rendezvous on July 9th.

Newell states:

> ... *met Drips with 4 Carts of Supplies from below held rendezvous I left with Mr F Ermatinger to fort hall left on the 9 of July arrived at fort hall on the 20 1839 Missionaries from the States Griffin and Monger with ladies.*[6]

Apparently Drips was in charge of the returning caravan while Moses Harris remained in the mountains during the winter of 1839-40.

Many of the trappers, including Newell, spent the winter in Brown's Hole of the Green River. The site had become a favorite wintering place for the mountainmen during the past few years.

GREEN RIVER (SISKEEDEE—AGIE) RENDEZVOUS
1840

Andrew Drips, assisted by his old friends, Jim Bridger and Henry Fraeb, directed the caravan to the 1840 Rendezvous. It left Westport on April 30th, the last caravan ever to leave the settlements and take supplies to the mounain rendezvous. Joel Walker, brother of Joseph Walker, gives the following details about the caravan:

> *About this time the Government of the United States offered emigrants six hundred and forty acres of land. The Congregational Missionaries came to Independence. Their names were Littlejohn, Harvey Clark and Smith with their families. I joined them with my wife and five children. I had two wagons and the missionaries had two, and for protection we traveled with the American Fur Company's men. They had thirty carts, and forty men.* [1]

Why the caravan was so much bigger than in 1839 is a mystery. The number of furs brought back in 1839 certainly did not warrant such a large caravan. This year's missionary group consisted of the Catholic Father, Pierre Jean DeSmet, and the Reverends Harvey Clark, P. B. Littlejohn, Alvin T. Smith and their wives.

On June 30th the caravan arrived at the rendezvous on Green River. Father DeSmet recorded the following concerning his trip to the mountains and the activities of the rendezvous:

> *On the 30th of April, (1840), I set out from Westport with the annual expedition of the American Fur Company, (Captain Andrew Drips) which was on its way to Green River, one of the branches of the Colorado. Until the 17th of May we traveled over immense plains, destitute of trees or shrubs, except along the streams, and broken by deep ravines, where our voyageurs lowered and raised the carts by means of ropes...* [2]

The trip for DeSmet was very difficult due to his illness. As he relates:

I had been no more than six days in the wilderness, when I was overcome by intermittent fever, with the chills that ordinarily precede the attacks of heat. This fever never left me until I reached the Yellowstone, on my way back from the mountains. I cannot give you any idea of my deplorable state. [3]

The travelers were amazed at the climate in the mountains. DeSmet states:

On the 19th, we descried the Wind or (Wind River) Mountains, in which is the rendezvous of the caravan and its point of separation as well; but we were still nine days' journey from the place. Every day we became aware that it was growing colder and colder, and on the 24th (June) we traversed plains covered with snow. [4]

Upon arrival at the rendezvous, DeSmet continued:

On the 30th I came to the rendezvous, where a band of Flatheads, who had been notified of my coming, were already waiting for me. This happened, as I said further back on Green river, a tributary of the Colorado; it is the place whither the beaver-hunters and the savages of different nations betake themselves every year to sell their peltries and procure such things as they need ...

The Shoshones, or Root-diggers called also Snakes, were present at the rendezvous in great number ... At the rendezvous they gave a parade to greet the whites that were there. Three hundred of their warriors came up in good order and at full gallop into the midst of our camp. They were hideously painted, armed with their clubs, and covered all over with feathers, pearls, wolves' tails, teeth and claws of animals, outlandish adornments, with which each one had decked himself out according to his fancy. Those who had killed the enemies of their tribe displayed their scars ostentatiously and waved the scalps they had taken on the ends of poles, after the manner of standards.

After riding a few times around the camp, uttering at intervals shouts of joy, they dismounted and all came to shake hands with the whites in sign of friendship. I was invited to a council by some thirty of the principal chiefs. Just as among the Cheyennes, we had first to go through all the ceremonies of the calument. To begin, the chief made a little circle on the ground, placed within it a small piece of burning dried cow-dung, and lit his pipe from it. Then he offered the pipe to the Great Spirit, to the sun, to the earth and the four cardinal points. All the others observed a most profound silence and sat motionless as statues. The calument passed from hand to hand, and I noticed that each one had a different way of taking it. One turned the calument around before putting the stem to his mouth; the next made a half-circle as he accepted it; another held the bowl in the air; a fourth lowered it to the ground, and so on. I am naturally inclined to laughter, and I must confess that on this occasion I had to make serious efforts not to brake out, as I watched the gravity observed by these poor savages in the midst of all these ridiculous affectations. These forms of smoking enter into their superstitious religious practices; each one has his own, from which he would never dare deviate all his life long, for fear of displeasing his Manitous...[5]

DeSmet records in his journal an event that took place at the rendezvous in regards to the Snake Indians preparing an expedition against the Blackfeet:

While I was in their camp, the Snakes were making ready for an expedition against the Blackfeet. As soon as the chief had announced to all the young warriors his resolution to carry the war into the enemy's country, all who proposed to follow him prepared their rations, moccasins, bows and arrows. The evening before their departure, the chief, at the head of his soldiers, performed his farewell dance at every lodge; everywhere he received a piece of tobacco or some other present. If they take any women prisoners on these expeditions, they carry them to camp and hand them over to their wives, mothers and sisters. These women immediately butcher them with their hatchets and knives, vomiting upon the poor wretches, in their frantic rage, the most crushing and outrageous language. "Oh, Blackfoot bitches," they cry: "If we could only eat the hearts of all your young ones, and bathe in the blood of your cursed nation!"[6]

Prior to leaving the rendezvous, DeSmet wrote:

I had stayed four days on Green River to allow my horses time to recover from their fatigue, to give good, wholesome advice to the Canadian hunters who seem to be in great need of it, and to talk with the Indians of various nations. On the 4th of July, I resumed my travels...[7]

In a letter written on February 4, 1841, to the Reverend F. J. Barbelm from St. Louis, DeSmet adds the following information:

> The Indians of different nations and the trappers had assembled at the rendezvous in great number, for the sake of the trade. On Sunday, the 5th of July, I had the consolation of celebrating the holy sacrifice of mass sub dio. The altar was placed on an elevation, and surrounded with boughs and garlands of flowers; I addressed the congregation in French and in English, and spoke also by an interpreter to the Flatheads and Snake Indians. It was a spectacle truly moving for the heart of missionary, to behold an assembly composed of so many different nations, who all assisted at our holy mysteries with great satisfaction. The Canadians sang hymns in French and Latin, and the Indians in their native tongue. It was truly a Catholic worship ... This place has been called since that time, by the French Canadians, la Prairie de la Messe.[8]

Joel Walker said of the rendezvous: "When we reached the head waters of Green River, we rendezvoised and there parted with the trappers ..."[9] Kit Carson, who did not attend the annual rendezvous, stated: "In the spring of 1840, Bridger and his party started for the rendezvous on Green River, while Jack Robinson and myself went to Robidoux's fort in Utah country, and there disposed of the furs we had caught ..."[10] Many trappers, like Carson, were taking their furs to such places as Fort Hall, Fort Crockett, or Fort Robidoux to obtain their supplies and dispose of their furs. Robert Newell's journal states that on February 7, 1840, he left Brown's Hole with 300 beaver pelts and traveled to Fort Hall to obtain supplies and sell his furs. The traders at Fort Crockett and Fort Robidoux were obtaining supplies from the forts on the South Platte, while Fort Hall was being supplied by Hudson's Bay Company from Vancouver.

Newell also indicates that the type of mountainmen was changing and not for the good. He claims, "The horse thieves about 10 or 15 are gone to California for the purpose of Robbing and Steeling such thing never had been Known till late."[11]

Newell went to Green River for the Rendezvous. He states,

"I went to the American randezvous Mr Drips Feab & Bridger from St Louis with goods but times was certainly hard no beaver and every thing dull some Missionaries came along with them for the Columbia Messers Clark Smith Littlejohn."[12]

With the close of the rendezvous, Newell guided the three missionary couples to Fort Hall. He continues his narrative:

I engaged to pilot them over the mountains with their waggons and succeeded in crossing to Fort hall thare I bought their waggons also of which I perchased and Sold them to the H Bay Co while at Rondezvous I had some difficulty with a man by the name of Moses Harris I think he intended murder he Shot at me about 70 or 80 yards but done no damage only to himself. I left the randezvous our little party consisted of 9 men and 3 women in 17 days we arrived at fort hall found all well and on the 27 of September 1840 with two waggons and my family I left fort hall for the Columbia and with Some little Difiqutly I arived at walla walla thare I left one waggon and the other I had took down in a boat to vancouver and have it at this time on my farm about 25 miles from vancouver west. [13]

Robert Newell eloquently summarizes the feelings of the old mountainmen toward the future of the fur trade, mountain life, and the new breed of lawlessness as he tells Joe Meek:

"Come," said Newell to Meek, "We are done with this life in the mountains — done with wading in beaver dams, and freezing or starving alternately — done with Indian trading and Indian fighting. The fur trade is dead in the Rocky Mountains, and it is no place for us now, if ever it was. We are young yet, and have life before us. We cannot waste it here; we cannot or will not return to the States. Let us go down to the Wallamet and take farms ... What do you say, Meek? Shall we turn American settlers?" [14]

Thus died an era of Western America. The rendezvous was dead, killed by many different enemies. The type of mountainmen who trapped the streams and rivers of the Rocky Mountains during the years of the rendezvous were vanishing and would soon be gone. They had no choice. The exchange of furry banknotes for supplies at the rendezvous was over, only to be remembered and to be glorified by writers and historians.

APPENDIX
BONNEVILLE'S ACCOUT
OF THE BATTLE OF PIERRE'S HOLE

On the 17th of July, a small brigade of fourteen trappers, led by *Milton Sublette, brother of the captain, set out with the intention of proceeding to the southwest. They were accompanied by Sinclair and his fifteen free trappers; Wyeth, also, and his New England band of beaver hunters and salmon fishers, now dwindled down to eleven, took this opportunity to prosecute their cruise in the wilderness, accompanied with such experienced pilots. On the first day, they proceeded about eight miles to the southeast, and encamped for the night, still in the valley of Pierre's Hole. On the following morning, just as they were raising their camp, they observed a long line of people pouring down a defile of the mountains. They at first supposed them to be Fontenelle and his party, whose arrival had been daily expected. Wyeth, however, reconnoitred them with a spyglass, and soon perceived they were Indians. They were divided into two parties, forming, in the whole, about one hundred and fifty persons, men, women, and children. Some were on horseback, fantastically painted and arrayed, with scarlet blankets fluttering in the wind. The greater part, however, were on foot. They had perceived the trappers before they were themselves discovered, and came down yelling and whooping into the plain. On nearer approach, they were ascertained to be Blackfeet.*

One of the trappers of Sublette's brigade, a half-breed named Antoine Godin, now mounted his horse, and rode forth as if to hold a conference. He was the son of an Iroquois hunter, who had been cruelly murdered by the Blackfeet at a small stream below the mountains, which still bears his name. In company with Antoine rode forth a Flathead Indian, whose once powerful tribe had been completely broken down in their wars with the Blackfeet. Both of them, therefore, cherished the most vengeful hostility against these marauders of the mountains. The Blackfeet came to a halt. One of the chiefs advanced singly and unarmed, bearing the pipe of peace. This overture was certainly pacific; but Antoine and the Flathead were predisposed to hostility, and pretended to consider it a treacherous movement.

"Is your piece charged?" said Antoine to his red companion.

"It is."

"Then cock it, and follow me."

They met the Blackfoot chief half-way, who extended his hand in friendship. Antoine grasped it.

"Fire!" cried he.

The Flathead levelled his piece, and brought the Blackfoot to the ground. Antoine snatched off his scarlet blanket, which was richly ornamented, galloped off with it as a trophy to the camp. The bullets of the enemy whistling after him. The Indians immediately threw themselves into the edge of a swamp, among willows and cotton-wood trees, interwoven with vines. Here they began to fortify themselves; the women digging a trench, and throwing up a breastwork of logs and branches, deep hid in the bosom of the wood, while the warriors skirmished at the edge to keep the trappers at bay.

The latter took their station in a ravine in front, whence they kept up a scattering fire. As to Wyeth, and his little band of "downeasters," they were perfectly astounded by this second specimen of life in the wilderness; the men especially unused to bush-fighting and the use of the rifle, were at loss how to proceed. Wyeth, however, acted as a skilful commander. He got all his horses into camp and secured them; then, making a breastwork of his packs of goods, he charged his men to remain in garrison, and not to stir out of their fort. For himself, he mingled with the other leaders, determined to take his share in the conflict.

In the meantime, an express had been sent off to the rendezvous for reinforcements. Captain Sublette, and his associate, Campbell, were at their camp when the express came galloping across the plain, waving his cap, and giving the alarm; "Blackfeet! Blackfeet! a fight in the upper part of the valley! — to arms! to arms!"

The alarm was passed from camp to camp. It was a common cause. Every one turned out with horse and rifle. The Nez Perces and Flatheads joined. As fast as horseman could arm and mount he galloped off; the valley was soon alive with white men and red men scouring at full speed.

Sublette ordered his men to keep to the camp, being recruits from St. Louis, and unused to Indian warfare. He and his friend Campbell prepared for action. Throwing off their coats, rolling up their sleeves, and arming themselves with pistols and rifles, they mounted their horses and dashed forward among the first. As they rode along, they made their wills in soldier-like style; each stating how his effects should be disposed of in case of his death, and appointing the other his executor.

The Blackfeet warriors had supposed the brigade of Milton Sublette all the foes they had to deal with, and were astonished to behold the whole valley suddenly swarming with horsemen, galloping to the field of action. They withdrew into their fort, which was completely hid from sight in the dark and tangled wood. Most of their women and children had retreated to the mountains. The trappers now sallied forth and approached the swamp, firing into the thickets at random; the Blackfeet had a better sight at their adversaries, who were in the open field, and a half-breed was wounded in the shoulder.

When Captain Sublette arrived, he urged to penetrate the swamp and storm the fort, but all hung back in awe of the dismal horrors of the place, and the danger of attacking such desperadoes in their savage den. The very Indian allies, though accustomed to bush-fighting, regarded it as almost impenetrable, and full of frightful danger. Sublette was not to be turned from his purpose, but offered to lead the way into the swamp. Campbell stepped forward to accompany him. Before entering the wood, Sublette took his brothers aside, and told them that in case he fell, Campbell, who knew his will was to be his executor. This done, he grasped his rifle and pushed into the thickets, followed by Campbell. Sinclair, the partisan from Arkansas, was at the edge of the wood with his brother and a few of his men. Excited by the gallant example of the two friends, he pressed forward to share their dangers.

The swamp was produced by the labors of the beaver, which, by damming up a stream, had inundated a portion of the valley. The place was all overgrown with woods and thickets, so closely matted and entangled that it was impossible to see ten paces ahead, and the three associates in peril had to crawl along, one after another, making their way by putting the branches and vines aside; but doing it with caution, lest they should attract the eye of some lurking marksman. They took the lead by turns, each advancing about twenty yards at a time, and now and then hallooing to their men to follow. Some of the latter gradually entered the swamp, and followed a little distance in their rear.

They had now reached a more open part of the wood, and had glimpses of the rude fortress from between the trees. It was a mere breastwork, as we have said, of logs and branches, with blankets, buffalo robes, and the leathern covers of lodges, extended round the top as a screen. The movements of the leaders, as they groped their way, had been descried by the sharp-sighted enemy. As Sinclair, who was in the advance, was putting some branches aside, he was shot through the body. He fell on the spot. "Take me to my brother," said he to Campbell. The latter gave him in charge to some of the men, who conveyed him out of the swamp.

Sublette now took the advance. As he was reconnoitering the fort, he perceived an Indian peeping through an aperture. In an instant his rifle was levelled and discharged, and the ball struck the savage in the eye. While he was reloading, he called to Campbell, and pointed out to him the hole: "Watching that place," said he, "and you will soon have a fair chance for a shot." Scarce had he uttered the words, when a ball struck him in the shoulder, and almost wheeled him around. His first thought was to take hold of his arm with his other hand, and move it up and down. He ascertained, to his satisfaction, that the bone was not broken. The next moment he was so faint that he could not stand. Campbell took him in his arms and carried him out of the thicket. The same shot that struck Sublette wounded another man in the head.

A brisk fire was now opened by the mountaineers from the wood, answered occasionally from the fort. Unluckily, the trappers and their allies, in searching for the fort, had got scattered, so that Wyeth, and a number of Nez Perces, approached the fort on the northwest side, while others did the same on the opposite quarter. A cross-fire thus took place, which occasionally did mischief to friends as well as foes. An Indian was shot down, close to Wyeth, by a ball which, he was convinced, had been sped from the rifle of a trapper on the other side of the fort.

The number of whites and their Indian allies had by this time so much increased by arrivals from the rendezvous, that the Blackfeet were completely overmatched. They kept doggedly in their fort, however, making no offer of surrender. An occasional firing into the breastwork was kept up during the day. Now and then, one of the Indian allies, in bravado, would rush up to the fort, fire over the ramparts, tear off a buffalo robe or a scarlet blanket, and return with it in triumph to his comrades. Most of the savage garrison that fell, however, were killed in the first part of the attack.

At one time is was resolved to set fire to the fort; and the squaws belonging to the allies were employed to collect combustibles. This, however, was abandoned; the Nez Perces being unwilling to destroy the robes and blankets, and other spoils of the enemy, which they felt sure would fall into their hands.

The Indians, when fighting, are prone to taunt and revile each other. During one of the pauses of the battle, the voice of the Blackfeet chief was heard.

"So long," said he, "as we had powder and ball, we fought you in the open field: When those were spent, we retreated here to die with our women and children. You may burn us in our fort; but, stay by our ashes, and you who are hungry for fighting will soon have enough. There are four hundred lodges of our brethren at hand. They will soon be here - their arms are strong - their hearts are big - they will avenge us!"

This speech was translated two or three times by Nez Perce and creole interpreters. By the time it was rendered into English, the chief was made to say that four hundred lodges of his tribe were attacking the encampment at the other end of the valley. Every one now was for hurrying to the defence of the rendezvous. A party was left to keep watch upon the fort; the rest galloped off to the camp. As night came on, the trappers drew out of the swamp, and remained about the skirts of the wood. By morning, their companions returned from the rendezvous with the report that all was safe. As the day opened, they ventured within the swamp and approached the fort. All was silent. They advanced up to it without opposition. They entered: It had been abandoned in the night, and the Blackfeet had effected their retreat, carrying off their wounded on litters made of branches, leaving bloody traces on the herbage. The bodies of ten Indians were found within the fort; among them the one shot in the eye by Sublette. The Blackfeet afterward reported that they had lost twenty-six warriors in this battle. Thirty-two horses were likewise found killed; among them were some of those recently carried off from Sublette's party, in the night; which showed that these were the very savages that had attacked him. They proved to be an advance party of the main body of Blackfeet which had been upon the trail of Sublette's party. Five white men and one half-breed were killed, and several wounded. Seven of the Nez Perces were killed, and six wounded. They had an old chief, who was reputed as invulnerable. In the course of the action he was hit by a spent ball, and threw up blood; but his skin was unbroken. His people were now fully convinced that he was proof against powder and ball.

A striking circumstance is related as having occurred the morning after the battle. As some of the trappers and their Indian allies were approaching the fort through the woods, they beheld an Indian woman, of noble form and features, leaning against a tree. Their surprise at her lingering here alone, to fall into the hands of her enemies, was dispelled when they saw the corpse of a warrior at her feet. Either she was so lost in grief as not to perceive their approach; or a proud spirit kept her silent and motionless. The Indians set up a yell, on discovering her, and before the trappers could interfere, her mangled body fell upon the corpse which she had refused to abandon. We have heard this anecdote discredited by one of the leaders who had been in the battle: but the fact may have taken place without his seeing it, and been concealed from him. It is all instance of female devotion, even to the death, which we are well disposed to believe and to record.[1]

FERRIS' ACCOUNT

On the 17th a party of trappers, of the Rocky Mountain Fur company, having received supplies for the fall hunt, left the company, and passed 10 miles up the valley intending to cross on to Lewis River, near the mouth of Salt River. The following morning they discovered a party of strange Indians near the margin of the stream, some distance above them, and several of the men immediately departed to ascertain who they were. As they approached, the chief advanced to meet them, armed with nothing but the calumet of peace; but he was recognized to be a Grosventre and in a twinkling was sent to eternity. At the same time the Indians, who perhaps numbered fifty men, besides women and children, entered a grove of cottonwood trees, and without loss of time proceeded to make a breastwork, or pen of trees impenetrable to balls. In the mean time an express was dispatched to inform us, and in a few minutes the plains were covered with whites, and friendly Indians, rushing to the field of battle. On their arrival, however, the enemy had completed an impenetrable fort, fifty feet square, within which they had fastened their horses. A general fire was immediately opened upon the fort, and was warmly kept up on both sides until dark. In the mean time a plan was formed by the whites to burn them up in their fort, and quantitites of dry wood and brush were collected for that purpose; but the Indians on our side object, on the ground that all the plunder would be lost, which they thought to appropriate to their own use. At length night came on, and the whites, who were provoked at the Indians, for not consented to annihilate the enemy at once, departed for their respective camps; the Indians soon followed, and left such of the enemy as survived, at liberty to depart and recount their misfortunes to their friends. We lost in this engagement, two men killed, one mortally wounded, and many others either severely or slightly. The Indians on our side, lost five killed, and many wounded, some supposed to be mortally. The following morning, a large party of both whites and Indians returned to the fort. In it were the dead bodies of three Grosventre Indians, a child, twenty-four horses, and several dogs. Our Indians followed the route of the fugitives several miles, and found their baggage, which they had concealed in divers places, as well as the bodies of five more Indians, and two young women, who were yet unhurt, though their heartless captures sent them to the shades, in pursuit of their relations without remorse. Amongst the dead horses were those lost by Mr. Fitzpatrick some days since; but those stolen from Sublett about the same time, were not among the number; hence we supposed that a larger party of Indians were yet behind.[2]

WYETH'S ACCOUNT

*On the 17th we put out and ste(e)red S.E. in direction to a pass
through the same mountains by which we entered the valley these Mts:
run E. & W. and the pass I refer to is the next E. of the one refer(r)ed to
and through it the waters of this valley reach Lewis River which is on the
S. side of this range at night we encamped within about 8 miles of the
commencement of the pass. On the 18th we did not leave camp when near
starting we observed 2 partys of Indians coming out of the pass about 200
in number with but few horses after securing our camp our riders went
out to meet them and soon found them to be Blackfeet a little skirmish
ensued one of the Blackfeet was killed and his Blankett and robe brought
into camp on this the Indians made for the timber the women and
children were seen flying to the mountains at this time only 42 men being
the party of Mess Milton Sublette & Frapp mine and a few independent
Hunters were in sight and the Indians were disposed to give us their
usual treatment when they meet us in small bodies but while the Indians
we(re) making their preparations we sent an express to camp which soon
brought out a smart force of Nez Perces Flatheads and whites the Indians
finding they were caught fortified themselves in a masterly manner in the
wood. We attacked them and continued the attack all day there were
probably about 20 of them killed and 32 horses were found dead They
decamped during the night leaving most of their utensils lodges &c and
many of the dead we have lost 3 whites killed 8 badly wounded among
which is Mr. Wm. Sublette who was extremely active in the battle about
10 of the Indians were killed or mortally wounded of the Nez Perces and
Flatheads in the morning we visited their deserted fort they had dug into
the ground to reach water and to secure themselves from our shot it was a
sickening scene of confusion and Blood shead one of our men who was
killed inside near the fort we found mutilated in a shocking manner on the
19th we removed back to our former ground to be near our whole force and
to recruit the wounded and bury the dead. We think that 400 lodges or
about 600 warriors of the Blackfeet are on the other side of the pass and if
they come they must be met with our whole force in which case the
contest will be a doubtful one We have mad(e) Horse pens and secured our
camp in as good a manner as we can and wait the result this affair will
detain us some days.*[3]

NIDEVER'S ACCOUNT

About the beginning of Aug. the trappers began to leave for their respective hunting grounds. Our party had decided to trap that season on Marys River, a small stream about South West of Salt Lake. We left Pierre's Hole in company with Frapp and Wyatt, our courses being the same for some distance. Frapp's company was mostly made up of Canadian French half-breeds. Our first camp was about 15 miles from the rendezvous. Frapp's and Wyatt's companies camped together, while we were a short distance in their rear.

The next morning about 8 o'clock we packed up and rode along to Wyatt's and Frapp's camp, only a few hundred yards ahead, and had hardly reached it when Indians were discovered coming towards us in large numbers, and we immediately recognized them as Blackfeet. They belonged to a village of some 400 warriors or more, that with their women, children, and camp baggage were moving north. They had discovered us before we did them, no doubt, and had resolved on attacking us. They were riding down on us at full speed and barely gave us time to prepare for them. We hurriedly formed a breastwork of our packs and despatched a young boy on our fleetest horse back to Pierre's Hole for aid. We saw from their numbers that we would need help, but by holding the Indians in check for two or three hours we knew reinforcements would reach us. As soon as the Indians arrived within range they began shooting, to which we replied. Conspicuous among them was a chief dressed in a bright scarlet coat, and he rode somewhat in advance of his men, who began to scatter and surround us upon arriving within shooting distance. On came the chief and out rode one of Wyatt's men, Goddar (Godin), a Canadian half-breed, to meet him. Across his saddle Goddar carried a short rifle which the chief did not see until, when within 40 or 50 yds. of him, Goddar raised it and shot. The chief fell from his saddle dead, and before his companions could come up to him his coat was stripped off by Goddar who amidst a heavy fire reached our camp in safety with his trophy. We continued to exchange shots, with a loss to the Indians of one or two killed, and to us of several wounded, until about ten o'clock, when the Indians suddenly took shelter in the heavy narrow belt of woods that lay between us and the river. We soon discovered the cause of this unexpected movement, in the coming of our reinforcements, that began to appear in sight and a few minutes later were among us to the number of about 250. Most of them were without saddles, having lost no time in setting out as soon as our messenger reached them. A council was held and Wm. Sublette was elected as our leader. Many were opposed to attacking them as, being posted in the heavy timber, we would find it difficult to drive them out, and our loss would be considerable. These objections were overruled by Sublette and others, who said we would have to fight them anyway and now that we had them at a disadvantage, we must profit by it.

The plan of attack was formed and the attacking party got into line, advanced, when the firing at once became general. Just after we entered the timber, our captain Alex. Sinclair was shot in the thigh, Phelps, a man who joined us at Pierre's Hole, was wounded in about the same place, and Wm. Sublette was shot in the arm. Our attacking party did not consist of much over 100 men, the rest refusing to join us. As we advanced and drove the Indians towards the river, the wings of our line gradually turned in until they rested on its bank and we had them surrounded.

Upon penetrating into timber we found that the Blackfeet had constructed a fort of logs on the bank of the river in the form of a half moon, the rear opening towards the river. We continued to advance, dodging and crawling from tree to tree and log to log, every foot stubbornly contested by the redskins, until almost sunset. Some of our men had succeeded in getting in the rear of the fort, which, however, afforded its inmates some shelter even on the open side, as it was filled with trees. One of the trappers of Frapp's company got very near the rear of the fort, almost up to it in fact, by crawling flat on the ground and pushing and rolling a large log so as to protect his head.

Several shots struck the log but the trapper got into the (rear) position and abandoned his log for a tree without being harmed.

Another one of Frapp's men, a Canadian half-breed, tried to distinguish himself by rashly crawling up to the very wall of the fort and then peeping over the top. He paid for his temerity when he received two bullets in his forehead. He was half drunk at the time, liquor having been distributed among the men during the early part of the fight. By sunset we had got so close to the fort that we determined to set it on fire, but before doing so it was agreed to give the Indians a chance to surrender. Accordingly, a renegade Blackfoot who was among Frapp's men was instructed to talk with them and try and induce them to surrender. They refused, however, and answered that, although they would all be killed that day, the next day it would be our turn, as they had sent word to a very large village of their nation, situated only a short distance from there, numbering some 1500 lodges.

It was well known that there was a very large village nearby, and that, should they send out all of their force after us, there would be some heavy fighting in which we would in all probability get worsted. Upon hearing the answer of the Indians, Frapp became alarmed and withdrew his men at once and this obliged the rest of us to retire, and those from Pierre's Hole having returned, we travelled on about 9 miles and went into camp with the same companies as the night previous. The next morning several of us went back to the scene of the fight. Within the fort and its immediate vicinity the ground was strewn with dead bodies mostly of women and children; but a very few warriors among them.

We counted 50 dead bodies, and inside of the fort were the bodies of 20 fine horses. Of the from 300 to 400 Indians which it was calculated the fighting men of the Blackfeet numbered, but very few escaped.

At the beginning of the engagement several got away, many of them being shot in attempting to swim the river. We afterwards learned through the Indians that when we withdrew our men only 6 Indians were left alive in the fort. The dead Indians were thrown into the river to prevent them from falling into our hands.

Many of the women were shot unintentionally as in the timber it was impossible to distinguish the women from the men; the children were killed no doubt by stray shots.

The Indians make a very poor fight on foot, their usual mode of fighting being to lay (lie) in ambush or to cut off small detached parties with such numbers as to make success sure.

We lost no time in getting out of this neighborhood, ...[4]

LEONARD'S ACCOUNT

After travelling a few miles this morning, some of the men, in taking a view of the country before us, discovered something like people upon horses, who appeared to be coming towards us. After continuing in the same direction for some time we came in view with the naked eye, when we halted — They advanced towards us displaying a British flag. This we could not comprehend; but on coming closer discovered them to be hostile Indians. We immediately despatched a messenger back to the rendezvous for reinforcements and prepared ourselves for defence. The Indians commenced building a fort in the timber on the bank of the river; but at the time we were not aware of what they were doing. After waiting here a few hours we were reinforced by 200 whites, 200 Flatheads, and 300 Nez Perces Indians. The Indians with the British flag, on seeing such a number of people galloping down the plain at full speed, immediately retreated within their fort, whither they were hotly pursued. The friendly Indians soon discovered them to belong to the Blackfeet tribe, who are decidedly the most numerous and warlike tribe in the mountains, and for this reason are not disposed to have any friendly intercourse with any other nation of an inferior number, unless they are good warriors and well armed with guns, &c. We thought we could rush right on them and drive them out of the brush into the plain and have a decisive battle at once. We advanced with all possible speed, and a full determination of success, until we discovered their fort by receiving a most destructive fire from the enclosure. This throwed our ranks into complete confusion, & we all retreated into the plain, with the loss of 5 whites, 8 Flatheads and 10 Nez Perces Indians killed, besides a large number of whites and Indians wounded. The formation of their fort astonished all hands. We had been within a few hundred yards of them all day and did not discover that they were building it. It was large enough to contain 500 warriors; and built strong enough to resist almost any attempt we might make to force it. After dressing the wounded, and having reconnoitered their fort, our forces were divided into several detachments, and sent in different directions with the intention of surrounding the fort and making them prisoners. This was done under the superintendance of Fitzpatrick, who acted as commander-in-chief.

In a case of this kind any man not evincing the greatest degree of courage, and every symptom of bravery, is treated as a coward; and the person who advances first, furthest and fastest, and makes the greatest display of animal courage, soon rises in the estimation of his companions. Accordingly with the hope of gaining a little glory while an opportunity offered, though not for any electioneering purpose, as a politician in the States would do – I started into the brush, in company with two acquaintances (Smith and Kean) and two Indians. We made a circuitous route and came towards the fort from a direction which we thought we would be least expected. We advanced closer and closer, crawling upon our hands and knees, with the intention of giving them a select shot; and when within about forty yards of their breast work, one of our Indians was shot dead. At this we all lay still for some time, but Smith's foot happening to shake the weeds as he was laying on his belly, was shot through. I advanced a little further, but finding the balls to pass too quick and close, concluded to retreat. When I turned, I found that my companions had deserted me. In passing by, Smith asked me to carry him out, which met my approbation precisely, for I was glad to get out of this unpleasant situation under any pretext – provided my reputation for courage would not be questioned. After getting him on my back, still crawling on my hands and knees, I came across Kean, lying near where the first Indian fell, who was also mortally wounded, and died soon after. I carried Smith to a place of safety and then returned to the seige. A continual fire was kept up, doing more or less execution on both sides until late in the afternoon, when we advanced to close quarters, having nothing but the thickness of their breast work between us, and having them completely surrounded on all sides to prevent any escaping. This position we maintained until sun-set, in the meantime having made preparations to set fire to the fort, which was built principally of old dry logs, as soon as night would set in, and stationed men at the point where we thought they would be most likely to make the first break, for the purpose of taking them on the wing, in their flight. Having made all these preparations, which were to put an end to all further molestation on the part of the Blackfeet, our whole scheme and contemplated victory was frustrated by a most ingenious and well executed device of the enemy. A few minutes before the torch was to be applied, our captives commenced the most tremendous yells and shouts of triumph, and menaces of defiance which seemed to move heaven and earth. Quick as thought a report spread through all quarters that the plain was covered with Blackfeet Indians coming to reinforce the besieged. So complete was the consternation in our ranks, created by this stratagem, that in five minutes afterwards, there was not a single white man, Flathead or Nez Perces Indian within a hundred yards of the fort. Every man thought only of his own security, and run for life without ever looking round, which would at once have convinced him of his folly. In a short time it was ascertained that it was only a stratagem, and our men began to collect together where our baggage was. I never shall forget the scene here exhibited. The rage of some was unbounded, and approached madness. For my own part, although I felt much regret at the result after so much toil and danger, yet I could not but give the savages credit for the skill they displayed in preserving their lives, at the very moment when desperation, as we thought, had seized the mind of each of them.

By the time we were made sensible of the full extent of our needless alarm, it had begun to get dark; and on ascertaining the extent of the injury which we received, (having lost 32 killed, principally Indians,) it was determined not to again attempt to surround the fort, which was a sore disappointment to some of the men who were keen for chastising the Indians for their trick. We then took up our march for the rendezvous; but on starting one of our party of 15 men, who had first started out the day before, could not be found. search was made, and he was found in the brush, severely wounded — After carrying him on a litter a few miles he died and was buried in the Indian style — which is by digging a hole in the ground, wrapping a blanket or skin round the body, placing it in the hole, and covering it with poles and earth. This is the manner of interring the dead in this country both by the Indians and whites, except in the winter season on account of the ground being frozen, when the Indians are in the habit of wrapping their dead in buffaloe robes, and laying them on poles *from one tree to another, on which poles the corpse is tied with cords. The next morning we raised another war party and went back to the battle ground, but no Indians could be found — They must have left the fort in great haste for we found 42 head of horses, together with Fitzpatrick's which they had taken on the mountain, two warriors and one squaw lying dead inside of their fort, besides a large quantity of their baggage, such as furs, skins, &c. There must have been a great number of them, from the holes they had dug in the ground around their dead horses and the edges of the fort, say from three to four hundred. I learned afterwards that the Nez Perces Indians shortly after found seven more dead Blackfeet, in some bush close by, where they had been secreted to save their scalps, which is the principal object with these Indians, in order to have their women dance. In the afternoon we returned to the rendezvous and presented Mr. Fitzpatrick with his long-lossed and highly valued horse, which seemed to compensate for all the sufferings and hardships which he had encountered.[5]*

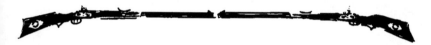

FOOTNOTES
1825

1. Dale L. Morgan, ed., **The West of William H. Ashley** (Denver: The Old West Publishing Co., 1964), p. 106.
2. Ibid., p. 107.
3. Ibid., pp. 112-13.
4. Ibid., pp. 113-14.
5. Ibid., p. 108.
6. Ibid.
7. Ibid., p. 118.
8. T. D. Bonner, **The Life and Adventures of James P. Beckwourth** (New York: Harper & Brothers, Publisher, 1856), p. 75.
9. Morgan, **William H. Ashley,** pp. 118-19.

1826
1. Dale L. Morgan, **Jedediah Smith and the Opening of the West** (Indianapolis: The Bobbs-Merrill Company, Inc.), 1953, p. 187
2. Maurice S. Sullivan, **The Travels of Jedediah Smith** (Santa Ana: The Fine Arts Press, 1934), p. 26.
3. George R. Brooks, **The Southwest Expedition of Jedediah S. Smith His Personal Account of the Journey to California** (Glendale: The Arthur H. Clark Company, 1977), pp. 39-40.
4. Gerald C. Bagley, "Daniel T. Potts, Chronicler of the Fur Trade 1822-1828 And the Earliest Confirmed Explorer of Yellowstone Park," Thesis Brigham Young University, 1964, p. 133.
5. Bonner, **James P. Beckwourth,** p. 107.

1827
1. Morgan, **William H. Ashley,** p. 152.
2. Bagley, "Daniel T. Potts," p. 135.
3. Bonner, **James P. Beckwourth,** pp. 108-11.
4. Morgan, **William H. Ashley,** p. 168.
5. Bagley, "Daniel T. Potts," pp. 137-38.
6. The winter of 1827-28 taught the mountainmen that it was next to impossible to transport the supplies to the mountains during the winter.

1828

1. Morgan, **William H. Ashley,** pp. 186-87.
2. Bagley, "Daniel T. Potts," p. 139.
3. Morgan, **William H. Ashley,** pp. 314-15.
4. Bonner, **James P. Beckwourth,** pp. 104-05.
5. Morgan, **William H. Ashley,** p. 182.
6. Ibid., p. 313.
7. Ibid., p. 182.

1829

1. Frances Fuller Victor, **The River of the West** (Hartford: Columbian Book Company, 1870), 48-49.
2. Ibid., pp. 49-50.
3. Ibid., pp. 58-59.
4. Ibid., pp. 83-84.

1830

1. Don Berry, **A Majority of Scoundrels** (New York: Harper & Brothers, 1961), pp. 235-36.
2. Ibid., p. 236.
3. Victor, **River of the West,** p. 89.

1831

1. Victor, **River of the West,** p. 99.
2. Paul C. Phillips, ed., **Life in the Rocky Mountains, A Diary of Wanderings on the Sources of the Rivers Missouri, Columbia, and Colorado From February 1830 to November 1835** (Denver: The Old West Publishing Company, 1940), p. 126.
3. Ibid.
4. Supplies were brought to the mountains by the American Fur Company in 1831. Etienne Provost delivered supplies to William Vanderburgh during the summer on Green River. Another supply train under the direction of Drips and Fontenelle left the settlements in Missouri, but were forced, due to the weather, to spend the winter at the mouth of Laramie Creek. The American Fur Company was learning the same lesson that Smith, Jackson and Sublette Company had experienced during the winter of 1827-28.

1832

1. Victor, **River of the West,** pp. 108-09.

2. F. G. Young, ed., "The Correspondence and Journal of Captain Nathaniel J. Wyeth 1831-6: A Record of Two Expeditions for the Occupation of the Oregon Country, with Maps, Introduction and Index," **Sources of The History of Oregon** (Eugene: University Press, 1899), I, p. 158.
3. Victor, **River of the West,** pp. 110-11.
4. Phillips, **Rocky Mountains,** p. 152.
5. Young, "Two Expeditions," p. 159.
6. Dorothy O. Johansen, ed., **Robert Newell's Memoranda: Travles in the Teritory of Missourie; Travle to the Kayuse War; together with a Report on the Indians South of the Columbia River** (Portland: Champoeg Press, 1959), p. 32.
7. W. F. Wagner, ed., **Adventures of Zenas Leonard Fur Trader and Trapper 1831-1836** (Cleveland: The Burrow Brothers Company, 1904), pp. 109, 112.
8. Washington Irving, **The Adventures of Captain Bonneville** (New York: G. P. Putnam, 1859), pp. 72-73.
9. William H. Ellison, ed., **The Life and Adventures of George Nidever (1802-1883)** (Berkeley: University of California Press, 1937), pp. 24-26.
10. Victor, **River of the West,** pp. 111-18.
11. Phillips, **Rocky Mountains,** pp. 184-85.

1833

1. The Crow word for the Green River had many variations in spelling — Siskadee, Siskede-azzeah, Sheetska dee and Seedskedee-agie. Its meaning was Prairie Hen River (Sage Grouse).
2. Young, "Two Expeditions," p. 205.
3. Irving, **Captain Bonneville,** pp. 180-83.
4. Phillips, **Rocky Mountains,** pp. 205-07, 209.
5. Victor, **River of the West,** pp. 142-43.
6. Wagner, **Zenas Leonard,** pp. 144-45.
7. Elliot Coues, ed., **Forty Years a Fur Trader on the Upper Missouri: The Personal Narrative of Charles Larpenteur 1833-1872** (New York: Francis P. Harper, 1898), I, pp. 30-39.
8. Young, "Two Expeditions," pp. 69-70.

9. Sir William Drummond Stewart, **Edward Warren** (London: Walker, 1854), p. 274.

10. Ellison, **George Nidever,** p. 32.

1834

1. John K. Townsend, **Narrative of a Journey Across the Rocky Mountains to the Columbia River** (Philadelphia: Henry Perkins, 1839), pp. 75-77.

2. Young, "Two Expeditions," p. 225.

3. Ibid.

4. Dale L. Morgan and Eleanor Towles Harris, ed., **The Rocky Mountain Journals of William Marshall Anderson** (San Marino: The Huntington Library, 1967), p. 137.

5. Ibid.

6. Ibid, pp. 27-28.

7. Young, "Two Expeditions," pp. 138-39.

8. Ibid., p. 141.

9. Berry, **Scoundrels,** p. 366.

10. Ibid., p. 367.

11. Young, "Two Expeditions," p. 225.

12. Morgan, **William Marshall Anderson,** p. 146.

13. Ibid., p. 148. June 29, 1834.

14. Cornelius J. Brosnan, **Jason Lee, Prophet of the New Oregon** (New York: The Macmillan Company, 1932), p. 59.

15. Morgan, **William Marshall Anderson,** p. 149.

16. Ibid., p. 146.

17. Ibid., p. 152.

18. Ibid., p. 156.

19. Ibid., p. 27.

20. John K. Townsend, **Narrative of Journey Across The Rocky Mountains to the Columbia River and a Visit to the Sandwich Islands, Chile, &c., With a Scientific Appendix** (Philadelphia: Henry Perkins, 1839), pp. 75-77.

21. Aubrey L. Haines, ed., **Journal of a Trapper** (Portland, Oregon: Oregon Historical Society, 1955), pp. 2-3.

22. Morgan, **William Marshall Anderson,** p. 32.

23. Brosnan, **Jason Lee,** p. 60.

24. Morgan, **William Marshall Anderson,** pp. 160, 162.

25. Ibid., p. 168.
26. Ibid., p. 172.
27. Hiram M. Chittenden, **The American Fur Trade of the Far West** (New York: Francis P. Harper, 1902), I, p. 305.

1835

1. Archer Butler Hulbert and Dorothy Printup Hulbert, ed., **Marcus Whitman Crusader** (Denver: The Denver Public Library, 1936), VI, p. 154.
2. Rev. Samuel Parker, **Journal of an Exploring Tour Beyond the Rocky Mountains** (Ithaca: Mack, Andrus, & Woodruff, 1840), pp. 79-80.
3. Haines, **Trapper,** pp. 13-14.
4. Hulbert, **Marcus Whitman,** pp. 154-55.
5. Parker, **Exploring Tour,** pp. 80-81.
6. Ibid., p. 82.
7. Ibid.
8. Ibid., pp. 83-85.
9. Milo M. Quaife, ed., **Kit Carson's Autobiography** (Lincoln: University of Nebraska Press, 1935), pp. 42-44.
10. Parker, **Exploring Tour,** p. 86.
11. Ibid., pp. 86-87.
12. Ibid., pp. 89-90.
13. Victor, **River of the West,** pp. 186-87.

1836

1. Hulbert, **Marcus Whitman,** p. 34.
2. Ibid., p. 230.
3. Clifford M. Drury, ed., **First White Women Over the Rockies** (Glendale: The Arthur H. Clark Company, 1963), I, pp. 51-53.
4. LeRoy R. Hafen, ed., **The Mountain Men and the Fur Trade of the Far West** (Glendale: The Arthur H. Clark Company, 1965), I, p, 152.
5. Ibid.
6. Victor, **River of the West,** p. 203.
7. Ibid., pp. 202-03, 205.
8. William H. Gray, **A History of Oregon, 1792-1849** (Portland: Harris, Holman, 1870), pp. 118-19.
9. Quaife, **Kit Carson,** p. 47.

10. Haines, **Trapper,** p. 41.
11. Victor, **River of the West,** pp. 205-09.
12. Gray, **History of Oregon,** pp. 121-23.
13. Ibid., p. 129.
14. Ibid.

1837

1. Marvin C. Ross, ed., **The West of Alfred Jacob Miller (1837)** (Norman: University of Oklahoma Press, 1951), p. 142.
2. Ibid., p. 139.
3. Ibid., p. 119.
4. Ibid., p. 76.
5. Ibid., p. 149.
6. Ibid., p. 177.
7. Ibid., p. 178.
8. Ibid., p. 4.
9. Ibid., p. 49.
10. Haines, **Trapper,** pp. 58-61.
11. Johansen, **Robert Newell's Memoranda,** p. 34.
12. William H. Gray, "The Unpublished Journal of William H. Gray," **The Whitman College Quarterly,** XVI (1913), pp. 55-63.
13. Ross, **Alfred J. Miller,** p. 199.
14. Ibid., p. 110.
15. Ibid., p. 175.
16. Ibid., p. 159.
17. Ibid., p. 127.
18. Ibid., p. 129.
19. Ibid., p. 12.
20. Ibid., p. 1.
21. Ibid., p. 111.
22. Johansen, **Robert Newell's Memoranda,** p. 36.

1838

1. Clifford M. Drury, ed., **First White Women Over the Rockies** (Glendale: The Arthur H. Clark Company, 1966), III, p. 273.
2. Ibid., p. 297.
3. Clifford M. Drury, ed., **The Diaries and Letters of Henry H. Spaulding and Asa Bowen Smith Relating to the Nez**

Perce Mission 1838-1842 (Glendale: The Arthur H. Clark Company, 1958), pp. 61-62.

4. Clifford M. Drury, ed., **First White Women Over the Rockies** (Glendale: The Arthur H. Clark Company, 1963), II, pp. 87-88.
5. Ibid., pp. 88-89.
6. Drury, **First White Women,** III, pp. 80, 82.
7. Ibid., pp. 272-273.
8. Drury, **Spaulding and Smith,** pp. 60-70, 73.
9. Drury, **First White Women,** III, pp. 89, 91-95.
10. Ibid., p. 302.
11. Drury, **First White Women,** II, pp. 94, 96-102.
12. Ibid.
13. Quaife, **Kit Carson,** p. 56.
14. Johansen, **Robert Newell's Memoranda,** p. 37.
15. Ibid., p. 47.
16. Ibid.
17. Drury, **First White Women,** III, p. 271.
18. Ibid., pp. 274-75.
19. Haines, **Trapper,** pp. 90-91.
20. Drury, **First White Women,** III, p. 90.
21. Ibid., pp. 300-01.
22. Drury, **First White Women,** II, p. 101.
23. Drury, **First White Women,** III, p. 301.
24. Haines, **Trapper,** p. 90.
25. Drury, **First White Women,** II, p. 101.

1839

1. F.A. Wislizenus, **A Journey to the Rocky Mountains in the Year 1839** (St. Louis: Missouri Historical Society, 1912), pp. 28-29.
2. Ibid., pp. 66-70.
3. Ibid., pp. 83-90.
4. Quaife, **Kit Carson,** p. 59.
5. Wislizenus, **Journey to the Rocky Mountains,** p. 88.
6. Johansen, **Robert Newell's Memoranda,** p. 38.

1840

1. Joel P. Walker, **A Pioneer of Pioneers: Narrative of Adventures Thro' Alabama, Florida, New Mexico,**

  Oregon, California, &c (Los Angeles: Glen Dawson, 1953), pp. 11-12.
2. Hiram M. Chittenden and Alfred Talbot Richardson, ed., **Life, Letters and Travels of Father Pierre-Jean DeSmet, S. J. 1801-1877** (New York: Francis P. Harper, 1905), I, p. 201.
3. Ibid., p. 202.
4. Ibid., p. 215.
5. Ibid., pp. 216-18.
6. Ibid., pp. 219-20.
7. Ibid., pp. 221.
8. Ibid., p. 262.
9. Walker, **Pioneer of Pioneers,** p. 13.
10. Quaife, **Kit Carson,** p. 62.
11. Johansen, **Robert Newell's Memoranda,** p. 39.
12. Ibid.
13. Ibid.
14. Victor, **River of the West,** pp. 264-65.

Appendix

1. Irving, **Captain Bonneville,** pp. 173-80.
2. Phillips, **Rocky Mountains,** pp. 153-55.
3. Young, "Two Expeditions," pp. 159-60.
4. Ellison, **George Nidever,** pp. 26-30.
5. Wagner, **Zenas Leonard,** pp. 112-18.

SELECTED BIBLIOGRAPHY
BOOKS, ARTICLES, THESES

Thousands of books and articles which have been written and published could be listed in a bibliography if it were to represent the total history of the American Fur Trade. However, the author's purpose in assembling the following bibliography is to present the literature pertaining only to the "rendezvous" and the role they played in Western America.

Abel, Annie Heloise, ed. **Journal At Fort Clark, 1834-1839.** Pierre, South Dakota: Department of History, State of South Dakota, 1932.

Alter, J. Cecil. **James Bridger, Trapper, Frontiersman, Scout and Guide: A Historical Narrative.** Salt Lake City: Shepherd Book Company, 1925.

——————. "W. A. Ferris in Utah," **Utah Historical Quarterly,** IX (1941).

Bagley, Gerald C. "Daniel T. Potts, Chronicler of the Fur Trade 1822-1828 and the Earliest Confirmed Explorer of Yellowstone Park." Unpublished Master's Thesis, Brigham Young University, Provo, Utah 1964.

Bancroft, Hubert H. **History of British Columbia 1792-1887.** San Francisco, History Company, 1887. XXXII.

——————. **History of Nevada, Colorado, and Wyoming, 1540-1888.** San Francisco: History Company, 1890. XXV.

——————. **History of Oregon.** San Francisco: History Company, 1886-88. XXIX-XXX.

——————. **History of the Northwest Coast.** San Francisco: A. L. Bancroft and Company, 1884. XXVII-XXVIII.

——————. **History of Utah, 1540-1886.** San Francisco: History Company, 1889. XXVI.

——————. **History of Washington, Idaho and Montana, 1845-1889.** San Francisco: History Company, 1890. XXXI.

Barker, Burt B., ed., **Letters of Dr. John McLoughlin, Written at Fort Vancouver 1829-1832.** Portland, Oregon: Binford & Mort, 1948.

——————. **The McLoughlin Empire and Its Rulers.** Glendale, California: The Arthur H. Clark Company, 1959.

Beidleman, Richard G. "Nathaniel Wyeth's Fort Hall," **Oregon Historical Quarterly,** *LVIII (1957).*

Berry, Don, **A Majority of Scoundrels, an Informal History of the Rocky Mountain Fur Company.** New York: Harper & Brothers, 1961.

Biebar, Ralph P., ed. **Wah-to-yah and the Taos Trail.** Glendale, California: The Arthur H. Clark Company, 1938.

Binns, Archie. **Peter Skene Ogden: Fur Trader.** Portland, Oregon: Binford & Mort, 1967.

Blassingame, Wyatt and Richard Glendinning. **The Mountain Men.** New York: F. Watts, 1962.

Bonner, T. D. **The Life and Adventures of James P. Beckwourth, Mountaineer, Scout, and Pioneer and Chief of the Crow Nation of Indians.** New York: Harper & Brothers, 1856.

Brooks, George R. **The Southwest Expedition of Jedediah S. Smith His Personal Account of the Journey to California.** Glendale, California: The Arthur H. Clark Company, 1977.

Brosnan, Cornelius J. **Jason Lee, Prophet of the New Oregon.** New York: The Macmillan Company, 1932.

Burger, Carl. **Beaver Skins and Mountain Men; the Importance of the Beaver in the Discovery, Exploration, and Settlement of the North American Continent.** New York: Dutton, 1968.

Burt, Olive W. **Mountain Men of the Early West.** New York: Hawthorne Books, 1937.

Camp, Charles L., ed. **George Yount and His Chronicles Of the West.** Denver: The Old West Publishing Company, 1966.

_____, ed. **James Clyman, American Frontiersman.** Portland, Oregon: Champoeg Press, 1960.

_____, ed. **The Plains and the Rockies.** Columbua, Ohio: Long's College Book Company, 1953.

Campbell, Robert. **The Rocky Mountain Letters of Robert Campbell.** New York: Frederick W. Beinecke, 1955.

Chittenden, Hiram M. **The American Fur Trade of the Far West.** 3 vols. New York: Francis P. Harper, 1902.

Chittenden, Hiram M. and Alfred T. Richardson, ed. **Life, Letters and Travels of Father Pierre-Jean DeSmet, 1901-1873.** 4 vols. New York: Francis P. Harper, 1905.

Cleland, Robert G. **This Reckless Breed of Men; the Trappers** and Fur Traders of the Southwest. New York; Knopf, 1963.

Cline, Gloria Griffen. **Exploring the Great Basin.** Norman: University of Oklahoma Press, 1963.

—————————. **Peter Skene Ogden and the Hudson Bay Company.** Norman; University of Oklahoma Press, 1974.

Coues, Elliot, ed. **Forty Years a Fur Trader on the Upper Missouri, the Personal Narrative of Charles Larpenteur 1833-1872.** 2 vols. New York: Francis P. Harper, 1898.

Dale, Harrison C., ed. **The Ashley-Smith Exploration and the Discovery of a Central Route to the Pacific 1822-1829.** Glendale, California: The Arthur H. Clark Company, 1941.

Davies, K.G., ed. **Peter Skene Ogden's Snake Country Journal 1826-27.** London: The Hudson's Bay Record Society, 1961.

Dee, Henry D. "An Irishman in the Fur Trade ... John Work," **British Columbia Historical Quarterly,** VII (1943).

De Jong, Thelma Bonham. "An Historical Narrative of the Explorations made by Fur Trappers in that Portion of the Oregon Country Which Later Became the State of Idaho." Unpublished Master's Thesis, Brigham Young University, Provo, Utah, 1957.

DeVoto, Bernard A. **Across the Wide Missouri.** Boston: Houghton Mifflin, 1964.

Drummond, Henry, ed. **The Journal of John Work, January to October, 1835.** Victoria, British Columbia: C. F. Banfield, 1945.

Drury, Clifford M., ed. **The Diaries and Letters of Henry H. Spalding and Asa Bowen Smith Relating the Nez Perce Mission, 1838-1842.** Glendale, California: The Arthur H. Clark Company, 1958.

—————————, ed. **First White Women over the Rockies.** 3 vols. Glendale, California: The Arthur H. Clark Company, 1963-66.

Dye, Eva E. **McLoughlin and Old Oregon.** Chicago: McClurg, 1913.

—————————. "Old Letters from Hudson's Bay Company Officials and Employees, 1829-1840," **Washington Historical Quarterly,** II (1909).

Eaton, W. Clement. "Nathaniel Wyeth's Oregon Expedition," **Pacific Historical Review, IV** (1955).

Elliott, Thompson C. "From Rendezvous to the Columbia," **Oregon Historical Quarterly, XXXVIII** (1937).

_____. "John McLoughlin, M.D.," **Oregon Historical Quarterly, XXXVI** (1935).

_____, ed. "Journal of E. Willard Smith While with the Fur Traders, Vasquez and Sublette, in the Rocky Mountain Region, 1839-1840 (and) Journal of John Work's Snake Country Expedition of 1830-31, Second Half," **Oregon Historical Quarterly, XIV** (1913).

_____, ed. "Journal of John Work's Snake Country Expedition, 1830-31," **Oregon Historical Quarterly, XIV** (1913).

_____. **Peter Skene Ogden, Fur Trader.** Portland, Oregon: Ivy Press, 1910.

_____. "Robert Newell," **Oregon Historical Quarterly, IX** (1908).

Ellison, William H., ed. **The Life and Adventures of George Nidever (1802-1883).** Berkeley: University of California Press, 1937.

Estergreen, M. Morgan. **Kit Carson, A Portrait in Courage.** Norman: University of Oklahoma Press, 1962.

Favour, Alpheus H. **Old Bill Williams, Mountain Man.** Chapel Hill, North Carolina: The University of North Carolina Press, 1936.

Frost, Donald M. **Notes on General Ashley, the Overland Trail and South Pass.** Barre, Massachusetts: Barre Gazette, 1960.

Gaul, R. Whorton. "Death of the Thunderbolt: Final Illness of Milton Sublette," **Montana Historical Society Bulletin, XVIII** (1961).

Ghent, William J. **The Road to Oregon, a Chronicle of the Great Emigrant Trail.** London: Longmans Green and Company, 1929.

Goetzmann, William H. **Army Exploration in the American West 1803-1863.** New Haven, Connecticut: Yale University Press, 1959.

Gray, William H. **A History of Oregon, 1792-1849.** Portland, Oregon: Harris & Holman, 1870.

_____. "The Unpublished Journal of William H. Gray," **The Whitman College Quarterly, XVI (1913).**

Green, T. V. "Scotts Bluffs, Fort John," **Nebraska Historical,** XVIII (1938).

Gregg, Kate L. and J. F. McDermott, ed. **Prairie and Mountain Sketches.** Norman: University of Oklahoma Press, 1957.

Hafen, LeRoy R., "Bean-Sinclair Party, 1830-1832,"**Colorado Magazine, XXX (1953).**

_____. **Broken Hand, The Life of Thomas Fitzpatrick: Mountain Man, Guide and Indian Agent.** Denver: The Old West Publishing Company, 1973.

_____. "Colorado Mountain Men of Fur Trade Days," **Westerner's Brand Book, Denver Posse, VIII (1952).**

_____. "Etienne Provost, Mountain Man and Utah Pioneer,"**Utah Historical Quarterly, XXXVI (1968).**

_____, ed. **Life in the Far West.** Norman: University of Oklahoma Press, 1964.

_____, ed. **Life in the Rocky Mountains, A Diary of Wanderings on the sources of the Rivers Missouri, Columbia, and Colorado 1830-1835 With Supplementary Writings and a Detailed Map of the Fur Country.** Denver: The Old West Publishing Company, 1983.

_____, ed. **The Mountain Men and the Fur Trade of the Far West.** 10 vols. Glendale, California: The Arthur H. Clark Company, 1965-1972.

_____. "Mountain Men as Explorers," **Westerner's Los Angeles Corral. Brand Book, XII (1966).**

_____. "Mountain Men Before the Mormons," Utah **Historical Quarterly, XXVI (1958).**

_____ and W. J. Ghent. **Broken Hand, The Life Story of Thomas Fitzpatrick Chief of the Mountain Men.** Denver: The Old West Publishing Company, 1931.

Haines, Aubrey L., ed. **Journal of a Trapper.** Portland, Oregon: Oregon Historical Society, 1955.

Haines, Francis D., Jr., ed. **The Snake Country Expedition of 1830-31: John Work's Field Journal.** Norman: University of Oklahoma Press, 1971.

Hill, Joseph J. "Ewing Young," **Oregon Historical Quarterly,** XXIV (1923).

_____. **Ewing Young in the Fur Trade of the Far Southwest, 1822-1834.** Eugene Oregon: Koke-Tiffany Company, 1923.

Holmes, Kenneth L. **Ewing Young, Master Trapper.** Portland, Oregon: Binford & Mort, 1967.

Hulbert, Archer B., ed., **Overland to the Pacific.** 8 vols. Denver: The Denver Public Library, 1932-41.

Humphreys, A. Glen. "The Expeditions, Trading, and Life of Thomas L. (Peg-leg) Smith." Unpublished Master's Thesis, Brigham Young University, Provo, Utah: 1964.

Irving, Washington, **The Adventures of Captain Bonneville, U.S.A., in the Rocky Mountains and the Far West.** New York: G. P. Putnam, 1859.

Johansen, Dorothy O., ed. **Robert Newell's Memoranda: Travels in the Teritory of Missourie Travle to the Kayuse War; together with a Report on the Indians South of the Columbia River.** Portland, Oregon: Champoeg Press, Inc. 1959.

Johnson, Robert C. **John McLoughlin: Patriarch of the Northwest.** Portland, Oregon: Metropolitan Press, 1935.

Kelly, Charles. "Antoine Robidoux," **Utah Historical Quarterly,** VI (1933).

Kittson, William. "Journal, Ogden's 1824-5 Snake Country Expedition," **Utah Historical Quarterly,** XXII (1954).

Laut, Anges, C. **The Fur Trade of America.** New York: The Macmillan Company, 1921.

_____. **The Story of the Trapper.** New York: D. Appleton and Company, 1902.

Lavender, David S. **The First In the Wilderness.** Garden City, New York: Doubleday, 1964.

Lewis, Oscar. **The Effects of White Contact Upon Blackfoot Culture, with Special Reference to the Role of the Fur Trade.** New York: J. J. Augustin, 1942.

Lewis, William S. and Paul C. Phillips, ed. **The Journal of John Work, A Chief-Trader of the Hudson's Bay Co., During His Expedition from Vancouver to the Flatheads and Blackfeet of the Pacific Northwest.** Cleveland: The Arthur H. Clark Company, 1923.

McDermott, John R., ed. **A Tour of the Prairies.** Norman: University of Oklahoma Press, 1956.

_____, ed. **The Western Journals of Washington Irving.** Norman: University of Oklahoma Press, 1944.

Mattes, Merrill J. **Fur Traders and Trappers of The Old West.** (n.p.) Yellowstone Library and Museum Association, (n.d.)

_____. "Jackson Hole, Crossroads of the Western Fur Trade 1807-1840 ...," **Pacific Northwest Quarterly,** XXXVII (1946), XXXIX (1948).

Merk, Frederick, ed. **Fur Trade and Empire; George Simpson's Journal.** Cambridge, Massachusetts: Harvard University Press, 1931.

Miller, David E., ed. "Journal of Expedition to Utah, 1825," **Utah Historical Quarterly,** XX (1952).

_____, ed. "The Journal of Peter Skene Ogden's Expedition to Utah, 1825," **Utah Academy of Sciences, Arts and Letters Proceedings,** (1952).

_____. "Ogden's Exploration in the Great Salt Lake Region," **Western Humanities Review,** VIII (1955).

_____. "Ogden's Trek into Utah, 1828-29," **Pacific Northwest Quarterly,** LI (1960).

Montgomery, Richard G. **The White-Headed Eagle, John McLoughlin, Builder of an Empire.** New York: Macmillan Company, 1934.

Morgan, Dale L. **The Great Salt Lake.** Indianapolis, Indiana: Bobbs-Merrill Co., 1947.

_____. **Jedediah Smith and the Opening of the West.** Indianapolis, Indiana: The Bobbs-Merrill Company, Inc., 1953.

_____, ed. **The West of William H. Ashley.** Denver: The Old West Publishing Company, 1964.

_____ and Carl I. Wheat. **Jedediah Smith and His Maps of the American West.** San Francisco: Historical Society, 1954.

_____ and Eleanor Towles Harris, ed. **the Rocky Mountain Journals of William Marshall Anderson, The West in 1834.** San Marino, California: The Huntington Library, 1967.

Mumey, Noley. **James Pierson Beckwourth, 1856-1866.** Denver: The Old West Publishing Company, 1957.

_____. **The Life of Jim Baker 1818-1898, Trapper, Scout, Guide and Indian Fighter.** Denver: The World Press, Inc., 1931.

Nadeau, Remi A. **Fort Laramie and the Sioux Indians.** Englewood Cliffs, New Jersey: Prentice-Hall, 1967.

Neihardt, John G. **The Splendid Wayfaring: The Story of the Exploits and Adventures of Jedediah Smith and His Comrades, the Ashley-Henry men, Discoverers and Explorers of the Great Central Route from the Missouri River to the Pacific Ocean, 1822-1831.** New York: The Macmillan Company, 1920.

Nunis, Doyce B., Jr. **Andrew Sublette, Rocky Mountain Prince, 1808-1853.** Los Angeles: Dawson's Book Shop, 1960.

_____. "The Fur Men: Key to Westward Expansion, 1822-30," **The Historian,** XXIII (1961).

_____. "Milton G. Sublette," **Montana Magazine,** XIII (1963).

Nute, Grace L. **Calendar of the American Fur Company's Papers.** Washington: United States Government Printing Office, 1945.

Ogden, Peter Skene. **Snake Country Journal 1824-5.** London: n.p., 1950.

Oswald, Delmont R., ed. **The Life and Adventures of James P. Beckwourth as Told to Thomas D. Bonner.** Lincoln: University of Nebraska Press, 1972.

Parker, Samuel. **Journal of an Exploring Tour Beyond the Rocky Mountains.** Ithaca, New York: Mack, Andrus, & Woodruff, Printers, 1840.

Phillips, Paul C. **The Fur Trade.** 2 vols. Norman: University of Oklahoma Press, 1961.

_____, ed. **Life in the Rocky Mountains, A Diary of Wanderings on the Sources of the Rivers Missouri, Columbia and Colorado From February, 1830 to November, 1835.** Denver: The Old West Publishing Company, 1940.

_____. "William H. Vanderburgh," **Missouri Valley Historical Review,** XXX (1943).

Porter, Mae Reed and Odessa Davenport. **Scotsman In Buckskin; Sir William Drummond Stewart and the Rocky Mountain Fur Trade.** New York: Hastings House, 1963.

Quaife, Milo M., ed. **Kit Carson's Autobiography.** Lincoln: University of Nebraska Press, 1935.

Rich, Edwin E. **The Fur Trade and the Northwest to 1857.** Toronto: McClelland and Stewart, 1967.

——————. **Hudson's Bay Company 1670-1870.** New York: Macmillan, 1960-61.

——————, ed. **Peter Skene Ogden's Snake Country Journals, 1824-25 and 1825-26.** London: The Hudson's Bay Record Society, 1950.

—————— and W. Kaye Lamb, ed. **The Letters of John McLoughlin from Fort Vancouver to the Governor and Committee.** Toronto: Champlain Society, 1941-44.

Robertson, Frank Chester. **Fort Hall, Gateway to the Oregon Country.** New York: Hastings House, 1963.

Ross, Marvin C. **The West of Alfred Jacob Miller (1837).** Norman: University of Oklahoma Press, 1951.

Rounds, Glen, ed. **Mountain Men: George Frederick Ruxton's First Hand Accounts of Fur Trappers and Indians in the Rockies.** New York: Holiday House, 1966.

Russell, Carl P. **Firearms, Traps and Tools of the Mountain Men.** New York: Knopf, 1967.

——————. **Guns on the Early Frontiers; a History of Firearms from Colonial Times Through the Years of the Western Fur Trade.** Berkeley: University of California Press, 1957.

——————. **Trapper Trails to the Sisk-Ke-Dee.** n.p., n.d.

——————. "Wilderness Rendezvous Period of the American Fur Trade," **Oregon Historical Society Quarterly,** XLII (1941).

Saum, Lewis O. **The Fur Trader and the Indian.** Seattle: University of Washington Press, 1965.

Skinner, Constance L. **Adventures of Oregon; A Chronicle of the Fur Trade.** New Haven, Connecticut: Yale University Press, 1921.

Smith, E. Willard. "Journal, While with Fur Traders Vasquez and Sublette," **Oregon Historical Quarterly,** XIV (1913).

Stewart, William Drummond. **Edward Warren.** London: Walker, 1854.

Sullivan, Maurice S. **The Travels of Jedediah Smith.** Santa Ana, California: The Fine Arts Press, 1934.

Sunder, John E. **Bill Sublette, Mountain Man.** Norman: University of Oklahoma Press, 1959.

_____. **The Fur Trade on the Upper Missouri, 1840-1865.** Norman: University of Oklahoma Press, 1965.

_____. **Joshua Pilcher, Fur Trader and Indian Agent.** Norman: University of Oklahoma Press, 1968.

Todd, Edgeley W., ed. **The Adventures of Captain Bonneville, U.S.A. in the Rocky Mountains and the Far West.** Norman: University of Oklahoma press, 1961.

Townsend, John K. **Narrative of a Journey Across the Rocky Mountains to the Columbia River.** Philadelphia: Henry Perkins, 1839.

Vandiveer, Clarence A. **The Fur-trade and Early Western Exploration.** Cleveland: The Arthur H. Clark Company, 1929.

Vestal, Stanley. **Joe Meek; the Merry Mountain Man.** Caldwell, Idaho: Caxton Printers, 1952.

_____. **Mountain Men.** Boston: Houghton Mifflin Company, 1937.

Victor, Frances F. **The River of the West.** Hartford, Connecticut: Columbian Book Company, 1870.

Wagner, W.F., ed. **Adventures of Zenas Leonard, Fur Trader and Trapper 1831-1836.** Cleveland: The Burrows Brothers Company, 1904.

Walker, Joel P. **A Pioneer of Pioneers: Narrative of Adventures Thro' Alabama, Florida, New Mexico, Oregon, California, &c.** Los Angeles: Glen Dawson, 1953.

Warner, Ted J. "Peter Skene Ogden and the Fur Trade of the Great Northwest," Unpublished Master's Thesis, Brigham Young University Provo, Utah, 1958.

Watson, Douglas S. **West Wind: The Life Story of Joseph Reddeford Walker.** Los Angeles: Percy H. Booth, 1934.

Weber, David J. **The Taos Trappers; the Fur Trade in the Far Southwest 1540-1846.** Norman: University of Oklahoma Press, 1971.

Wheat, Carl I. **Mapping the Transmississippi West, 1540-1861.** 6 vols. San Francisco: Institute of Historical Cartography. 1957-1963.

Whitman, Marcus. "Journal and Report by Dr. Marcus Whitman of his Tour of Exploration with Reverend Samuel Parker in 1835 Beyond the Rocky Mountains," **Oregon Historical Quarterly,** XXVIII (1927).

Williams, Glyndwr, ed. **Peter Skene Ogden's Snake Country**

Journals, 1827-28 And 1828-29. London: The Hudson's Bay Record Society, 1971.

Wishart, David J. **The Fur Trade of the American West 1807-1840, A Geographical Synthesis.** Lincoln: University of Nebraska Press, 1979.

Wislizenus, F. A. **A Journal to the Rocky Mountains in the Year 1839.** St. Louis: Missouri Historical Society, 1912.

Woodward, Arthur, ed. **The Autobiography of a Mountain Man, 1805-1889.** Pasadena, California: G. Dawson, 1948.

Wyeth, John B. **Oregon; Or a Short History of a Long Journey.** Ann Arbor, Michigan: University Microfilms, 1966.

Young, F. G., ed. "The Correspondence and Journal of Captain Nathaniel J. Wyeth 1831-36: A Record of Two Expeditions for the Occupation of the Oregon Country, with Maps, Introduction and Index," **Sources of the History of Oregon.** Vol. I, Eugene, Oregon: University Press, 1899.

INDEX

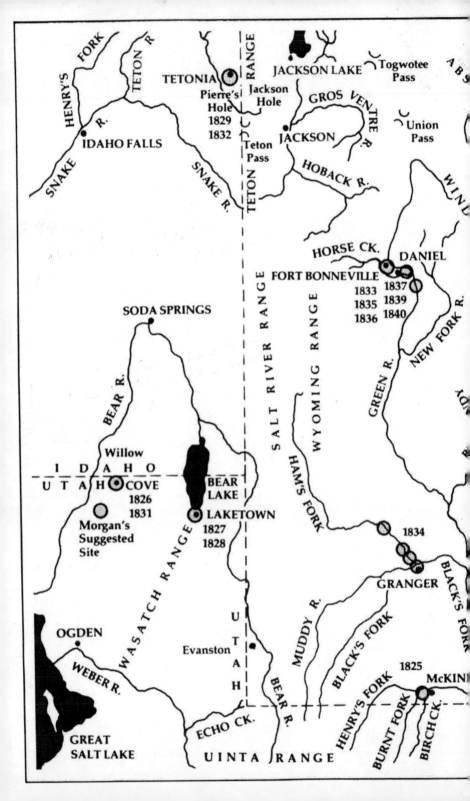